The Canterbury and York Society

GENERAL EDITOR: DR P. HOSKIN

ISSN 0262–995X

DIOCESE OF LINCOLN

CANTERBURY AND YORK SOCIETY VOL. XCIX

The Register of

Richard Fleming

BISHOP OF LINCOLN

1420–1431

VOLUME II

EDITED BY

N.H. BENNETT

The Canterbury and York Society

The Boydell Press

2009

First published 2009

A Canterbury and York Society publication
published by The Boydell Press
an imprint of Boydell & Brewer Ltd
PO Box 9, Woodbridge, Suffolk IP12 3DF, UK
and of Boydell & Brewer Inc.
668 Mt Hope Avenue, Rochester, NY 14620, USA
website: www.boydellandbrewer.com

ISBN 978–0–90723–971–0

A CIP catalogue record for this book is available
from the British Library

Details of previous volumes are available from Boydell & Brewer Ltd

This publication is printed on acid-free paper

Typeset by Pru Harrison, Hacheston, Suffolk
Printed in Great Britain by
CPI Antony Rowe, Chippenham, Wiltshire

CONTENTS

PREFACE

This second volume of the register of Richard Fleming, bishop of Lincoln from 1420 until 1431, appears more than twenty years after the first, a delay for which the editor offers his apologies. His thanks are due to the successive General Editors of the Society during that time for their exemplary patience. The thanks of the Society are again due to the Bishop of Lincoln, and to Derek M. Wellman, the Lincoln Diocesan Registrar, for permission to publish this calendar.

Folios 88–204 of the register are covered here, including the institutions for the archdeaconries of Leicester, Huntingdon, Bedford, Oxford and Buckingham, collations of dignities and prebends, ordinations, and the acts of Archbishop Chichele during his visitation of the diocese in 1424–5.

EDITORIAL METHOD

The institution entries are usually calendared; it may be assumed that the original entries are in memoranda form and that they include (unless otherwise stated) a mandate for induction by the appropriate archdeacon or his official. In the case of exchanges, where an institution is made to a benefice in another diocese, it may be assumed that induction to that benefice is reserved to the bishop of that diocese.

In the ordination lists, where a title is specified, it may be assumed that it was conferred for all orders, unless otherwise stated.

The historical year, beginning on 1 January, has been used throughout. Place-names have been modernised; where unusual variant forms occur in the manuscript they are given in round brackets and italicised. Personal names are given in the form in which they are found in the manuscript, except that where a principal surname is followed by an identifiable toponymic, the latter is given in its modern form.

Where entries have been transcribed in full, punctuation and capitalisation have been modernised; 'c' and 't' and 'u/v' have been employed in accordance with their English equivalents.

GENERAL ABBREVIATIONS

A. and C.	abbot/abbess and convent
archbp	archbishop
archdn	archdeacon
archdnry	archdeaconry
B.A.	Bachelor of Arts
B.Cn. & C.L.	Bachelor of Canon and Civil Law
B.Dec.	Bachelor of Decrees
B.Th.	Bachelor of Divinity or Theology
bp	bishop
br.	brother
cath.	cathedral
cess.	cession
D. and C.	dean and chapter
D.Dec.	Doctor of Decrees
decd	deceased
dioc.	in/of the diocese of
D.M.	Doctor of Medicine
D.Th.	Doctor of Divinity or Theology
Ind.	Induction by
fo.	folio
kt	knight
Lic.C. & Cn.L.	Licentiate of Civil and Canon Law
LL.B.	Bachelor of Laws
LL.D.	Doctor of Laws
M.	Master
M.A.	Master of Arts
P. and C.	prior/prioress and convent
preb.	prebend/prebendary
res.	resignation
s.	son of
sr	sister
t.	title
vac.	vacant

BIBLIOGRAPHICAL ABBREVIATIONS

BRUO   A. B. Emden, *A Biographical Register of the University of Oxford to 1500* (3 vols, Oxford, 1957–9)

Complete Peerage   G. E. Cokayne, *Complete Peerage of England, Scotland, Ireland, Great Britain and United Kingdom, extant, extinct, or dormant*, new edn, revised and much enlarged, by V. Gibbs *et al.* (13 vols in 14, London, 1910–98)

CPL   *Calendar of Papal Letters* (HMSO, London, 1893–)

CPR   *Calendar of Patent Rolls* (HMSO, London, 1891–)

Fasti Parochiales   A. Hamilton Thompson, C. T. Clay, N. A. H. Lawrence, N. K. M. Gurney and D. M. Smith (eds), *Fasti Parochiales* (5 vols, Yorkshire Archaeological Society, Record Series 85, 107, 129, 133, 143, 1933–85)

Le Neve 1300–1541   H. P. F. King, J. M. Horn and B. Jones (eds), *John Le Neve, Fasti Ecclesiae Anglicanae 1300–1541* (12 vols, London, 1962–67)

Reg.   Lincolnshire Archives, Bishop's Register

Reg. Chichele   E. F. Jacob (ed.), *The Register of Henry Chichele, Archbishop of Canterbury, 1414–1443* (4 vols., Oxford, 1943–7)

Reg. Fleming   N. H. Bennett (ed.), *The Register of Richard Fleming, Bishop of Lincoln, 1420–31*, Vol. I (Canterbury and York Society 73, 1984)

Reg. Hallum   Joyce Horn (ed.), *The Register of Robert Hallum, Bishop of Salisbury, 1407–17* (Canterbury and York Society 72, 1982)

Reg. Spofford   A. T. Bannister (ed.), *Registrum Thome Spofford, episcopi Herefordensis* (Canterbury and York Society 23, 1919)

VCH   *Victoria County History*

Visitations   A. Hamilton Thompson (ed.), *Visitations of Religious Houses* (3 vols., Lincoln Record Society 7, 14, 21 and Canterbury and York Society 17, 24, 33, Horncastle and London, 1914–29)

[Archdnry of Leicester institutions. Throughout this section, it may be assumed that each institution entry includes a mandate to induct addressed to the archdn of Leicester or his official, unless otherwise stated. See introductory note on editorial practice above.]

Quarto kalendas Maii anno domini millesimo quadringentesimo vicesimo incipit annus primus consecrationis reverendi in Christo patris et domini domini Ricardi dei gracia Lincolniensis episcopi.

1. Institution of John Herford, priest, to vicarage of Ab Kettleby, vac. by res. of John Paunton; patron, P. and C. of Launde. Lincoln, 10 June 1420.

Johannes Herford' presbiter presentatus per Priorem et Conventum de Landa ad vicariam perpetuam ecclesie parochialis de Apeketelby Lincolnien' diocesis per resignationem domini Johannis Paunton' ultimi vicarii eiusdem in manibus domini Lincoln' episcopi factam et per ipsum admissam vacantem, ad eandem decimo die mensis Junii anno domini millesimo CCCC^mo xx^mo apud Lincoln' fuit admissus et vicarius perpetuus secundum formam constitutionum legatinarum in hoc casu editarum juratus institutus canonice in eadem nulla inquisitione previa quia etc. jurata canonica obediencia ut in forma. Scriptum fuit archidiacono Leycestr' seu ipsius Officiali ad inducendum eundem.

2. Institution of David Michell, priest, to church of Aston, Herts., vac. by death of Thomas Bowedon; patron, A. and C. of Reading. Ind. archdn of Leicester.[1] Langtoft, 28 August 1420.

3. Institution of Thomas Durnell, clerk, in person of John Claybroke, his proctor, to church of Shenley, Herts., vac. by death of Richard atte Yate; patron, John Pulteney kt. Ind. archdn of Leicester.[2] Stamford, 25 August 1420.

4. Institution of William Barwell, priest, in person of William Exham, clerk, his proctor, to vicarage of Hungarton, vac. by death of John Halfwayn; patron, A. and C. of St Mary, Leicester. Langtoft, 5 September 1420.

5. Institution of William Edrych, priest, to church of Hoby, vac. by death of John Frekylton; patron, Anthony Howby, lord of Hoby, *domicellus*. Note that an inquiry was carried out by the archdn of Leicester, by which it was found that the said Anthony had the right of presentation, by inheritance, at alternate turns, and that Margaret, countess of Norfolk, had presented at the last vacancy. Langtoft, 5 September 1420.

6. Institution of John Upryght, priest, to vicarage of Packington; patron, P. and C. of Coventry. Langtoft, 11 September 1420.

---

[1]　Presumably an error for 'Huntingdon'.
[2]　Presumably an error for 'Huntingdon'.

7.   Institution of Richard Osteler, priest, to vicarage of Plungar, vac. by res. of Thomas Meysam; patron, P. and C. of Belvoir. By exchange with vicarage of St Mary, Torksey. Langtoft, 18 September 1420.

8.   [fo. 88v] Institution of William atte Kyrk, chaplain, to vicarage of Ratby; patron, P. and C. of Nuneaton. Langtoft, 23 September 1420.

9.   Institution of John Freman, priest, to church of Bottesford, vac. by death of Thomas Clyff; patron, Margaret, lady of Roos. Langtoft, 27 September 1420.

10.   Institution of Henry Cope, priest, to church of Beeby; patron, A. and C. of Crowland. Langtoft, 27 September 1420.

11.   Institution of Richard Baker, priest, in person of M. John Ernesby, clerk, his proctor, to church of Hathern, vac. by death of William Bulkyngton; patron, treasurer and canons of the collegiate church of St Mary *iuxta castrum*, Leicester (the sacrist being absent). Langtoft, 4 October 1420.

12.   Institution of William Clement, priest, to vicarage of King's Norton, vac. by res. of William Nutt; patron, A. and C. of Owston. By exchange with church of Whitwell. Langtoft, 4 October 1420.

13.   Institution of Thomas Kybbeworth, priest, to vicarage of Queniborough, vac. by res. of Roger Hyklyng; patron, King Henry. Langtoft, 14 October 1420.

14.   Institution of William Holme, priest, to church of Swepstone; patron, William Trussell kt. Langtoft, 22 October 1420.

15.   Institution of William Lychefeld, priest, to church of Carlton Curlieu; patron, P. and C. of Jesus of Bethlehem, Sheen. Fotheringhay, 1 November 1420.

16.   Collation of church of Asfordby, vac. by res. of John Duffeld, to Alan Humbreston, chaplain. By exchange with church of Branston. Note that no mandate for induction was issued because, immediately after his institution, Humbreston resigned the church. Fineshade, 5 November 1420.

17.   Collation of church of Asfordby, vac. by res. of Alan Humbreston, to John Humberston, priest. Fineshade, 5 November 1420.

18.   [fo. 89r] Institution of Robert Gene, clerk, to church of Nether Broughton, vac. by res. of Thomas Mye; patron, P. and C. of Lenton. Fineshade, 3 November 1420.

19.   Institution of Richard Broun of *Calcote*, priest, to vicarage of Frisby on the Wreake, vac. by res. of Richard Wibtoft; patron, P. and C. of Launde. Fineshade, 6 November 1420.

20.   Certificate of Robert [Nouesle], abbot of Owston. In accordance with a commission of Bp Fleming, addressed to him jointly with M. John Annore, sequestrator in the archdnry of Leicester, and William Irby, rector of Medbourne, and dated at Langtoft, 31 October 1420, he has held an inquiry, on Monday after the feast of All Saints [4 November] in the church of St Leonard, Leicester, into the election of br. William Sadyngton as abbot of St Mary, Leicester. Finding no impediment, he has confirmed the election. Owston, 8 November 1420.

21. [fo. 89v] Institution of William Mey, priest, to church of Pickwell, vac. by death of Thomas Curson; patron, John Curson, lord of Pickwell, *domicellus*. Fineshade, 16 November 1420.

22. Institution of Thomas Graunt, priest, to church of Edmondthorpe; patron, King Henry, by reason of his duchy of Lancaster. Fineshade, 17 November 1420.

23. Institution of Richard Grene, priest, to vicarage of Peatling Magna, vac. by res. of Roger Rycard; patron, P. and C. of Jesus of Bethlehem, Sheen. Note that an inquiry was carried out by M. John Annore, commissary-general in archdnry of Leicester, by which it was found that the prior and convent were true patrons by reason of the appropriation by the king of the priory of Ware to the said priory of Sheen. Fineshade, 21 December 1420.

24. Institution of John Claypole, priest, in person of M. William Hexham, clerk, his proctor, to church of Rearsby, vac. by death of M. William Belton; patron, John Folvyle, *domicellus*. Note that an inquiry was carried out by the official of the archdn of Leicester, by which it was found that John Folvyle was true patron by hereditary right, and that he presented at the last vacancy. Fineshade, 23 December 1420.

25. Institution of Thomas Fraunceys, clerk, to church of Blaby; patrons, Ralph Fraunceys and Elizabeth his wife. London, 14 December 1420.

26. Institution of M. Gilbert Kymere, D.M., M.A., LL.B., clerk, to church of Lutterworth, vac. by death of Robert Ashehurst; patron, William, lord Ferrers of Groby. London, 16 December 1420.

27. Institution of Thomas Whyte, clerk, to church of Swepstone; patron, Ralph Sherley kt. Note that an inquiry was carried out by M. John Annore, commissary in archdnry of Leicester, by which it was found that Ralph Sherley was the true patron by reason of a dimission to him of the manor and advowson of Swepstone by John Pavy. Dunstable, 20 December 1420.

28. Institution of Thomas Herryson of Great Dalby, priest, to vicarage of Hungarton, vac. by death of William Barewell; patron, A. and C. of St Mary, Leicester. Fineshade, 3 January 1421.

29. [fo. 90r] Collation of chantry in church of Wigston, vac. by institution of Richard Broune to vicarage of Frisby on the Wreake, to John Grymmesby, chaplain. Fineshade, 23 January 1421.

30. Institution of Henry Andrewe, priest, to vicarage of Slawston, vac. by res. of

William Boveton; patron, A. and C. of Owston. By exchange with vicarage of Tallington. Fineshade, 19 February 1421.

31.   Institution of John Bate, clerk, to mediety of church of Sheepy, vac. by res. of John Brokhampton; patron, Thomas Asteley, lord of Sheepy. Note that an inquiry was carried out by the official of the archdn of Leicester, by which it was found that the said Thomas was true patron by hereditary right, and that he presented John Brokhampton at the last vacancy. Wykeham, 14 March 1421.

32.   Institution of John Whyte, priest, in person of William Hexham, clerk, his proctor, to the fourth prebend in the new collegiate church of St Mary, Leicester, vac. by death of William Almanbury; patron, King Henry. Ind. dean of the said church. Wykeham, 19 April 1421.

[fo. 90v]

Quarto kalendas Maii anno domini millesimo CCCC^{mo} vicesimo primo incipit annus secundus consecrationis reverendi in Christo patris et domini domini Ricardi dei gracia Lincolniensis episcopi.

33.   Certificate of Henry, prior of St Mary Overy, Southwark. In accordance with a commission of Bp Fleming (dated at Old Temple, 7 May 1421), he has examined the election of br. William Kilpesham, canon of Owston, as abbot of the same and, finding no impediment, he has confirmed the same. Southwark, 20 May 1421.

34.   [fo. 91r] Institution of M. John Sylby *alias* Beby to church of Coston; patron, Richard, earl of Warwick – and of M. John Play to church of Kingweston, dioc. Bath and Wells; patron, A. and C. of St Saviour, Bermondsey. Exchange, by authority of commission of Nicholas [Bubwith], bp of Bath and Wells (dated at London, 4 June 1421). Buckden, 10 June 1421.

35.   Institution of John Howys, priest, to vicarage of Hinckley, vac. by death of John Katour; patron, P. and C. of Mount Grace. Buckden, 11 June 1421.

36.   [fo. 91v] Institution of John Morell, clerk, to mediety of church of Sheepy; patron, William Assheby of Welby, esquire. Note that an inquiry was carried out by M. John Annore, commissary-general in archdnry of Leicester, by which it was found that the said mediety was vac. by res. of John Kyng by reason of his institution to church of Pleasley, dioc. Coventry and Lichfield, and that the said William was patron by right of a feoffment to him by Francis Meryng who presented at the last vacancy. Buckden, 27 June 1421.

37.   Institution of William Dorkyng, priest, to church of Coleorton, vac. by death of John Baull; patrons, John de Grey of Ruthin and Constance, countess Marschall, his wife. Buckden, 2 July 1421.

38.   Institution of William Heyne, priest, to church of Rearsby, vac. by death of John Claypole; patron, John Folvyll, *domicellus*. Buckden, 10 July 1421.

39.   Institution of William Bolton, priest, to church of Nether Broughton, vac. by res. of Robert Grene; patron, P. and C. of Holy Trinity, Lenton. By exchange with church of Hardwick. Buckden, 10 July 1421.

40.   Institution of John s. Richard de Cottesmore, priest, to vicarage of King's Norton; patron, A. and C. of Owston. Buckden, 18 July 1421.

41.   Institution of Richard Strynsall, priest, to vicarage of St Margaret, Leicester, vac. by death of Nicholas Godyer; patron, M. Thomas More, preb. of Leicester St Margaret in Lincoln cath. Ind. D. and C. of Lincoln. Buckden, 9 August 1421.

42.   Institution of Robert Wattes, priest, to vicarage of St Leonard, Leicester; patron, A. and C. of St Mary, Leicester. Buckden, 20 August 1421.

43.   Institution of John Gaddesby, priest, to tenth prebend in collegiate church of St Mary, Leicester, vac. by death of John Claypole; patron, King Henry. Ind. dean of collegiate church. Stamford, 10 September 1421.

44.   Institution of John Colynson, priest, to vicarage of Eaton, vac. by death of John Smyth; patron, A. and C. of St Mary, Leicester. Sleaford, 12 September 1421.

45.   [fo. 92r] Institution of William Tayllour, priest, to vicarage of Welham; patron, P. and C. of Launde. Sleaford, 15 September 1421.

46.   Institution of Henry Radclyff, priest, to vicarage of Loddington, vac. by res. of Nicholas Colman; patron, P. and C. of Launde. Kirby Bellars, 7 October 1421.

47.   Institution of John Brounyng to church of Rotherby; patron, Thomas Assheby of Lowesby, esquire – and of John Baxster to church of Rampton, dioc. Ely; patron, Margaret, widow of Richard le Scrop. Exchange, by authority of commission of John [Fordham], bp of Ely (dated at Downham, 16 October 1421). Cottingham, 22 October 1421.

48.   [fo. 92v] Institution of Richard Martell B.A., priest, in person of Thomas Charite, his proctor, to church of Glenfield; patron, P. and C. of Jesus of Bethlehem, Sheen. Cottingham, 22 October 1421.

49.   Institution of John Grenelowe, bp *Soltoniensis*, to church of Long Whatton; patron, A. and C. of St Mary, Leicester – and of M. Walter Fouler, in person of William Northburgh, *literatus*, his proctor, to mediety of church of Cotgrave, dioc. York; patron, P. and C. of Holy Trinity, Lenton. Exchange, by authority of commission of Henry [Bowet], archbp of York (dated at Bishopthorpe, 1 November 1421). Swerford, 10 November 1421.

50.   Collation, by M. Robert Iwardeby, canon of Lincoln, of vicarage of Dalby on the Wolds to Richard Woulsy of *Graynby*, priest. By lapse. 15 November 1421.[3]

---

[3]   Place not specified.

51. [fo. 93r] Institution of John Gybbe, priest, in person of William Tatersale, literate, his proctor, to vicarage of Ab Kettleby, vac. by res. of John Hareford; patron, P. and C. of Launde. London, 4 December 1421.

52. Institution of William Bode, priest, to vicarage of Croxton Kerrial, vac. by res. of Thomas Roger; patron, A. and C. of Croxton. By exchange with vicarage of Aylesbury. London, 9 December 1421.

53. Institution of John s. William Mason of Swayfield, priest, in person of M. Richard Aldenham, clerk, his proctor, to church of Edmondthorpe, vac. by res. of Thomas Graunt; patron, King Henry, by reason of his duchy of Lancaster. London, 17 December 1421.

54. Institution of Robert Warde, priest, to vicarage of Bringhurst, vac. by res. of Richard Brencher; patron, John Sutton, rector of Bringhurst, clerk. Hertford, 20 December 1421.

55. Institution of William Hayhyrst, priest, to vicarage of St Martin, Leicester, vac. by res. of Henry Whyghthede; patron, A. and C. of St Mary, Leicester. Hertford, 20 December 1421.

56. Institution of William Mayhewe, priest, to vicarage of Shackerstone, vac. by death of Robert Hulcok; patron, P. and C. of Harrold. Fenny Stratford, 9 January 1422.

57. Institution of Richard Brygham, priest, to vicarage of Peatling Magna, vac. by res. of Richard Grene; patron, P. and C. of Jesus of Bethlehem, Sheen. Buckden, 30 January 1422.

58. [fo. 93v] Certificate of William [Heyworth], bp of Coventry and Lichfield. In accordance with commission of Bp Fleming (dated at Huntingdon priory, 23 January 1422), he had instituted William Tryve to vicarage of Glen Magna, vac. by res. of Thomas Wystowe; patron, A. and C. of Alcester. Exchange with vicarage of Marton, dioc. Coventry and Lichfield. Eccleshall, 29 January 1422. Received at Huntingdon, 11 February 1422.

59. Institution of Robert Dykys B.Th. to church of Glenfield, vac. by res. of Richard Martell; patron, P. and C. of Jesus of Bethlehem, Sheen. London, 10 February 1422.

60. Certificate of subdean and chapter of Lincoln (the dean being absent). In accordance with commission of Bp Fleming (dated at Buckden, 1 February 1422), they had instituted William Corbrygg to vicarage of Lowesby, vac. by res. of Henry Bilburgh; patron, master and brethren of Burton Lazars. Exchange with a chantry of John de Buckyngham, late bp of Lincoln, in jurisdiction of D. and C. of Lincoln. Lincoln, 12 February 1422. Received at Huntingdon, 16 February 1422.

[Institutions carried out by Robert Leek, Vicar-General.]

61. [fo. 94r] Certificate of Walter Cook, canon of St Paul's and official of London *sede vacante*. In accordance with commission of Robert Leek LL.D., canon of Lincoln and vicar-general of Bp Fleming *in remotis* (dated at Liddington, 7 March 1422), he had instituted Henry Gyles to vicarage of North Kilworth, vac. by res. of Thomas Curteys; patron, A. and C. of St Mary, Leicester. Exchange with vicarage of All Saints and St Peter, Maldon, dioc. London. London, 18 March 1422. Received at Liddington, 14 March 1422.[4]

62. Institution of John Bateman, in person of John Bradegate, literate, his proctor, to church of St Peter and St Paul, Belgrave, vac. by death of Thomas Hanley; patron, P. and C. of Jesus of Bethlehem, Sheen. Liddington, 15 March 1422.

63. [fo. 94v] Certificate of Richard Crosby, prior of Coventry. In accordance with commission of Robert Leek LL.D., canon of Lincoln and vicar-general of Bp Fleming *in remotis* (dated at Liddington, 17 March 1422), he had instituted Roger Wylkyns to church of Cadeby, vac. by res. of Thomas Ganvyll; patron, P. and C. of Dunstable. Exchange with chantry of St Thomas the Martyr in Coventry cath. Coventry, 20 March 1422. Received at Liddington, 23 March 1422.

64. Institution of Thomas Robert, clerk, in person of M. Thomas Juster, clerk, his proctor, to free chapel of Kibworth Harcourt, vac. by death of Thomas Hanley; patron, warden and scholars of Merton College, Oxford. Liddington, 3 April 1422.

65. Institution of Robert Jors, priest, to vicarage of Little Dalby, vac. by res. of John Brampton; patron, P. and C. of Langley. Liddington, 4 June 1423.

[fo. 95r]

Quarto kalendas Maii anno domini millesimo quadringentesimo vicesimo secundo incipit annus tertius consecrationis reverendi in Christo patris et domini domini Ricardi dei gracia Lincolniensis episcopi.

66. Institution of William Typp, priest, to church of Sibson, vac. by res. of William Spon; patron, P. and C. of Jesus of Bethlehem, Sheen. By exchange with church of Towcester. Liddington, 6 June 1422.

67. Institution of Nicholas Burton, priest, to church of Bringhurst, vac. by res. of John Sutton; patron, A. and C. of Peterborough. Liddington, 1 March 1422.

68. Institution of John Wyllyamson of Frisby, priest, to church of Rotherby, vac. by res. of John Brounyng; patron, Thomas Assheby of Lowesby, *domicellus*. Liddington, 25 June 1422.

---

[4] Either the date of the certificate or that of its receipt is wrong.

69. Institution of John Bower, priest, to vicarage of Wardley, vac. by res. of William Holbek; patron, P. and C. of Launde. Ind. archdn of Leicester.[5] Liddington, 17 August 1422.

70. Institution of John Leuche to church of Appleby; patron, P. and C. of Lytham – and of William Goldryng, in person of John Fower, literate, his proctor, to vicarage of Stoke by Nayland, dioc. Norwich; patron, P. and C. of St Mary, Prittlewell. Exchange, by authority of commission of John [Wakering], bp of Norwich (dated at Thorpe by Norwich, 4 August 1422). Liddington, 12 August 1422.

71. [fo. 95v] Institution of John de Stonesby, priest, to church of Elmesthorpe, vac. by res. of John Brydlyngton; patrons, Thomas Maureward kt, William Holme, John Wevere, John Charnels and Walter Swane, clerks. Note that an inquiry was carried out by M. William Aslokby, commissary-general in archdnry of Leicester, by which it was found that the patrons presented by reason of a feoffment made to them by William Trussell kt of all his lands with the advowsons thereto pertaining. Liddington, 29 August 1422.

72. Certificate of the rector of Cottesmore. In accordance with a commission of the vicar-general (addressed to him jointly with the vicar of Melton Mowbray and dated at Liddington, 14 August 1422), he has carried out an inquiry into the resignation of John s. Robert s. Richard, rector of Waltham on the Wolds, and into the presentation, by P. and C. of Nuneaton, of Henry Fenton to that benefice. Finding no impediment, he has accepted the resignation and has instituted Henry, who is of honest life and has the first tonsure, to the living. Cottesmore, 20 August 1422.

73. [fo. 96r] Admission of br. John Botyler, canon of Repton, as prior of Charley; patron, William Ferrers (*de Ferrariis*) of Groby kt. Liddington, 30 August 1422.

74. Admission of br. William Horbery, canon of Nostell, as prior of Breedon; patron, King Henry, by reason of his duchy of Lancaster. Old Temple, 26 November 1422.

75. Certificate of William [Heyworth], bp of Coventry and Lichfield. In accordance with a commission of the vicar-general (dated at Pytchley, 19 August 1422), he has instituted William Cook to church of Croft, vac. by res. of William Tonworth; patron, A. and C. of Leicester. Exchange with church of Stretton Baskerville, dioc. Coventry and Lichfield. Beaudesert, 27 August 1422. Received at Liddington, 10 September 1422.

76. [fo. 96v] Institution of Robert Benebruk, priest, to church of Withcote, vac. by res. of John Cook; patron, A. and C. of Owston. Liddington, 15 September 1422.

---

5 Presumably an error for 'Northampton'.

77. Institution of John Helsdoun, priest, to church of Fenny Drayton, vac. by res. of John Brystowe; patron, P. and C. of Jesus of Bethlehem, Sheen. Liddington, 22 September 1422.

78. Institution of Richard Wartre, priest, in person of Thomas Gregory literate, his proctor, to church of Glooston; patron, John Beaufo kt – and of William Spenser, priest, to chantry or wardenship of Sapcote; patron, Robert Moton kt. By exchange. Liddington, 6 October 1422. Note that an inquiry was carried out by M. William Aslakby, commissary-general in archdnry of Leicester, by which it was found that the said John Beaufo was the true patron of Glooston by the hereditary right of his wife,[6] heiress of Robert Haryngton who presented William Spenser at the last vacancy. It was also found that lord Grey of Codnor and Robert Moton were true patrons of the chantry of Sapcote, presenting to the same at alternate turns, and that Robert Moton was patron at this turn because Richard lord Grey, decd, had presented at the last vacancy.

[fo. 97r] **Hic incipiunt institutiones facte per reverendum in Christo patrem et dominum dominum Ricardum dei gracia Lincoln' episcopum post reditum suum in diocesim suam Lincolniensem.**

79. Institution of Robert Overton, priest, to vicarage of Thornton, vac. by res. of Robert Louershale; patron, A. and C. of St Mary, Leicester. Liddington, 17 October 1422.

80. Institution of William Rooke, priest, to church of Lutterworth, vac. by res. of M. Gilbert Kymer; patron, William de Ferrers, lord of Groby. Old Temple, 4 December 1422.

81. Institution of Thomas Halywell to church of Sileby; patron, John Mowbray, earl Marshal, earl of Nottingham and lord Segrave – and of Nicholas Gylle to church of Stow cum Quy, dioc. Ely; patron, Thomas Dengayn esquire. Exchange, by authority of commission of John [Fordham], bp of Ely (dated at Downham, 20 February 1423). Liddington, 15 February 1423.[7]

82. [fo. 97v] Institution of John Bromburgh, priest, to sixth prebend in collegiate church of St Mary, Leicester, vac. by death of John Noeburgh; patron, Queen Katherine. Ind. dean of collegiate church. Liddington, 23 February 1423.

83. Institution of Richard Barker, priest, to church of Ashby Parva, vac. by res. of William Kywe; patron, br. Henry Crounhale, lieutenant of br. William Hulles, prior of Hospitallers in England. Liddington, 2 March 1423.

84. Institution of William Bedale, priest, to second prebend in collegiate church

---

6 John Beaufo married Margaret (J. S. Roskell, Linda Clark and Carole Rawcliffe, *The History of Parliament: The House of Commons 1386–1421*, II (Stroud, 1993), 163–4). See also *VCH Leicester* v. 113.

7 The date of the commission is presumably an error.

of St Mary, Leicester, vac. by res. of William Cir; patron, Queen Katherine. Ind. dean of collegiate church. Liddington, 6 March 1423.

85. [fo. 98r] Institution of M. John Dyke *alias* Langton B.Dec. to church of Langton; patrons, Henry [Chichele], archbp of Canterbury, Henry [Beaufort], bp of Winchester, Thomas [Langley], bp of Durham, Thomas duke of Exeter, Ralph earl of Westmorland, Henry FitzHugh kt, Walter Hungerford kt, John Wodehous esquire and John Leventhorp esquire, feoffees of certain properties of the duchy of Lancaster – and collation of church of Fen Ditton, dioc. Ely, to M. John Nichole *alias* Sudbury B.Th. Exchange, by authority of commission of John [Fordham], bp of Ely (dated at Downham, 9 March 1423). Liddington, 20 March 1423.

86. Institution of William Hauberk to vicarage of Tugby; patron, A. and C. of St Mary, Croxden – and of William Heyne to church of Harston; patron, A. and C. of St Mary, Leicester. By exchange. Liddington, 31 May 1423.

[fo. 98v]

Hic incipiunt institutiones facte per honorabilem virum magistrum Robertum Leek legum doctorem ecclesie Lincolniensem canonicum reverendi in Christo patris et domini domini Ricardi dei gratia Lincolniensis episcopi in remotis agentis vicarium in spiritualibus generalem.

Quarto kalendas Maii anno domini millesimo CCCC^mo vicesimo tertio incipit annus quartus consecrationis reverendi in Christo patris et domini domini Ricardi dei gratia Lincolniensis episcopi.

87. Institution of William Byngham, priest, to church of Carlton Curlieu, vac. by res. of William Lychefeld; patron, P. and C. of Jesus of Bethlehem, Sheen. Liddington, 23 June 1423.

88. Institution of John How, priest, to vicarage of Cosby, vac. by death of John Morell; patron, A. and C. of St Mary, Leicester. Liddington, 18 June 1423.

89. Certificate of John Arundell, dean of royal chapel of St George within castle of Windsor. In accordance with a commission of the vicar-general (addressed to him jointly with M. Robert Gilbert D.Th., canon of Lincoln, and dated at Liddington, 28 May 1423), he had instituted John Tuwe, priest, in person of Henry Haunsard, chaplain, his proctor, to church of Wymondham; patron, Queen Katherine. Note that an inquiry was carried out, by which it was found that Queen Katherine was the true patron by reason of her dower. Windsor, 13 June 1423. Received 19 June 1423.

90. [fo. 99r] Institution of John Smyth, priest, to church of Ashby Parva, vac. by res. of Richard Barker; patron, br. Henry Crounhale, lieutenant of br. William Hulles, prior of Hospitallers in England. Liddington, 9 August 1423.

91. Institution of John Boteler, priest, to church of Laughton, vac. by res. of

Walter Douffe; patron, William Lovell, lord Lovel and Holand. Liddington, 15 August 1423. Note that an inquiry was carried out by M. William Aslokby, commissary-general in archdnry of Leicester, by which it was found that the advowson of Laughton belonged to William, lord Lovel and Holand, by hereditary right, and that Maud, lady Lovel and Holand (now decd) presented Walter Douffe at the last vacancy.[8]

92.   Institution of John Thymelby to vicarage of Evington; patron, A. and C. of Leicester – and of John Gynger to vicarage of Beeston, dioc. York; patron, P. and C. of Holy Trinity, Lenton. Exchange, by authority of commission of Henry [Bowet], archbp of York (dated at Cawood, 3 September 1423). Liddington, 8 September 1423.

93.   [fo. 99v] Institution of John Smyth, priest, to vicarage of Croxton Kerrial; patron, A. and C. of Croxton. Liddington, 10 September 1423.

94.   Certificate of official of archdn of Leicester. In accordance with a commission of the vicar general (dated at Liddington, 16 August 1423), he has instituted M. William Aslakby, priest, to church of Walton on the Wolds, vac. by res. of John Burton; patron, King Henry. He had first held an inquiry, by which it was found that the right of presentation belonged to the Crown for this turn, by reason of the minority of lord Beaumont, and that King Henry V presented John Burton at the last vacancy. Leicester, 27 August 1423.

95.   [fo. 100r] Certificate of William [Heyworth], bp of Coventry and Lichfield. In accordance with a commission of the vicar general (dated at Liddington, 1 October 1423), he has instituted Thomas Crull to church of Croft, vac. by res. of William Cook; patron, A. and C. of St Mary, Leicester. By exchange with vicarage of Mickleover, dioc. Coventry and Lichfield. Haywood, 7 October 1423. Received at Liddington, 11 October 1423.

96.   [fo. 100v] Institution of Nicholas Boney, priest, in person of John Boney, literate, his proctor, to church of Ashby Parva, vac. by res. of John Smyth; patron, br. Henry Crounehale, lieutenant of br. William Hulles, prior of Hospitallers in England. By exchange with vicarage of Riby. Liddington, 12 November 1423.

97.   Institution of John Hykelyng, priest, to church of Thurlaston, vac. by res. of John Smyth of Barkby; patron, John Gra kt. By exchange with church of Claycoton. Liddington, 25 October 1423. Note that an inquiry was carried out by M. William Aslakby, commissary-general in archdn of Leicester, by which it was found that the right of presentation to the church of Thurlaston belonged to Baldwin Bug (by hereditary right) and to John Gra kt (by hereditary right of his wife Joan, daughter of Roger Swylyngton kt, decd), by alternate turns, and that Edmund Bug, father of the said Baldwin Bug, presented John Smyth of Barkby at the last vacancy.

---

[8]   Maud, lady Lovel and Holand, died on 7 May 1423 and was succeeded by her grandson, William. See *Complete Peerage* viii (1932), pp. 221–2.

98.   Institution of Henry Rose, priest, to the seventh prebend in the new collegiate church of St Mary, Leicester, vac. by death of John Clyff; patron, Queen Katherine. Ind. dean of the said church. Liddington, 18 November 1423.

99.   Certificate of abbot of Owston. In accordance with a commission of the vicar general (dated at Liddington, 31 July 1423), he has held an inquiry, on 5 August in the parish church of Owston, into the election of br. William Northampton, canon of Launde, as prior of the same, having first ordered the citation, by M. William Irby B.Dec., on Sunday 1 August in the conventual church of St John Baptist, Launde, of any wishing to object. In the presence of the prior-elect and of br. Robert Stoke, proctor of the subprior and convent, he has examined the election and, finding no impediment, he has confirmed the same. Owston, 7 August 1423.

100.   [fo. 101r] Institution of M. William Bonetemps, in person of Stephen Cuton, deacon, his proctor, to church of Glenfield; patron, P. and C. of Jesus of Bethlehem, Sheen – and of M. Robert Dykes, in person of Thomas Brydwode, his proctor, to church of Wethersfield, dioc. London; patrons, Henry [Chichele], archbp of Canterbury, Henry [Beaufort], bp of Winchester, Thomas [Langley], bp of Durham, Ralph earl of Westmorland, Henry lord Fitzhugh, Walter Hungarford, John Wodehous and John Leventhorp (by reason of a feoffment to them of manors and advowsons belonging to the duchy of Lancaster). Exchange, by authority of commission of John [Kempe], bp of London (dated at London, 5 December 1423). Liddington, 10 December 1423.

101.   [fo. 101v] Institution of William Averham to vicarage of Shepshed; patron, A. and C. of St Mary, Leicester – and of William, s. Henry Watson, to church of Keyworth, dioc. York; patron, Elizabeth Barry of *Sancto Botulpho*. Exchange, by authority of commission of chapter of York, *sede vacante* (dated at York, 3 February 1423/4), the dean being *in remotis*. Liddington, 9 February 1423/4.

102.   [fo. 102r] Institution of Richard Dyngdale, priest, to vicarage of Little Dalby, vac. by res. of Robert Jors; patron, P. and C. of Langley. Liddington, 17 March 1423/4.

103.   Institution of Thomas Sutton, priest, to church of Skeffington (*Skevyngton'*), vac. by death of Thomas Tilton; patron, John Merbury of Weobley, esquire. Liddington, 24 March 1423/4. Note that an inquiry was carried out by M. William Aslakby, commissary-general in archdnry of Leicester, by which it was found that the said John Merbury was true patron by right of Agnes, lady Devereux (*Deveros*), now his wife, which Agnes presented Thomas Tilton at the last vacancy.[9]

104.   Institution of Thomas Harey, priest, to chantry in chapel of St Giles, Great Stretton, vac. by death of John Brys; patron, Robert Nevyll kt. Liddington, 17 April 1424. Note that an inquiry was carried out by M. William Aslokby,

---

[9]   The wills of John Merbury of Weobley and Agnes Devereux his wife are printed in *Reg. Spofford*, pp. 225–7.

commissary-general in archdnry of Leicester, by which it was found that the said Robert was patron for this turn by reason of a feoffment of the manor of Great Stretton, together with the advowson of the said chantry, made to him in writing by Ralph Nevyll kt, his brother, working overseas; and that the said Ralph presented John Brys at the last vacancy.

[fo. 102v]

Quarto kalendas Maii anno domini millesimo CCCC^{mo} xxiiij^{to} incipit annus quintus consecrationis reverendi in Christo patris et domini domini Ricardi dei gracia Lincolnien' episcopi.

105. Institution of William Heyne to church of Blaby; patron, A. and C. of Leicester, on nomination of William Babthorp, William Belgrave, John Fraunceys and John Marschall of Upton – and of Thomas Fraunceys to church of Rearsby; patron, John Folvyll. By exchange. Liddington, 5 May 1424.

[fo. 103r]

Duodecimo die mensis Februarii anno domini millesimo CCCC^{mo} xxiiij^{to} incipiunt institutiones expedite per honorabilem virum magistrum Robertum Leek legum doctorem officialem et commissarium in hac parte per dominum Cantuar' sufficienter deputatum sicut planius patet in simili rubrica in quaterno archidiaconatus Lincoln'.

106. Institution of Richard Stryngsale, priest, to vicarage of Eaton, vac. by res. of John Colyns; patron, A. and C. of St Mary, Leicester. Liddington, 20 April 1425.

107. Certificate of William Admoundestone B.Cn. & C.L., canon of Lichfield, official of bp's consistory of Lichfield, and vicar-general of William [Heyworth], bp of Coventry and Lichfield. In accordance with a commission of vicar-general (dated at Thame, 15 April 1425), he has instituted Robert Baron to vicarage of Tugby, vac. by res. of Thomas Flynderkyn; patron, A. and C. of Croxden. By exchange with vicarage of Leek Wootton, dioc. Coventry and Lichfield. Lichfield, 18 April 1425. Received at Liddington, 26 April 1425.

108. Institution of M. Thomas Hill, priest, to twelfth prebend in collegiate church of St Mary, Leicester, vac. by death of M. William Broune; patron, Queen Katherine. Ind. dean of collegiate church. Liddington, 19 June 1425.

109. [fo. 103v] Institution of Robert Yerburgh, priest, to vicarage of Swinford, vac. by res. of Robert Bolton; patron, br. Henry Crounhale, preceptor of Eagle and lieutenant of br. William Hulles, prior of Hospitallers in England, *in remotis*. Liddington, 29 June 1425.

[fo. 104r]

Huntyngdon' (Archdnry of Huntingdon institutions. Throughout this section, it may be assumed that each institution entry includes a mandate to induct addressed to the archdn of Huntingdon or his official, unless otherwise stated. See introductory note on editorial practice above.)

Quarto kalendas Maii anno domini millesimo CCCC^{mo} vicesimo incipit annus primus consecrationis reverendi in Christo patris et domini domini Ricardi dei gracia Lincolniensis episcopi.

110.   Institution of Thomas Mye, priest, to church of Houghton cum Wyton, vac. by res. of Thomas Balne; patron, A. and C. of Ramsey. Grantham, 6 July 1420.

Thomas Mye presbiter presentatus per abbatem et conventum monasterii Rameseye ad ecclesiam parochialem de Houghton' cum Wytton' Lincoln' diocesis per resignationem domini Thomas Balne ultimi Rectoris eiusdem in manibus domini Lincoln' episcopi factam et per ipsum admissam vacantem, ad eandem sexto die mensis Julii anno domini supradicto apud Grantham fuit admissus et Rector institutus canonice in eadem, nulla inquisitione previa quia etc. jurata canonica obediencia ut in forma communi. Scriptum fuit archidiacono Huntyngdon' seu ipsius Officiali ad inducendum eundem.

Decimo nono die mensis Maii anno domini millesimo CCCC^{mo} vicesimo incipiunt institutiones facte per venerabilem virum magistrum Johannem Southam ecclesie Lincolniensis canonicum archidiaconum Oxonie in eadem prefati reverendi in Christo patris et domini domini Ricardi dei gracia Lincolniensis episcopi extra suas civitatem et diocesim in remotis agentis vicarium in spiritualibus generalem.

111.   Institution of Walter Wylmot to church of Wood Walton; patron, A. and C. of Ramsey – and of John Jonysson to vicarage of Hoxne, dioc. Norwich; patron, bp of Norwich. Exchange, by authority of commission of John [Wakering], bp of Norwich (dated at Thorpe, 28 June 1420). Lincoln, 10 June 1420.

112.   [fo. 104v] Institution of John Vantort, priest, in person of M. John Metham, his proctor, to church of Kelshall, vac. by res. of Richard Vantort; patron, John [Fordham], bp of Ely. Lincoln, 10 July 1420.

113.   Institution of Edmund Thrapston, priest, in person of John Boton, literate, his proctor, to vicarage of Hemel Hempstead, vac. by res. of John Bateman; patron, rector and convent of Ashridge. Lincoln, 13 July 1420.

114.   Institution of Richard Heth, priest, to church of Stibbington, vac. by res. of M. William Burton; patron, A. and C. of Thorney. Lincoln, 20 July 1420.

115.   Institution of William Ryley B.Dec. to church of Hemingford Abbots, vac. by res. of John Escheton; patron, A. and C. of Ramsey. Lincoln, 10 August 1420.

[fo. 105r]

Hic incipiunt institutiones facte per reverendum in Christo patrem et dominum dominum Ricardum dei gracia Lincolniensis episcopum post accessum suum in diocesim suam Lincoln'.

116.   Institution of Thomas Broune, priest, to vicarage of Stow Longa with Spaldwick, vac. by death of Henry Clyfton; patron, John Dalton, preb. of Stow Longa in Lincoln cath. Ind. subdean and chapter of Lincoln (dean being absent). Fineshade, 12 February 1421.

117.   Institution of John Thomas, in person of William Nicoll, *domicellus*, his proctor, to church of Kings Ripton; patron, King Henry – and of Edmund Nicoll, in person of Richard Prentys, literate, his proctor, to archdnry of St David's; patron, bp of St David's. Exchange, by authority of commission of Benedict [Nicholl], bp of St David's (dated at Lamphey, 20 July 1420). Langtoft, 23 August 1420.

118.   [fo. 105v] Institution of M. Peter de Alcobasse, in person of William Bastchirch, literate, his proctor, to church of Watton at Stone; patron, Philip Botiler kt, lord of Watton – and of Richard Chaundeler to church of St Mary Woolchurch, London; patron, A. and C. of St John, Colchester. Exchange, by authority of commission of Richard [Clifford], bp of London (dated at London, 20 August 1420). Crowland, 23 August 1420.

119.   [fo. 106r] Institution of Thomas Bose, priest, to chantry of chapel of St Thomas in church of Eynesbury Hardwick (*Puttokherdwyk'*), vac. by res. of Robert Sherman; patron, Margaret, widow of Roger Trumpyngton kt. Langtoft, 12 September 1420.

120.   Institution of Adam Perys, priest, to chantry in church of St John, Huntingdon, vac. by death of Robert Ive; patron, P. and C. of Huntingdon. Langtoft, 11 October 1420.

121.   Institution of Henry Hanslape, priest, to church of Graveley, vac. by res. of William Gaunstede; patron, William Assh and Elizabeth his wife, and John Muslee and Christiana his wife. Langtoft, 14 October 1420.

122.   Institution of John Roo, priest, to church of Great Munden (*Munden' Furnevale*); patron, Walter Pejon and Margaret his wife. Langtoft, 21 October 1420.

123.   Institution of John Reve, priest, to chantry of St Mary in church of Orton Waterville, vac. by death of John Hull; patron, Roger Hunte. Langtoft, 22 October 1420.

124.   Institution of John Eston, priest, in person of William Hill, literate, his proctor, to church of Conington, vac. by res. of William Islepe; patron, M. Henry Welles clerk, William Babyngton, Richard Peveryll, Thomas Bevyll of Walton, Roger Louthe, William Paston and John Godefelowe, feoffees of Thomas Wesonhame, late lord of Conington, in the manor and advowson of Conington. By exchange with church of Kettering. Langtoft, 23 October 1420.

125.   Institution of Robert Fossard, priest, to vicarage of St Leonard, Bengeo, vac. by res. of Robert Everyngham; patron, A. and C. of Bermondsey. Fineshade, 30 October 1420.

126.   Institution of Robert Kirkeby, priest, to vicarage of Waresley, vac. by res. of John Aldham; patron, warden and fellows of Valence Marie [Pembroke] Hall, Cambridge. By exchange with vicarage of Flitton with chapel of Silsoe. Langtoft, 29 October 1420.

127.   [fo. 106v] Institution of John Bukden, priest, to church of Woolley, vac. by res. of William Rande; patron, John Laurence and Stephen Plavys, clerks. Fineshade, 20 November 1420. Note that an inquiry was carried out by M. John Garton, commissary-general in archdnries of Huntingdon and Bedford, by which it was found that John Laurence and Stephen Plavys presented for this turn as feoffees of John Styvecle, and that they presented the said William Rande at the last vacancy.

128.   Institution of Thomas Skele, priest, to vicarage of Winwick, vac. by res. of William Croxton; patron, P. and C. of Huntingdon. Huntingdon, 27 November 1420.

129.   Institution of M. Thomas Malton, priest, to church of Essendon with chapel of Bayford; patron, King Henry, by reason of his duchy of Lancaster. London, 30 November 1420.

130.   Certificate of John s. John Depyng LL.B., rector of Market Overton, reciting commission of bp (addressed to him jointly with M. John Garton, sequestrator in archdnries of Huntingdon and Bedford, and dated at Westminster, 4 December 1420) to inquire into vacancy and patronage of church of Hatfield, to which Robert Wetheryngsete had been presented by John [Fordham], bp of Ely. An inquiry had been held in full chapter in Hatfield church, attended by John Cobtoe rector of Ayot St Peter (*Mochet Ayot*),[10] John Barkworth rector of Little Berkhamsted, John Stevenes rector of Digswell, Walter Wylcok rector of Welwyn, Robert Beuchamp rector of Hertingfordbury and Roger Gobbe chaplain of Totteridge. They had stated that the church was vac. by the appointment of M. Thomas Polton, the last incumbent, as bp of Hereford; that John, bp of Ely, was patron and had presented Polton at the last vacancy; that Robert Wetheryngsete was of honest life, in priest's orders, and held one other benefice with cure, namely

---

[10] John Cobbeto of Great Bowden, instituted 31 July 1419 (Reg. 14, fo. 371r).

the archdnry of Ely. Depyng had therefore instituted Wetheryngsete, in person of Richard Pyghtesley his proctor. Hatfield, 17 December[11] 1420.

131. [fo. 107r] Institution of John Burgeys, priest, to vicarage of North Mimms; patron, P. and C. of Charterhouse, London. Westminster, 10 December 1420.

132. Institution of Thomas Chace, priest, to hospital of St John Baptist, Huntingdon, vac. by res. of John Caston; patron, Robert Pecke and John Fette, bailiffs and burgesses of the town of Huntingdon. Westminster, 13 December 1420.

133. Institution of John Heylie, priest, to vicarage of Great Gransden, vac. by res. of M. William Wymbyll; patron, master and scholars of Clare Hall, Cambridge. Westminster, 16 December 1420.

134. Institution of William Mathewe, priest, to church of King's Ripton, vac. by res. of John Thomas; patron, King Henry. Fineshade, 26 January 1421.

135. Institution of John Tesedale, priest, to vicarage of Great Staughton; patron, P. and C. of Charterhouse, London. Old Temple, 22 February 1421.

136. [fo. 107v] Institution of John Drewe, clerk, in person of M. Thomas Colstone, clerk and notary public, his proctor, to church of Therfield, vac. by death of M. William Taverham; patron, John Wodehous esquire, by grant for this turn from A. and C. of Ramsey. Wykeham, 27 April 1421.

137. Certificate of br. John Alcumbury, prior of St Ives, reciting commission of bp (dated at Langtoft, 20 September 1420, and addressed to Alcumbury and M. James Walsyngham Lic.C. & Cn.L.) to examine election of br. John Madyngley, canon of Huntingdon, as prior of the same. The examination was held in the parish church of St Ives on 23 September 1420, attended by br. Thomas Huntyngdon, canon of Huntingdon and proctor of the same in this business. Finding no impediment, Alcumbury had confirmed the election. St Ives, 23 September 1420. The official of the spiritual jurisdiction of Ramsey had attached his seal to the certificate.

[fos 107r–108r]

138. Certificate of M. John Aldewyk B.Cn. & C.L., reciting commission of bp (dated at Huntingdon, 27 November 1420, and addressed to Aldewyk and the prior of Huntingdon) to examine election of sr Anna Brynkle, nun of Hinchingbrooke, as prioress of the same. The examination was held in the parish church of St John, Huntingdon, on 4–5 December 1420, attended by John Almot, rector of the said church, as proctor of the prioress-elect and convent. Finding no

---

[11] MS 'Septembris'. Polton received the temporalities of Hereford on 9 November 1420 (see *Le Neve 1300–1541* ii. 2).

impediment, Aldewyk had confirmed the election. Huntingdon, 5 December 1420. The dean of Huntingdon had attached his seal to the certificate.

[fo. 108v] **Quarto kalendas Maii anno domini millesimo CCCC^mo vicesimo primo incipit annus secundus consecrationis reverendi in Christo patris et domini domini Ricardi Flemmyng dei gracia Lincolniensis episcopi.**

139. Institution of Thomas Pygott, priest, in person of Thomas Tyntachell, literate, his proctor, to vicarage of Fenstanton, vac. by death of Henry Rosyngton; patron, D. and C. of royal free chapel of St Stephen, Westminster. Buckden, 6 July 1421.

140. Institution of William Basse of Hitchin, priest, to vicarage of Ippollitts (*Dynesley*), vac. by res. of William Colyns; patron, A. and C. of Elstow. Buckden, 28 July 1421.

141. Institution of Stephen Noble to church of Therfield; patron, A. and C. of Ramsey – and of John Drewe to church of Northwold, dioc. Norwich; patron, John [Fordham], bp of Ely. Exchange, by authority of commission of John [Wakering], bp of Norwich (dated at Thorpe, 9 September 1421). Sleaford, 13 September 1421.

142. [fo. 109r] Institution of Robert Stok, priest, to church of Caldecote; patron, Joan, countess of Kent. Sleaford, 24 September 1421.

143. Institution of John Hull, priest, to vicarage of Waresley, vac. by res. of Robert Kyrkeby; patron, master and fellows of Valence Marie [Pembroke] Hall, Cambridge. Sleaford, 5 October 1421.

144. Institution of William Taillour, priest, to vicarage of Stagsden, vac. by res. of John Normanton; patron, P. and C. of Newnham. Leicester, 12 October 1421. Ind. archdn of Huntingdon.[12]

145. Certificate of institution, by Reginald Kentwode, Official of London *sede vacante*, of Thomas Aldesworth to vicarage of Great Paxton, vac. by res. of John Bees of Pinchbeck; patron, subdean and chapter of Lincoln (the dean being absent). Exchange by authority of commission of bp of Lincoln (dated at Whiston, 31 October 1421), with church of East Horndon, dioc. London. London, 4 November 1421. Received at Old Temple, 2 December 1421.

[fo. 109v]

146. Institution of John Malberthorp, priest, in person of John Hoggesthorp, clerk, his proctor, to church of Denton; patron, Nicholas [Bubwith], bp of Bath and Wells, by custody of the lands and tenements of Thomas Greneham, son and

[12] Presumably an error; Stagsden was in the archdnry of Bedford.

heir of William Greneham decd, and Ralph Joce. Canons Ashby, 6 November 1421.

147. Institution of William Felys to church of St Nicholas, Hertford; patron, King Henry – and of John Whytyng, in person of John Swerston, his proctor, to vicarage of Morden, dioc. Winchester; patron, A. and C. of Westminster. Exchange, by authority of commission of Henry [Beaufort], bp of Winchester (dated at Southwark, 8 November 1421). Old Temple, 4 December 1421.

148. [fo. 110r] Institution of Peter Aumner, clerk, to church of St Mary, Baldock; patron, King Henry. London, 4 December 1421.

149. Institution of John Wardele, priest, to church of Clothall; patron, Robert Hoke, citizen and grocer of Lincoln. London, 8 December 1421.

150. Institution of Roger Byrne, clerk, to church of Sacombe; patron, Robert Babthorp, kt. London, 12 December 1421.

151. Institution of Walter Cheyle, priest, to vicarage of Great Wymondley, vac. by res. of William Colwyk; patron, A. and C. of Elstow. Wymondley, 21 December 1421.

152. Institution of William de Rasyn, priest, to church of St Mary, Hertford; patron, A. and C. of Holy Cross, Waltham. Buckden, 27 December 1421.

153. Institution of Simon Dallyng B.Cn & C.L. to church of Broughton; patron, A. and C. of Ramsey. Dunstable, 15 January 1421/2.

154. Institution of William Haldenby, priest, to church of Botolph Bridge, vac. by death of last rector; patron, br. Henry Crounehale, lieutenant of br. William Hulles, prior of Hospitallers in England. Elstow, 17 January 1421/2.

155. Certificate of institution, by Simon Northewe, canon of Chichester and vicar-general of John [Kempe], bp of Chichester, of William Buckyngham to church of Catworth, vac. by res. of John Buckyngham; patron, Thomas Bekeryng, esquire. Exchange with church of St Thomas, Winchelsea, dioc. Chichester, by authority of commission of bp of Lincoln (dated at Caldwell Priory, 18 January 1421/2). Chichester, 2 February 1421/2. Received at London, 7 February 1421/2.

156. [fo. 110v] Institution of Robert Vyntefer, priest, to church of St Andrew, Huntingdon, vac. by res. of Stephen Monynden; patron, A. and C. of Ramsey. Huntingdon, 13 February 1421/2.

157. Institution of Giles Chaunceys, priest, to church of Conington, vac. by death of John Eston; patron, John Colepepyr, esquire. Liddington, 14 March 1421/2. Note that an inquiry was carried out by M. Stephen Monynden, commissary-general in archdnries of Huntingdon and Bedford, by which it was found that John Colepepyr was the true patron for this turn, that the advowson belonged to him on alternate turns by hereditary right, and that Thomas Wesenham, lord of the manor of Conington, presented at the last vacancy.

158.   Institution of William Crosse, priest, in person of John Screche esquire, his proctor, to church of Alwalton, vac. by res. of Alan Kyrketon; patron, A. and C. of Peterborough. Liddington, 20 March 1421/2.

159.   Institution of William Martyn B.A. to vicarage of Everton, vac. by death of Thomas Stokkyng; patron, P. and C. of St Neots. Liddington, 28 March 1422.

160.   Institution of Richard Lyng, priest, to vicarage of prebendal church of Leighton Bromswold, vac. by res. of Walter Claver; patron, M. Richard Leyot, preb. of Leighton Ecclesia in Lincoln cath. Liddington, 27 March 1422. Ind. D. and C. of Lincoln.

[fo. 111r] **Quarto kalendas Maii anno domini millesimo CCCC^mo vicesimo secundo incipit annus tertius consecrationis reverendi in Christo patris et domini domini Ricardi dei gracia Lincoln' episcopi.**

161.   Institution of John Buckeworth, priest, to church of Washingley, vac. by res. of William Bonage; patron, Joan Wassyngle. Liddington, 14 May 1422. Note that an inquiry was carried out by M. Stephen Monynden, commissary-general in archdnries of Huntingdon and Bedford, by which it was found that the said Joan Wassyngle was the true patron, by reason of a feoffment of a croft in Washingley with the advowson of the said church, and that the Chancellor of King Edward II last presented to the same.[13]

162.   Institution of Nicholas Northgate, priest, to church of Caldecote, vac. by res. of Robert Stocke; patron, Joan, countess of Kent, lady Wake. Liddington, 29 May 1422.

Hic incipiunt institutiones facte per honorabilem virum magistrum Robertum Leek legum doctorem ecclesie Lincoln' canonicum reverendi in Christo patris et domini domini Ricardi dei gracia Lincolnien' episcopi in remotis agentis vicarium in spiritualibus generalem.

163.   Certificate of M. John Depyng LL.B., reciting commission of vicar-general (dated at Liddington, 8 May 1422) to inquire into vacancy and patronage of church of Warboys, to which M. John Nowell had been presented by A. and C. of Ramsey. An inquiry had been held in full chapter in Warboys church, by which it was found that the church was vac. by res. of John Langevyll, made by reason of his great age, loss of sight (*carencia visus*) and his absence from this cure through his continual residence in the college of Windsor, of which he was a canon. It was also

---

[13] The institution of William Bonage is not recorded in the Lincoln registers. It must have taken place after the institution of William de Fodrynggeye in 1372 [Reg. 10, fo. 304r] and the patron was presumably the Chancellor of King Edward III or King Richard II.

found that M. John Nowell was of good fame, in priest's orders, and held no more than one other benefice (namely the church of Stanwick, dioc. Lincoln). Depyng had therefore accepted the resignation of Langevyll and instituted Nowell, in person of Ralph Benyngton, clerk, his proctor. Warboys, 12 May 1422.

164. [fo. 111v] Institution of Hugh Wowet, priest, to church of Ayot St Lawrence, vac. by death of M. Stephen Brake; patron, King Henry. Liddington, 22 July 1422. Note that an inquiry was held by M. Stephen Monynden, commissary-general in archdnries of Huntingdon and Bedford, by which it was found that the King was true patron for this turn by reason of his guardianship of John Barr, s. Thomas Barre kt, decd, and that the said Thomas Barr kt presented at the last vacancy.

165. [fo. 112r] Institution of Thomas Cook, priest, to church of Steeple Gidding; patron, A. and C. of Ramsey. Liddington, 29 November 1422.

Hic incipiunt institutiones facte per reverendum in Christo patrem et dominum dominum Ricardum dei gracia Lincolnien' episcopum post reditum suum in Angliam et diocesim suam Lincolnien'.

166. Institution of Richard Baker, priest, to perpetual chantry of St Mary the Virgin in church of St John Baptist, Huntingdon, vac. by res. of Adam Pers; patron, P. and C. of Huntingdon. Liddington, 30 October 1422.

167. Institution of Thomas Greveley, clerk, to church of Stibbington, vac. by res. of M. Richard Hethe; patron, A. and C. of Thorney. Old Temple, 7 November 1422.

168. Institution of Edmund Nicoll, in person of William Mathu, chaplain, his proctor, to church of Hemingford Abbots; patron, A. and C. of Ramsey – and collation of archdnry of St David's to M. William Ryley. Exchange, by authority of commission of Benedict [Nichols], bp of St David's (dated at London '*in hospicio nostro*', 12 November 1422). Old Temple, 24 November 1422.

169. [fo. 112v] Collation, by authority of William [Barrow], bp of Bangor (dated at London '*in hospicio nostro*', 22 November 1422) to M. William Ryley of prebend in Bangor cath., which Thomas Knyght lately held, vac. by res. of Edmund Nicoll. By exchange with church of Hemingford Abbots. Old Temple, 24 November 1422.

170. [fo. 113r] Institution of John Baldok, priest, to vicarage of Hemel Hempstead, vac. by res. of Edmund Thrapston; patron, rector and convent of Ashridge. Old Temple, 8 December 1422.

171. Institution of Thomas Upton, priest, to church of Folksworth, vac. by res. of John Crowlee; patron, A. and C. of Crowland. Liddington, 12 February 1422/3.

Quarto kalendas Maii anno domini millesimo CCCC^mo vicesimo tertio incipit annus quartus consecrationis reverendi in Christo patris et domini domini Ricardi dei gracia Lincoln' episcopi.

[fo. 113v] **Hic incipiunt institutiones facte per honorabilem virum magistrum Robertum Leek legum doctorem ecclesie Lincolnien' canonicum reverendi in Christo patris et domini domini Ricardi dei gracia Lincolnien' episcopi in remotis agentis vicarium in spiritualibus generalem.**

172.   Institution of John Walyngton, priest, to church of Baldock; patron, King Henry. Liddington, 5 May 1423.

173.   Institution of Richard Henris to church of Wood Walton; patron, A. and C. of Ramsey – and of Walter Wylmott to church of Fulmodestone with chapel of Croxton annexed, dioc. Norwich; patron, P. and C. of Castle Acre. Exchange, by authority of commission of John [Wakering], bp of Norwich (dated at Norwich, 20 May 1423). Liddington, 29 May 1423.

174.   [fo. 114r] Institution of John Becclys, clerk, to church of Stanton Harcourt [Oxon.], vac. by res. of John Play; patron, A. and C. of Reading. Ind. archdn of Huntingdon.[14] Thame, 11 June 1423.

175.   Institution of John Crane, priest, to church of Little Gidding, vac. by death of John Longe; patron, br. Henry Crounehale, lieutenant of prior of Hospitallers in England. Liddington, 16 June 1423.

176.   Certificate of institution, by subdean and chapter of Lincoln (the dean being absent), of Henry Bilburgh to church of Coppingford, vac. by res. of William Suplet; patron, Thomas Bevyle, lord of Wood Walton, and John Colles of Huntingdon. Exchange with chantry of John Buckyngham, sometime bp of Lincoln, in Lincoln cath, by authority of commission of vicar-general (dated at Liddington, 2 August 1423). Lincoln, 6 August 1423. Received at Liddington, 7 August 1423.

177.   Certificate of institution, by John, prior of St Albans, commissary-general of John [Wheathampstead], abbot of the same, *in remotis*, of Robert Barowe to vicarage of Great Paxton, vac. by res. of Thomas Allesworth; patron, subdean and chapter of Lincoln (the dean being absent). Exchange with vicarage of Newnham, dioc. Lincoln and jurisdiction of St Albans, by authority of commission of vicar-general (dated at Liddington, 12 August 1423). St Albans, 16 August 1423. Received at Liddington, 25 August 1423.

178.   [fo. 114v] Institution of Robert Wetheryngsete, priest, in person of M. John Depyng his proctor, to church of Somersham, vac. by death of M. Walter Cook; patron, John [Fordham], bp of Ely. Liddington, 12 September 1423.

---

14 Presumably an error for 'Oxford'.

179. Institution of John Horley, priest, to chantry of Colney, vac. by res. of John Tryll; patron, Thomas Pulteney esquire, John Frey recorder of London, William Buson and Edward Bybworth esquires. By exchange with church of Little Kimble. Liddington, 7 October 1423. Note that an inquiry was carried out by M. Stephen Monynden, commissary-general in archdnries of Huntingdon and Bedford, by which it was found that the presenters were true patrons by reason of a feoffment made to them by John Pulteney kt, and that the said John Pulteney kt presented John Tryll at the last vacancy.

180. Institution of Thomas Stodele, priest, to vicarage of Great Stukeley, vac. by death of Richard Thernyng; patron, P. and C. of Huntingdon. Liddington, 15 October 1423.

181. Institution of Thomas Bekyngton LL.D., priest, to church of Hatfield, vac. by res. of M. Robert Wetheryngsete; patron, John [Fordham], bp of Ely. Old Temple, 22 October 1423.

182. [fo. 115r] Institution of Simon Dullyng, priest, to church of Holywell, vac. by res. of Thomas Pulter; patron, A. and C. of Ramsey. Liddington, 28 November 1423.

183. Institution of John Clampayn, priest, to church of St Andrew, Hertford; patron, Queen Katherine. Liddington, 3 December 1423.

184. Institution of Peter Alcobasse, in person of William Bassechyrche literate, his proctor, to church of Datchworth; patron, Anne, lady Morley – and of John Hogge to church of Watton at Stone; patron, King Henry, by reason of the minority of Philip, son and heir of Philip Boteler kt, decd, who held of the king in chief. By exchange. Liddington, 6 December 1423.

185. Institution of Walter Barbur, in person of John Pakell, literate, the substitute of John Herde his original proctor, to vicarage of St John Evangelist, Hertford; patron, P. and C. of St Mary, Hertford – and of Thomas Smyth to vicarage of St Michael, Marden, dioc. Canterbury; patron, A. and C. of Lesnes. Exchange, by authority of commission of Henry [Chichele], archbp of Canterbury (dated at Lambeth, 24 November 1423). Liddington, 9 December 1423.

186. [fo. 115v] Institution of Robert Sutton, clerk, in person of William Kyrkeby, clerk, the substitute of M. William Hoper LL.D. his original proctor, to church of Broughton, vac. by res. of M. Simon Dallyng; patron, A. and C. of Ramsey. Liddington, 17 January 1423/4.

187. Institution of John Tailliour, priest, to vicarage of Rushden, vac. by res. of George Tailliour; patron, subdean and chapter of Lincoln (the dean being absent). Liddington, 20 January 1423/4.

188. Institution of William Toly, in person of M. Robert Somersete, clerk, his proctor, to wardenship of free chapel of St Mary, Watton at Stone; patron, William Phelipp, kt – and of Thomas Ryby to church of Boxwell, dioc. Worcester; patron,

A. and C. of St Peter, Gloucester. Exchange, by authority of commission of Philip [Morgan], bp of Worcester (dated at London, 29 January 1423/4). Liddington, 6 February 1423/4.

189. [fo. 116r] Institution of John Wyltonherst, priest, to church of Steeple Gidding, vac. by res. of Thomas Cook; patron, A. and C. of Ramsey. By exchange with church of Wing. Liddington, 7 February 1423/4.

190. Institution of Richard Edows, priest, to church of Offord Darcy, vac. by death of Henry Brytt; patron, John Harpeden kt. Liddington, 1 February 1423/4. Note that an inquiry was carried out by M. Stephen Monenden, commissary-general in archdnries of Huntingdon and Bedford, by which it was found that John Harpeden kt, lord Cobham, had the right of presentation for this turn, and that Hugh Lotrell kt, Peter le Pole and William Spenser presented Henry Brytt at the last vacancy.

191. Institution of John Whitchyrche, priest, to church of Datchworth, vac. by res. of M. Peter Alcobasse; patron, Ann, lady Morley. Liddington, 17 March 1423/4.

192. Institution of John Thomson, priest, in person of Richard Barton literate, his proctor, to chantry at the altar of St Anne in church of Hatfield, vac. by res. of Roger Gube; patron, Robert de Luda. Liddington, 31 March 1424. Note that an inquiry was carried out by M. Stephen Monenden, commissary-general in archdnries of Huntingdon and Bedford, by which it was found that the said Robert was the true patron by hereditary right, and that he presented at the last vacancy.

[fo. 116v] **Quarto kalendas Maii anno domini millesimo CCCC^{mo} xxiiij^{to} incipit annus quintus consecrationis reverendi in Christo patris et domini domini Ricardi dei gracia Lincolnien' episcopi.**

193. Institution of Richard Wellys, priest, in person of William Grenelane clerk, the substitute of John Turvey clerk his original proctor, to church of Flamstead, vac. by res. of M. William Blakamore; patron, Richard de Beauchamp, earl of Warwick. By exchange with church of Potterspury. Liddington, 8 May 1424.

194. Institution of Hugh Beuerych, priest, to vicarage of Abbotsley, vac. by res. of M. William Wyllesthorp; patron, master and fellows of Balliol College, Oxford. Liddington, 25 May 1424.

[fo. 117r] **Duodecimo die mensis Februarii anno domini millesimo CCCC^{mo} xxiiij^{to} incipit institutiones expedite per honorabilem virum magistrum Robertum Leek legum doctorem officialem consistorii Linc' ac commissarium per dominum Cantuarien' in hac parte sufficienter deputatum ut planius patet in simili rubrica in quaterno archidiaconatus Lincoln'.**

195. Institution of Thomas Tayllour, priest, to church of Caldecote, vac. by death of William Maxey; patron, abbot of St Albans. Liddington, 12 March 1424/5.

196. Memorandum of commission to official of archdn of Huntingdon to inquire into vacancy of vicarage of St John, Hertford, and the merits of John Nicoll, presented to the same by P. and C. of St Mary, Hertford, and to institute him if nothing hinders. Liddington, 14 March 1424/5.

197. Institution of John Chaumberleyn, priest, to vicarage of Great Paxton; patron, subdean and chapter of Lincoln (the dean being absent). Liddington, 23 March 1424/5.

198. Institution of John Bailly, priest, in person of Richard Pyghtesley clerk, his proctor, to church of St Andrew, Huntingdon, vac. by res. of Robert Vynter; patron, A. and C. of Ramsey. Liddington, 29 March 1425.

199. Institution of John Tychemersh, priest, in person of John Ward literate, his proctor, to church of Broughton, vac. by res. of Thomas Pulter; patron, A. and C. of Ramsey. Liddington, 19 April 1425.

200. Institution of William Malberthorp, priest, in person of William Port literate, his proctor, to church of Denton, vac. by res. of John Malberthorp; patron, Thomas Grenham, *domicellus*. Liddington, 28 April 1425.

201. Certificate of M. Stephen Monynden, commissary-general in archdnries of Bedford and Huntingdon, reciting commission of M. Robert Leek, official and archbp's commissary (dated at Liddington, 15 March 1424/5) to inquire into vacancy and patronage of church of Yelling, to which John Dally, bp *Stephanensis*, had been presented by P. and C. of Merton. An inquiry had been held, attended by Edmund Hungerford rector of Offord Cluny, Richard Edhos rector of Offord Darcy, John Almot rector of St John Huntingdon, Thomas Blakebourne rector of St Benedict Huntingdon, William Ade vicar of Godmanchester and John Wadenho vicar of Hemingford Grey, by which it was found that the church was vac. by the death of John Penreth, the last rector, at Yelling on 10 March 1424/5. Finding no impediment, Monynden had therefore instituted Dally. Huntingdon, 20 March 1424/5.

202. [fo. 117v] Memorandum of commission to prior of Huntingdon, M. Stephen Wilton D.Dec., and M. Stephen Monynden, commissary-general, to inquire into vacancy of church of Abbots Ripton and if expedient to admit Thomas Pulter, presented by A. and C. of Ramsey, to the same. Liddington, 3 April 1425.

203. Institution of John Wright, priest, to church of Denton, vac. by res. of William Malberthorp; patron, Thomas Grenham, *domicellus*. Liddington, 29 June 1425.

[fos 118 and 119 have been excised.]

[fo. 120r]

Bedford (Archdnry of Bedford institutions. Throughout this section, it may be assumed that each institution entry includes a mandate to induct addressed to the archdn of Bedford or his official, unless otherwise stated. See introductory note on editorial practice above.)

Quarto kalendas Maii anno domini millesimo CCCC^{mo} vicesimo incipit annus primus consecrationis reverendi in Christo patris et domini domini Ricardi Flemmyng' dei gracia Lincolnien' episcopi.

Vicesimo nono die mensis Maii anno domini millesimo CCCC^{mo} vicesimo incipiunt institutiones facte per honorabilem virum magistrum Johannem Southam in legibus licentiatum ecclesie Lincoln' canonicum archidiaconum Oxon' in eadem reverendi in Christo patris et domini domini Ricardi Flemmyng' dei gracia Lincoln' episcopi in remotis agentis vicarium in spiritualibus generalem.

204. Institution of Robert Horewode, priest, in person of John Marom literate, his proctor, to vicarage of prebendal church of Leighton Buzzard, vac. by death of Thomas Wykys; patron, M. Thomas Walton, preb. of Leighton Buzzard in Lincoln cath. Ind. D. and C. of Lincoln. Lincoln, 5 June 1420.

Robertus Horewode presbiter presentatus per magistrum Thomam Walton' ecclesie Lincoln' canonicum ac prebendarium prebende de Leghton' Bozard' in eadem ad vicariam perpetuam ecclesie prebendalis de Leghton' predictam per mortem domini Thome Wykys ultimi vicarii eiusdem vacantem, ad eandem quinto die mensis Junii anno domini supradicto apud Lincoln' fuit admissus et vicarius perpetuus secundum formam constitutionum legatinarum in hac parte editarum juratus institutus canonice in eadem in personam Johannis Marom' literati procuratoris sui sufficienter in hac parte constituti, nulla inquisitione previa quia etc. jurata canonica obediencia ut in forma consueta. Scriptum fuit decano et capitulo ecclesie Lincoln' ad inducendum.

205. Institution of Richard Sampton to vicarage of Felmersham; patron, warden and fellows of King's Hall, Cambridge – and of John Stokes to portion of St Mary in church of Toddington; patron, Thomas Peyure. By exchange. Lincoln, 20 June 1420.

206. Institution of William Clerk, priest, to church of Aspley Guise, vac. by death of Nicholas Fulburn; patron, P. and C. of Newnham. Note that an inquiry was held by M. John Newerk, commissary-general in archdnries of Huntingdon and Bedford, by which it was found that the prior and convent were true patrons and presented at the last vacancy. Lincoln, 14 July 1420.

207. Institution of John Halby, priest, to church of Turvey, vac. by death of M. John Caundyssh; patron, P. and C. of St Neots. Lincoln, 19 July 1420.

208. Institution of John Myryell, priest, to chantry in the parish church of Sandy, vac. by death of Thomas Penreth; patron, King Henry. Lincoln, 20 June 1420. Note that an inquiry was first held by official of archdn of Bedford, by which it was found that King Henry was patron for this turn by reason of the minority of John Barnak, heir of the lord of Sandy, and that the archbp of Canterbury presented by lapse at the last vacancy.

209. [fo. 120v] Institution of br. Thomas Burre, canon of Dunstable, priest, in person of Thomas Blounham his proctor, to vicarage of Flitwick, vac. by res. of br. Roger Stevenache; patron, P. and C. of Dunstable. Lincoln, 13 August 1420. Note that an inquiry was first held by M. John Newerk, commissary-general in archdnries of Huntingdon and Bedford, by which it was found that the P. and C. were true patrons and held a spiritual privilege to present one of their canons to the vicarage.

Hic incipiunt institutiones facte per reverendum in Christo patrem et dominum dominum Ricardum dei gracia Lincolnien' episcopum post accessum suum in diocesim suam Lincolnien'.

210. Institution of Laurence atte Wode, priest, in person of Gilbert Smyth his proctor, to vicarage of Renhold, vac. by death of William Stoghton; patron, P. and C. of Newnham. Langtoft, 8 October 1420.

211. Certificate of institution, by Thomas More dean and chapter of St Paul's, London, of William Acastre to church of Astwick, vac. by res. of William Smyth; patron, P. and C. of Chicksands. Exchange with vicarage of Albury, dioc. London, by authority of commission of bp of Lincoln (dated at Langtoft, 10 October 1420). Chapter house of St Paul's, 15 October 1420. Received at Langtoft, 19 October 1420.

212. [fo. 121r] Institution of John Aldham, priest, to vicarage of Flitton with chapel of Silsoe, vac. by res. of Robert Kyrkeby; patron, A. and C. of Elstow. By exchange with vicarage of Waresley. Langtoft, 29 October 1420.

213. Institution of Henry Syreston, clerk, to church of Marston Moretaine, vac. by death of Walter Pappele; patron, Elizabeth Morteyn. Fineshade, 3 November 1420.

214. Institution of Richard Valdryan, priest, to church of Colmworth; patron, Gerard Braybrok kt. Fotheringhay, 31 October 1420.

215. Institution of John Clardon, priest, to vicarage of Willington, vac. by death of Bartholomew Holygoste; patron, P. and C. of Newnham. Fineshade, 31 December 1420.

216. Certificate of Thomas Hore B.Dec. In accordance with bp's commission (dated at Langtoft, 13 October 1420), he has held an inquiry into the election of br. Thomas Bole, canon of the priory of SS John Baptist and John Evangelist, Caldwell, as prior of the same. Finding no impediment, he has confirmed the election at the petition of br. Thomas Beckeford, canon of Caldwell and proctor of the subprior and convent of the same. Instal. official of archdn. Caldwell Priory, 20 October 1420.

217. [fo. 121v] Institution of Richard Kellowe, priest, to church of Tilbrook, vac. by res. of M. Thomas Malton; patron, King Henry. London, 1 December 1420.

218. Institution of Richard Camelyn to church of Tingewick; patron, warden and fellows of New College, Oxford – and of M. John Grene B.Th. to vicarage of Dorking, dioc. Winchester; patron, P. and C. of Reigate. Exchange, by authority of commission of Henry [Beaufort], bp of Winchester (dated at manor of Southwark, 7 December 1420). London (*in hospitio nostro iuxta Westm'*), 8 December 1420.

219. [fo. 122r] Institution of John Drake to vicarage of Sundon; patron, P. and C. of Holy Trinity of *Bosco*, Markyate – and of Richard Julyan to vicarage of Caldecote, dioc. Ely; patron, P. and C. of Barnwell. Exchange, by authority of commission of John [Fordham], bp of Ely (dated at his manor of Somersham, 10 December 1420). London ('*in hospitio nostro iuxta Westm'* '), 10 December 1420.

220. [fo. 122v] Institution of Robert Lety, priest, to vicarage of Caddington, vac. by res. of William Stretle; patron, M. Walter Cook, clerk, perpetual farmer of church of Caddington. Old Temple, 16 February 1420/1.

221. Institution of John Aylyff, priest, to church of Wrestlingworth, vac. by death of Robert Tymworth; patron, P. and C. of Newnham. London, 16 February 1420/1.

222. Institution of John Beauchamp, priest, to vicarage of Sharnbrook, vac. by res. of John Waterson; patron, A. and C. of Leicester. Wykeham, 26 March 1421.

Quarto kalendas Maii anno domini millesimo CCCC^{mo} vicesimo primo incipit annus secundus consecrationis reverendi in Christo patris et domini domini Ricardi dei gracia Lincolnien' episcopi.

223. Institution of John Broune, priest, to church of Sutton, vac. by res. of John Crouche; patron, King Henry. London, 8 May 1421.

224. Institution of William Hendysson, priest, in person of John Russell clerk, his proctor, to church of Farndish, vac. by res. of William Talbot; patron, John Reynes of Clifton kt, Peter Hynwyk and William Campyon clerks, and John Everton, feoffees in all lands and tenements formerly held by Eleanor, late wife of John Tyryngham esquire decd. By exchange with church of St Giles, Northampton. London, 9 May 1421.

225. [fo. 123r] Institution of Robert Calyser, priest, in person of Gilbert Smyth priest, his proctor, to vicarage of Willington, vac. by res. of John Clardon; patron, P. and C. of Newnham. London, 16 May 1421.

226.   Institution of Roger Dryver, priest, to vicarage of Segenhoe, vac. by death of William Dylney; patron, P. and C. of Dunstable. London, 24 May 1421.

227.   Institution of John Wynslowe, priest, to vicarage of Great Barford, vac. by death of John Baldywell; patron, P. and C. of Newnham. London, 27 May 1421.

228.   Institution of Laurence Stafford, clerk, to church of Tilbrook, vac. by res. of Richard Kellowe; patron, King Henry. London, 29 May 1421.

229.   Institution of Thomas Wryght, priest, to vicarage of Clophill; patron, P. and C. of Beaulieu. Buckden, 7 June 1421.

230.   Institution of John Wryght to vicarage of Goldington; patron, P. and C. of Newnham – and of John Brotherton to vicarage of Ravensden; patron, P. and C. of Newnham. By exchange. Buckden, 20 June 1421.

231.   Institution of Richard Pabenham, priest, to vicarage of Stotfold, vac. by res. of Richard Brodred; patron, P. and C. of Chicksands. By exchange with canonry in collegiate church of Irthlingborough. Buckden, 5 July 1421.

232.   Institution of William Lymyngton to church of Wymington; patron, Thomas Bronneflete kt – and of William Weston to church of Warmwell, dioc. Salisbury; patron, Nicholas Coker esquire. Exchange, by authority of commission of John [Chaundler], bp of Salisbury (dated at Ramsbury, 8 April 1421). Buckden, 16 July 1421. Certificate dated at Buckden, 11 July 1421.[15]

233.   [fo. 123v] Institution of William Burnell, priest, to church of All Saints, Bedford, vac. by res. of John Malcote; patron, P. and C. of Newnham. Buckden, 16 July 1421.

234.   Institution of William Collys, priest, in person of Gilbert Smyth his proctor, to vicarage of Salford, vac. by res. of Walter Cheyle; patron, P. and C. of Newnham. Buckden, 5 August 1421.

235.   Institution of M. Richard Heth, priest, to church of Shillington; patron, M. William Lassels, clerk. Old Temple, 15 December 1421.

236.   Certificate of institution, by Reginald Kentwode, Official of London *sede vacante*, of Richard Raufe to portion at altar of St Mary in church of Toddington, vac. by res. of John Stokes; patron, Thomas Peyver, esquire. Exchange, by authority of commission of bp of Lincoln (dated at Old Temple, 12 December 1421), with church of Shellow Bowells, dioc. London. London, 13 December 1421. Received at London, 16 December 1421.

---

[15] The surname of William Lymyngton is variously given as Lymyngton or Wymyngton. For his previous institution to Warmwell, see *Reg. Hallum*, p. 70. The date of the certificate is presumably an error.

237. [fo. 123ᵃr] Institution of Stephen Monynden, priest, to church of Astwick, vac. by res. of William Acastre; patron, P. and C. of Chicksands. Hitchin, 22 December 1421.

238. Institution of Thomas Pellycan to church of Wilden; patron, Richard Archer, esquire – and collation to Thomas Gyles of church of Bromley, dioc. Rochester. Exchange, by authority of commission of Henry [Chichele], archbp of Canterbury, exercising spiritual jurisdiction of bp of Rochester *sede vacante* (dated at Lambeth, 6 December 1421). Buckden, 3 January 1421/2.[16]

239. [fo. 123ᵃv] Institution of Robert Hyne, priest, to church of Chellington, vac. by res. of John Hyne; patron, William Bozum, John Goldyngton and John Hyne chaplain. Bletsoe, 8 January 1421/2.

240. Collation of chantry next to bridge of Biddenham, vac. by res. of John Coke. Newnham, 19 January 1421/2.[17]

241. Institution of Robert Wysebeche, priest, to vicarage of Salford, vac. by res. of John Collys;[18] patron, P. and C. of Newnham. Old Temple, 21 February 1421/2.

242. Institution of John Tymkas, priest, to vicarage of Podington, vac. by res. of William Mayewe; patron, P. and C. of Canons Ashby. Old Temple, 21 February 1421/2.

243. Certificate of Thomas Hore B.Dec. In accordance with bp's commission (dated at Old Temple, 4 February 1421/2), he has examined the resignation of William Pychelesthorn, vicar of Eaton Socon, made on the grounds of age and bodily weakness. Finding no impediment, he has admitted William's resignation and has instituted Richard Couper of *Rothele*, chaplain; patron, br. Henry Crounhale, preceptor of Eagle and lieutenant of br. William Hulles, prior of Hospitallers in England, *in remotis*. He has also assigned a suitable annual portion of the fruits of the vicarage as a pension for the retiring incumbent during his life. Bedford, 28 February 1421/2.

244. [fo. 124r] Certificate of M. Stephen Monynden, commissary-general in archdnries of Huntingdon and Bedford. In accordance with bp's commission (dated at Huntingdon, 21 February 1421/2), he has held an inquiry into the vacancy of the church of Tempsford, and the presentation, by William Trystour, citizen and cellarer of London, of Thomas Bole to the same. The inquiry found that the church became vac. at Tempsford, on the Sunday before the feast of SS Fabian and Sebastian [18 January], by the death of Edmund the last incumbent;

---

16 Thomas Gyles is also described as canon of St Asaph and preb. of Portio David (Llanfair, Second Comportion) in the same. Although this benefice is not mentioned in the actual exchange, Thomas Pellycan was holding it by 1427. See *CPL* VII (1417–1431), p. 496.

17 The name of the new chaplain is not given.

18 Collys's forename was given as William at his institution: see no 234 above.

that the said William Trystour was the true patron by reason of a certain glebe lying in the fields of *Crandouerfeld'* in *le dychefurlong'* in the parish of Tempsford, which he acquired together with the advowson by charter and livery of seisin; that Henry Pomfrett, citizen of London, presented the said Edmund at the last vacancy; that the said Thomas Bole is of good fame, in priest's orders, and is not beneficed elsewhere. He has therefore instituted Thomas to the church. Tempsford, 4 March 1421/2.

245. [fo. 124v] Institution of John Throbber, priest, to vicarage of Oakley, vac. by res. of John Forster; patron, P. and C. of Caldwell. By exchange with vicarage of Little Houghton. Liddington, 30 July 1422.

246. Institution of William Edenham, late monk of Vaudey, to vicarage of Flitton with chapel of Silsoe, vac. by res. of John Aldham; patron, A. and C. of Elstow. By exchange with vicarage of Southwick. Liddington, 24 September 1422.

Quarto kalendas Maii anno domini millesimo CCCC^{mo} vicesimo secundo incipit annus tertius consecrationis reverendi in Christo patris et domini domini Ricardi dei gracia Lincoln' episcopi.

247. Institution of M. John Blome alias Therford to church of Higham Gobion; patron, P. and C. of Markyate – and of Alexander Denny alias Smyth to vicarage of Finchingfield, dioc. London; patron, P. and C. of St Mary, Thetford. Exchange, by authority of commission of David Pryce, canon of Lincoln and vicar-general of John [Kempe], bp of London, *in remotis* (dated at London, 18 September 1422). Liddington, 21 September 1422.[19]

248. [fo. 125r] Institution of Aunger Tymberland to church of Stondon; patron, P. and C. of Merton – and collation to John Syward of vicarage of North Weald, dioc. London. Exchange, by authority of commission of John [Kempe], bp of London (dated at London, 30 January 1422/3). Liddington, 6 February 1422/3.

249. [fo. 125v] Institution of John Lee to portion of chapel of St Mary in church of Toddington; patron, Thomas Pevyr, esquire – and of Richard Rauff to church of Ibberton, dioc. Salisbury; patron, King Henry. Exchange, by authority of commission of John [Chaundler], bp of Salisbury (dated at Potterne, 5 March 1420/1). Old Temple, 9 March 1422/3.[20]

250. Institution of M. Thomas Delham, priest, to church of Tilbrook, vac. by res. of Laurence Stafford; patron, Anne countess of Stafford. London, March 1422/3 or 1423.[21]

---

[19] This exchange was carried out by M. Robert Leek, vicar-general of bp Fleming *in remotis agente.*
[20] The date of the commission is evidently an error for 5 March 1422/3; the royal presentation to Ibberton was dated 6 February 1422/3. See *CPR 1422–1429*, p. 39.
[21] The day of the month is not specified.

251. [fo. 126r] Institution of William Spechell, priest, to church of Astwick, vac. by res. of Stephen Monynden; patron, P. and C. of Chicksands. By exchange with church of Colsterworth. Liddington, 12 March 1422/3.

252. Confirmation, by M. Robert Leek LL.D., canon of Lincoln and vicar-general of Bp Fleming *in remotis*, of election, *per viam spiritus sancti*, by William Chorleton, Simon Paxsweyn, John Bampton and John Newman, chaplains of collegiate church of St Mary, Northill, of M. Richard Heth, rector of Shillington, as master of the said church, vac. by death of John Warde. The decree of the election was exhibited to the vicar-general in prebendal church of Liddington; the confirmation, dated 5 July 1422, is given in full.

253. Collation of hospital of Hockliffe, vac. by res. of M. Thomas Chace, last master, to M. Adam Symond B.Dec. Old Temple, 3 December 1422.

Hic incipiunt institutiones facte per honorabilem virum magistrum Robertum Leek legum doctorem ecclesie Lincolnien' canonicum reverendi in Christo patris et domini domini Ricardi dei gracia Lincoln' episcopi in remotis agentis vicarium in spiritualibus generalem.

[fo. 126v] **Quarto kalendas Maii anno domini millesimo CCCC^mo vicesimo tertio incipit annus quartus consecrationis reverendi in Christo patris et domini domini Ricardi dei gracia Lincolnien' episcopi.**

254. Institution of Thomas Dalton, priest, to vicarage of Potsgrove, vac. by res. of Henry Gustard; patron, prior of St Albans, commissary-general of abbot of St Albans *in remotis*. Liddington, 26 July 1423.

255. Institution of William Lopyngton, in person of John Lopyngton his proctor, to church of Meppershall; patron, P. and C. of Holy Trinity, Lenton – and of John Hale, in person of John Hoggesthorp his proctor, to church of All Hallows Gracechurch Street, London, in immediate jurisdiction of archbp of Canterbury; patron, P. and C. of Canterbury. Exchange, by authority of commission of Henry [Chichele], archbp of Canterbury (dated at Slindon, 14 August 1423). Liddington, 19 August 1423.

256. [fo. 127r] Institution of John Broke, priest, to vicarage of Streatley; patron, P. and C. of Holy Trinity, Markyate. Liddington, 16 September 1423.

257. Institution of Richard Sampton, priest, in person of Gilbert Smyth his proctor, to church of All Saints, Bedford, vac. by res. of William Burnell; patron, P. and C. of Newnham. Liddington, 28 November 1423.

258. Institution of Thomas Pulter, priest, in person of Luke Coterell, literate, his proctor, to church of Cranfield, vac. by death of William Calandre; patron, John Pulter the younger. Liddington, 28 November 1423.

259. Institution of William Cosyn, priest, to vicarage of Felmersham, vac. by res. of Richard Sampton; patron, warden and fellows of King's Hall (*Aule Regie*), Cambridge. Liddington, 11 December 1423.

260. Institution of John Brygge, priest, in person of Richard Barton, clerk, his proctor, to church of St Cuthbert, Bedford, vac. by res. of John Cantyng; patron, P. and C. of Dunstable. Liddington, 31 March 1424.

261. Institution of William Hampton, in person of William Halle, literate, his proctor, to church of Cockayne Hatley; patron, P. and C. of Newnham – and of Thomas Boteler to church of Great Hallingbury, dioc. London; patron, Anne, lady Morley. Exchange, by authority of commission of David Pryce, canon of Lincoln, vicar-general of John [Kempe], bp of London *in remotis* (dated at London, 13 March 1423/4). Liddington, 8 April 1424.

262. [fo. 127v] Institution of br. John Eyton, canon of Dunstable, priest, to vicarage of Flitwick, vac. by res. of br. Thomas Burre; patron, P. and C. of Dunstable. Liddington, 18 April 1424.

[fo. 128r] **Quarto kalendas Maii anno domini millesimo CCCC^mo vicesimo quarto incipit annus quintus consecrationis reverendi in Christo patris et domini domini Ricardi dei gracia Lincoln' episcopi.**

263. Institution of Thomas Hill, in person of M. Richard Kyrkeby, clerk, his proctor, to church of Tingrith; patron, John Brokkele, lord of the manor of Tingrith – and of Henry More to church of Alphamstone, dioc. London; patron, A. and C. of Holy Cross, Waltham. Exchange, by authority of commission of John [Kempe], bp of London (dated at Fulham, 11 February 1423/4). Note that an inquiry was held by M. Stephen Monenden, commissary-general in archdnries of Huntingdon and Bedford, by which it was found that John Brokkele was true patron of Tingrith, and that Thomas Pevere of Toddington, esquire, presented the said Henry at the last vacancy. Liddington, 26 May 1424.

264. [fo. 128v] Institution of John Dauntre, priest, to church of Edworth, vac. by death of John Asty; patron, Roger Hunt,[22] John Legat, citizen and fishmonger of London, and John Bullok. London, 22 May 1424. Note that an inquiry was first held by official of archdn of Bedford, by which it was found that Roger Hunt, John Legat and John Bullok had the right to present to Edworth, which they had acquired from P. and C. of St Neots, and that King Richard II presented at the last vacancy.

[fos 129–130 are missing]

---

[22] For Hunt's career, see J. S. Roskell, Linda Clark and Carole Rawcliffe, *The History of Parliament: The House of Commons 1386–1421*, III (Stroud, 1993), 455–460.

[fo. 131r]

Oxon' (Archdnry of Oxford institutions. Throughout this section, it may be assumed that each institution entry includes a mandate to induct addressed to the archdn of Oxford or his official, unless otherwise stated. See introductory note on editorial practice above.)

Quarto kalendas Maii anno domini millesimo CCCC^mo vicesimo incipiunt institutiones facte per venerabilem virum magistrum Johannem Southam ecclesie Lincolnien' canonicum archidiaconum Oxonie in eadem reverendi in Christo patris et domini domini Ricardi dei gracia Lincoln' episcopi extra suas civitatem et dioc' in remotis agentis vicarium in spiritualibus generalem.

265. [fo 131r] Institution of John Potter, priest, in person of John Payn his proctor, to church of Standlake, vac. by death of Thomas Myll alias Myller; patron, John Grevell, esquire. Lincoln, 5 June 1420. Note that an inquiry was first held by official of archdn of Oxford, by which it was found that the said John Grevell was true patron for this turn by right of a certain manor which he held in the town of Standlake by hereditary right of Sybil his wife.

Johannes Potter presbiter presentatus per honestum virum Johannem Grevell' armigerum ad ecclesiam parochialem de Stanlake Lincoln' diocesis per mortem domini Thome Myll' alias Myller ultimo rectoris eiusdem vacantem, ad eandem quinto die mensis Junii anno domini supradicto apud Lincoln' fuit admissus et rector in personam Johannis Payn' procuratoris sui sufficienter et legitime in hac parte constituti institutus canonice in eadem, capta prius inquisitione super jure presentantis etc. per officialem archidiaconi Oxon' per quam compertum est quod prefatus Johannes Grevell' nunc presentans est verus eiusdem ecclesie hac vice patronus et quod jure cuiusdam manerii sive dominii quod idem Johannes habet in villa de Stanlak' jure hereditario Sibille uxoris sue debet ad dictam ecclesiam presentare etc. deinde jurata canonica obediencia ut in forma communi. Scriptum fuit archidiacono Oxon' seu eius officiali ad inducendum eundem vel procuratorem suum eius nomine.

266. Institution of Richard Hawkeslowe to vicarage of Churchill; patron, P. and C. of St Frideswide, Oxford – and of John Fyzt to church of Spernall, dioc. Worcester; patron, P. and C. of Cook Hill. Exchange, by authority of commission of John, prior of Worcester, vicar-general of Philip [Morgan], bp of Worcester *in remotis* (dated at Worcester, 15 May 1420). Lincoln, 31 May 1420.

267. [fo. 131v] Institution of Thomas Arkynden, priest, to vicarage of St Giles, Oxford, vac. by res. of Thomas Olyver; patron, prioress and convent of Godstow.[23] Lincoln, 27 June 1420.

---

[23] Although Godstow was an abbey, the abbess is not mentioned in the presentation.

268. Institution of Walter Blanket to church of Warpsgrove; patron, A. and C. of Dorchester – and of John Dalbert to church of Nuneham Courtenay; patron, King Henry. By exchange. London, 2 July 1420.

269. Institution of M. Nicholas Cosyn, in person of M. Thomas Colston, clerk, his proctor, to church of Warpsgrove, vac. by res. of Walter Blanket; patron, A. and C. of Dorchester. Lincoln, 13 July 1420.

270. Institution of Walter Blanket, priest, in person of M. John Swanswyche his proctor, to perpetual chantry of Holy Trinity in church of All Saints, Oxford, vac. by res. of M. Nicholas Cosyn; patron, warden and fellows of New College, Oxford. Lincoln, 13 July 1420.

271. [fo. 132r] Institution of John Bateman, in person of John Boton literate, his proctor, to church of Taynton, vac. by death of John Pekke; patron, P. and C. of Deerhurst. Lincoln, 13 July 1420.

272. Institution of Robert Slynge, priest, to vicarage of prebendal church of Langford, vac. by death of John Brownyng; patron, M. Roger Westwode, preb. of Langford in Lincoln cath.. Lincoln, 16 July 1420.

273. Institution of William Cursun, clerk, to church of Hethe, vac. by death of Thomas Weston; patron, P. and C. of St Mary, Kenilworth. Lincoln, 2 August 1420.

274. Institution of William Prayns, priest, to church of Ipsden; patron, warden and scholars of Merton College, Oxford. Lincoln, 28 June 1420.

Hic incipiunt institutiones facte per reverendum in Christo patrem et dominum dominum Ricardum dei gracia Lincolnien' episcopum post reditum suum in diocesim suam Lincolnien' anno consecrationis sue primo.

275. Institution of John Grene, priest, to church of Ewelme, vac. by death of Geoffrey Prentys; patron, Thomas Chaucer, esquire. Willingham,[24] 17 August 1420.

276. Institution of John Shypston, priest, in person of Walter Landesdale, clerk, his proctor, to vicarage of Steeple Barton; patron, A. and C. of Osney. Langtoft, 6 September 1420.

277. [fo. 132v] Institution of John Franke, clerk, in person of William Dorsete, literate, his proctor, to church of Stanton Harcourt, vac. by death of M. Geoffrey Crakeadan; patron, A. and C. of Reading. Langtoft, 4 October 1420.

---

[24] South Willingham in Lincolnshire: see *Visitations* I, p. xx.

278. Institution of John Brokehampton, priest, in person of Thomas Rawlyn, literate, his proctor, to church of Ducklington; patron, Maud, lady Lovel and Holand. Langtoft, 24 October 1420.

279. Institution of Robert Jordan, priest, to church of Hampton Poyle, vac. by [cause not specified] of M. Ralph Thorp; patron, John de la Poyle. Langtoft, 24 October 1420. Note that an inquiry was first held by M. John Merbury, commissary-general in archdnries of Oxford and Buckingham, by which it was found that John de la Poyle was true patron by reason of his demesne in the town of Hampton Poyle together with the advowson, by hereditary right.

280. Institution of William Drie, clerk, to church of 'Henton'; patron, King Henry. Fineshade, 4 November 1420.[25]

281. Institution of Henry Emmot, priest, in person of John Turvey, clerk, his proctor, to church of Godington, vac. by res. of John Ryvelowe; patron, A. and C. of Elstow. By exchange with vicarage of Weedon Bec. Fineshade, 17 November 1420.

282. Certificate of institution, by John, prior of Worcester, vicar-general of Philip [Morgan], bp of Worcester *in remotis*, of John Gase to vicarage of Broadwell, vac. by res. of John Walscheborne; patron, br. Henry Crounehale, lieutenant of br. William Hulles, prior of Hospitallers in England. Exchange, by authority of commission of bp of Lincoln (dated at Langtoft, 28 October 1420), with church of Great Comberton, dioc. Worcester. Worcester, 15 December 1420. Received at Fineshade, 30 December 1420.

283. [fo. 133r] Institution of Walter Blanket, in person of M. John Gouteby, clerk, his proctor, to vicarage of Ambrosden; patron, rector and convent of Ashridge – and of Robert Lardener to chantry of Holy Trinity in church of All Saints, Oxford; patron, warden and fellows of New College, Oxford. By exchange. London, 9 December 1420.

284. Certificate of institution, by John, prior of Worcester, vicar-general of Philip [Morgan], bp of Worcester *in remotis*, of John More to vicarage of Black Bourton, vac. by res. of Peter Willerzey; patron, A. and C. of Osney. Exchange, by authority of commission of bp of Lincoln (dated at Westminster, *in hospicio nostro*, 17

---

[25] The identification of this church is uncertain. There is no church of Henton or Hinton in Oxfordshire. The chapel of St James at Henton was a dependency in the parish of Chinnor and no institutions are recorded in the Lincoln registers either to this chapel or to the chantry established there in 1321 by Henry de Malyns, although the 'advowson' of Henton chapel was included in the property conveyed in 1485 by Sir Thomas Danvers to William of Waynflete and thence to Magdalen College, Oxford. It is possible that the institution refers to the church of Hinton in the Hedges, just outside the county in Northamptonshire. The presentation of William Drie does not appear to be recorded on the Patent Rolls. See *VCH Oxon* viii. 63, 74; R. R. Sharpe (ed.), *Calendar of Wills Proved and Enrolled in the Court of Husting, London*, I (1889), 295–303; *CPR 1416–1422*.

December 1420), with church of Spetchley, dioc. Worcester. Worcester, 23 December 1420. Received at Fineshade, 31 December 1420.

285. [fo. 133v] Certificate of institution, by John, prior of Worcester, vicar-general of Philip [Morgan], bp of Worcester *in remotis*, of John Chalowe to vicarage of Weston on the Green, vac. by res. of Ralph Phylypp; patron, A. and C. of Osney. Exchange, by authority of commission of bp of Lincoln (dated at Westminster, *in hospicio nostro*, 15 December 1420), with church of Eccleshall, dioc. Worcester. Worcester, 20 December 1420. Received at Fineshade, 14 January 1420/1.

286. Institution of William Reve, priest, to vicarage of Kirtlington, vac. by res. of Robert Copyn; patron, P. and C. of St Anne, Coventry. Fineshade, 18 January 1420/1.

287. [fo. 134r] Institution of Roger Baker to vicarage of Churchill; patron, P. and C. of St Frideswide, Oxford – and of Richard Haukeslowe to vicarage of Winterbourne Monkton, dioc. Salisbury; patron, A. and C. of Cirencester. Exchange, by authority of commission of John [Chaundler], bp of Salisbury (dated at Sonning, 18 January 1420/1). Old Temple, 9 February 1420/1.

288. Institution of John Bonde, priest, in person of Robert Cardemaker, chaplain, his proctor, to chantry in chapel of St Cecilia in churchyard of the parish church of Minster Lovell; patron, Maud, lady Lovel and Holand. Old Temple, 7 March 1420/1.

[fo. 134v]

Quarto kalendas Maii anno domini millesimo cccc^{mo} vicesimo primo incipit annus secundus consecrationis reverendi in Christo patris et domini domini Ricardi dei gracia Lincolnien' episcopi.

289. Institution of Robert Colas to church of Alvescot; patron, King Henry – and of William Humberston, in person of John Sheryff, literate, his proctor, to church of Broadwell, dioc. Worcester; patron, A. and C. of Evesham. Exchange, by authority of commission of Philip [Morgan], bp of Worcester (dated at London, 17 May 1421). London, 19 May 1421.[26]

290. [fo. 135r] Institution of Thomas Louthburgh, priest, in person of Richard Kyrkeby, clerk, his proctor, to vicarage of Cowley; patron, A. and C. of Osney. Buckden, 20 June 1421.

291. Institution of Robert Dyer, priest, in person of Richard Kyrkeby, clerk, his proctor, to church of Britwell Salome, vac. by res. of Walter Colswayn; patron, Isabell Malyns, lady of Henton. By exchange with vicarage of Great Kimble. Buckden, 26 June 1421.

[26] The certificate is dated in error at London, 19 June 1421.

292. Institution of Thomas Whytyngton, priest, in person of Richard Kyrkeby, clerk, his proctor, to vicarage of Minster Lovell, vac. by res. of Robert Cardemaker; patron, King Henry. Buckden, 31 July 1421.

293. Institution of Ralph Wooston, priest, to church of Wilcote, vac. by res. of William Pate; patron, Elizabeth, widow of William Wylcotes, esquire. Buckden, 3 September 1421.

294. Institution of John Broune, priest, to vicarage of Preston Deanery [Northants.], vac. by death of William Colette; patron, P. and C. of St Andrew, Northampton. Sleaford, 18 September 1421.

295. [fo. 135v] Institution of Thomas Whytchurche, priest, to church of Finmere, vac. by res. of M. Geoffrey Damport; patron, A. and C. of St Augustine, Bristol. Sleaford, 18 September 1421.

296. Institution of John Haselere, priest, to vicarage of North Stoke, vac. by res. of John Pomfreyt; patron, P. and C. of Broomhall. Langton, 16 October 1421.

297. Certificate of institution, by Reginald Kentwode, Official of London *sede vacante*, of John Rossen to church of Begbroke, vac. by res. of M. William Burreth; patron, Thomas Chetewode kt. Exchange, by authority of commission of bp of Lincoln (dated at Sleaford Castle, 1 October 1421), with vicarage of Ardleigh, dioc. London. London, 15 October 1421. Received at Raunds, 19 October 1421.

298. Institution of Thomas Wylle, priest, to perpetual chantry of St Mary the Virgin in church of St Aldate, Oxford, vac. by res. of Lewis Frewchirche; patron, Thomas Gybbus, citizen and alderman of Oxford. Whiston, 30 October 1421.

299. Institution of John Andrewe, priest, to vicarage of Spelsbury, vac. by res. of Nicholas Bateman; patron, D. and C. of St Mary, Warwick. By exchange with vicarage of Norton by Daventry. Witney, 11 November 1421.

300. [fo. 136r] Certificate of institution, by John [Wheathampstead], abbot of St Albans, of William Mayhewe to vicarage of North Stoke, vac. by res. of John Haselere; patron, P. and C. of Broomhall. Exchange, by authority of commission of bp of Lincoln (dated at Oxford, 17 November 1421), with vicarage of Abbots Langley, dioc. Lincoln and in jurisdiction of St Albans. St Albans, 21 November 1421. Received at Notley, 28 November 1421.

301. Institution of M. Thomas Nassh, priest, in person of John North, literate, his proctor, to church of Chinnor, vac. by res. of John Hayworth; patron, P. and C. of Wallingford. By exchange with preb. of Welton Ryval in Lincoln cath. London, 14 December 1421.

302. [fo. 136v] Institution of William Martyn, in person of John Swanwych, clerk, his proctor, to church or chapel of Warpsgrove; patron, A. and C. of Dorchester – and of Nicholas Cosyn to church of Bighton, dioc. Winchester; patron, A. and C. of Hyde. Exchange, by authority of commission of Henry

[Beaufort], bp of Winchester (dated at manor of Southwark, 30 November 1421). Old Temple, 12 December 1421.

303. Certificate of institution, by Thomas More, dean, and chapter of St Paul's, London, of Robert Colston, in person of William Pyrye his proctor, to church of Nuneham Courtenay, vac. by res. of John Dalbert; patron, King Henry, by custody of land and heir of John Drayton kt, decd. Exchange, by authority of commission of bp of Lincoln (dated at Old Temple, 3 December 1421), with mastership of free chapel of St Radegund in St Paul's cath., London. Chapter house of St Paul's, London, 12 December 1421. Received at London, 14 December 1421.

304. [fo. 137r] Institution of M. John Play to church of Stanton Harcourt; patron, A. and C. of Reading – and of John Frank, in person of William Dorset, literate, his proctor, to church of Kingweston, dioc. Bath and Wells; patron, A. and C. of Bermondsey. Exchange, by authority of commission of Nicholas [Bubwith], bp of Bath and Wells (dated in manor of Wookey, 30 December 1421). Dunstable, 14 January 1421/2.

305. [fo. 137v] Institution of Robert Rolleston, priest, in person of William Multon, clerk, his proctor, to prebendal church of Shipton under Wychwood in Salisbury cath., vac. by death of Thomas More; patron, John [Chaundler], bp of Salisbury, on nomination of Queen Katherine. No date. The presentation deed (dated at Sherborne castle, 4 January 1421/2) is given in full.

306. Institution of John Wellys, priest, to perpetual chantry of Holy Trinity in church of All Saints, Oxford, vac. by res. of Thomas Lardyner;[27] patron, warden and fellows of New College, Oxford. London, January 1421/2.[28]

307. Institution of John Graunger, priest, to vicarage of Chesterton, vac. by res. of Robert Sawelle; patron, rector and brethren of Ashridge. Old Temple, 19 February 1421/2.

308. Collation of church of Rousham to Richard Randolf, priest. By lapse. Old Temple, 20 February 1421/2.

309. Certificate of M. Richard Burneham, canon of Lincoln. In accordance with commission of Bp Fleming (dated at High Wycombe, 1 December 1421), he has confirmed, on 3 December 1421 in church of St Mary, Oxford, the election of M. Henry Kayll as provost of Oriel College in the university of Oxford. Oxford, Feast of St Nicholas [6 December], 1421.

310. [fo. 138r] Collation of church of St Mildred, Oxford, to M. John Carpenter, priest. Barton le Clay, 15 January 1421/2.

---

[27] Lardyner's forename was given as Robert at his institution: see no 283 above.
[28] The day of the month is not specified.

[fo. 138v]

Quarto kalendas Maii anno domini millesimo quadringentesimo vicesimo secundo incipit annus tertius consecrationis reverendi in Christo patris et domini domini Ricardi dei gracia Lincolnien' episcopi.

311.   Certificate of institution, by John [Wheathampstead], abbot of St Albans, of John Albyn to church of Albury, vac. by res. of Peter Braunch; patron, Joan, widow of William Baldyndon esquire, decd. Exchange, by authority of commission of bp of Lincoln (dated at Liddington, 16 March 1422/3), with vicarage of Winslow, dioc. Lincoln and jurisdiction of St Albans. St Albans, 20 March 1422/3.

[Note: Two folios have been cut out between fo. 138 and fo. 139.]

[fo. 139r]

Hic incipiunt institutiones facte per honorabilem virum magistrum Robertum Leek legum doctorem ecclesie Lincoln' canonicum reverendi in Christo patris et domini domini Ricardi Flemmyng dei gracia Lincolnien' episcopi extra suas civitatem et diocesim in remotis agentis vicarium in spiritualibus generalem.

312.   Institution of Peter Bysshop to portion of Motons in church of Waddesdon, Bucks.; patron, King Henry – and of Nicholas Dounscombe, in person of John Baker alias Twygyshayes, chaplain, his proctor, to church of Clayhidon, dioc. Exeter; patron, Robert Maynard and Thomas Hertescote. Exchange, by authority of commission of Edmund [Lacy], bp of Exeter (dated in his manor of St Breoke (*Pawton*), 17 March 1422/3). Liddington, 19 April 1423. Note that an inquiry was first held by M. William Symond, commissary-general in archdnries of Oxford and Buckingham, by which it was found that King Henry was true patron of the said portion for this turn, by reason of the minority of Thomas Courteney, earl of Devon, and that Edward Courteney, grandfather of the said Thomas, presented M. Nicholas Dounscomb at the last vacancy.[29]

313.   [fo. 139v] Institution of John Smart priest to the vicarage of Watlington; patron, A. and C. of Osney. Liddington, 9 March 1421/2.

314.   Institution of Walter Bell M.A., priest, in person of William Spenser B.A., his proctor, to the church of Bletchingdon, vac. by the death of M. John Malvern; patron, provost and scholars of Queen's Hall (*Aule Regine*), Oxford. Liddington, 23 March 1421/2.

---

[29] Although this exchange is entered in the archdnry of Oxford section, and the mandate for induction is stated to be issued to the archdn of Oxford or his official, the parish of Waddesdon is in fact situated in the archdnry of Buckingham.

315. Institution of Richard Astewode priest to the church of Hardwicke (*Hardewyk' Awdeley*), vac. by the res. of Ralph Philipp; patron, br. Henry Crounhale, preceptor of Eagle, lieutenant of br. William Hulles, prior of Hospitallers in England. Liddington, 27 March 1422.

316. Institution of John Clifford priest, in person of Thomas Ilderton, clerk, his proctor, to the church of Taynton, vac. by the res. of John Bateman; patron, P. and C. of Deerhurst. Liddington, 2 April 1422.

317. Institution of John Bonde priest to the vicarage of Minster Lovell; patron, King Henry. Liddington, 3 April 1422.

318. Institution of John Thomas priest to the church of Heythrop, vac. by the res. of Thomas Leukenore; patron, William Kynwolmerssh, William Felmersham and Thomas Frankeleyn. Liddington, 15 April 1422.

319. [fo. 140r] Certificate of Thomas Southam, commissary-general in archdnries of Oxford and Buckingham. In accordance with a commission of vicar-general (dated at Liddington, 18 March 1421/2), he has instituted Thomas Leukenour to the church of Whitchurch; patron, King Henry. Oxford, 4 April 1422.

320. Institution of Robert Beverley priest to chantry of St Anne in church of All Saints, Oxford, vac. by res. of M. John Lygh; patron, William Brampton, mayor of Oxford. Liddington, 2 June 1422.

321. Institution of John Mathewe priest to church of Ipsden, vac. by res. of William Prawns; patron, warden and scholars of Merton College, Oxford. Liddington, 18 July 1422.

322. Institution of Thomas Manyn priest, in person of M. Thomas Chace, clerk, his proctor, to church of Crowell, vac. by res. of Robert Parfyt; patron, Humfrey Stafford kt. Liddington, 27 July 1422.

323. [fo. 140v] Institution of Robert Berndesley priest to vicarage of Lewknor, vac. by res. of Thomas Moweton; patron, A. and C. of Abingdon. By exchange with church of Hardwick. Liddington, 13 August 1422.

324. Institution of William Hoper LL.D., priest, in person of John Batyn, clerk, his proctor, to church of St Michael at the South Gate, Oxford, vac. by death of M. Thomas Pannall; patron, P. and C. of St Frideswide, Oxford. Liddington, 12 August 1422. Note that an inquiry was first held by M. Thomas Southam, commissary-general in archdnries of Oxford and Buckingham, by which it was found that the Prior and Convent were true patrons and presented M. Thomas at the last vacancy.

325. Certificate of M. Thomas Southam, commissary-general in archdnries of Oxford and Buckingham. In accordance with a commission of vicar-general (dated at Liddington, 27 July 1422), he has instituted Walter Chycon to church of

Grendon Underwood; patron, Eleanor de Sancto Amando, widow of Almaric de Sancto Amando kt, decd. Grendon Underwood, 2 August 1422.[30]

[fo. 141r]

Hic incipiunt institutiones facte per reverendum in Christo patrem dominum Ricardum Flemmyng dei gracia Lincolnien' episcopum post reditum suum in diocesim suam Lincolnien'.

326. Institution of John Neuton priest to church of Shelswell, vac. by death of Robert Dormer; patron, Thomas Stokkes, lord of Shelswell, *domicellus*. Liddington, 21 September 1422. Note that an inquiry was first held by M. Thomas Southam, commissary-general in archdnries of Oxford and Buckingham, by which it was found that the said Thomas Stokkes was the true patron.

327. Institution of br. Thomas Thornebury, canon of St Frideswide, Oxford, priest, in person of Walter Clerk his proctor, to vicarage of Headington, vac. by death of br. Andrew de Hanovia; patron, P. and C. of St Frideswide, Oxford. Liddington, 22 September 1422.

328. Collation of church of St Michael at the North Gate (*ad portam borialem*), Oxford, to Richard Babthorp clerk. Liddington, 16 October 1422.

329. Certificate of institution, by Simon Sydenham, dean of Salisbury, of William Carles to church of Souldern, vac. by res. of John Pagrave alias Offord; patron, A. and C. of Eynsham. Exchange, by authority of commission of bp of Lincoln (dated at Liddington, 16 October 1422), with vicarage of prebendal church of Faringdon (*Chepyngfaryndon*), dioc. Salisbury and in the dean's jurisdiction. Salisbury, 23 October 1422. Received at Liddington, 30 October 1422.

330. [fo. 141v] Institution of Nicholas Blake priest to vicarage of Merton, vac. by res. of Thomas Fysshe; patron, A. and C. of Eynsham. London, December 1422.[31] Note that an inquiry was first held by M. William Symond, commissary-general in archdnries of Oxford and Buckingham, by which it was found that A. and C. of Eynsham were true patrons and presented at the last vacancy.

331. Certificate of institution, by John [Wheathampstead], abbot of St Albans, of Robert Bateman to vicarage of Spelsbury, vac. by res. of John Cook; patron, Dean and Chapter of St Mary, Warwick. Exchange, by authority of commission of bp of Lincoln (dated at Liddington, 4 February 1422/3), with vicarage of Aston Abbots, dioc. Lincoln and jurisdiction of St Albans. St Albans, 11 February 1422/3. Received at Liddington, 16 February 1422/3.

---

[30] Although this institution is entered in the archdnry of Oxford section, and the mandate for induction is stated to be issued to the archdn of Oxford or his official, the parish of Grendon Underwood is in fact situated in the archdnry of Buckingham.
[31] The day of the month is not specified.

332. [fo. 142r] Institution of William Mathewe priest, in person of Thomas Kyrkeby, literate, his proctor, to vicarage of North Stoke; patron, P. and C. of Broomhall. Liddington, 5 March 1422/3.

333. Institution of br. Theobald Wynchestre, canon of St Frideswide, Oxford, in person of John Appelton, literate, his proctor, to vicarage of Marston, vac. by res. of Thomas Thornebury.[32] Liddington, 14 March 1422/3.

334. Institution of John Kent priest to church of Waterstock, vac. by death of Thomas Derecors; patron, John Danvers, esquire. Liddington, 16 March 1422/3. Note that an inquiry was first held by M. William Symond, commissary-general in archdnries of Oxford and Buckingham, by which it was found that the said John Danvers was patron for this turn by reason of a feoffment to him of the manor and advowson of Waterstock by William Bruly who presented at the last vacancy.[33]

335. Institution of Henry Nevyll, priest, in person of Henry Trycarell, clerk, his proctor, to vicarage of Crowmarsh Gifford, vac. by death of William Northbury; patron, P. and C. of Goring. Liddington, 18 March 1422/3.

336. Collation of church of St Michael at the North Gate, Oxford, to John Beke M.A., priest. Old Temple, 11 November 1422.

Quarto kalendas Maii anno domini millesimo CCCC^mo vicesimo tertio incipit annus quartus consecrationis reverendi in Christo patris et domini domini Ricardi Flemmyng' dei gracia Lincoln' episcopi.

[fo. 142v]

Hic incipiunt institutiones facte per honorabilem virum Magistrum Roberti Leek' legum doctorem ecclesie Lincoln' canonicum reverendi in Christo patris et domini domini Ricardi Flemmyng dei gracia Lincoln' episcopi extra suas civitatem et diocesim in remotis agentis vicarium in spiritualibus generalem.

337. Institution of William Stok, clerk, in person of Richard Sudbury, clerk, his proctor, to church of Garsington, vac. by res. of Robert Espele; patron, P. and C. of Wallingford. Liddington, 10 May 1423.

338. Institution of Richard Nayler B.Dec., priest, to vicarage of prebendal church of Banbury, vac. by res. of John Ratherby; patron, John Forest, preb. of Banbury in Lincoln cath. By exchange with vicarage of Great Kimble. Liddington, 15 May 1423. Ind. D. and C. of Lincoln.

339. Institution of William Eston priest to vicarage of Crowmarsh Gifford, vac.

---

[32] The name of the patron is not specified.
[33] Danvers married Joan, granddaughter of William Bruley: see *VCH Oxon* vii. 223.

by death of Henry Nevyll; patron, P. and C. of Goring. Liddington, 26 May 1423.

340. Institution of John Hogges, priest, in person of William Wale, literate, his proctor, to perpetual chantry of St Mary the Virgin in church of Chipping Norton, vac. by res. of William Crowton; patron, John Wale of Chipping Norton. Liddington, 18 May 1423. Note that an inquiry was first held by M. William Symond, commissary-general in archdnries of Oxford and Buckingham, by which it was found that the said John Wale had the right of presentation for this turn by hereditary right, by reason of a certain tenement commonly called Wales in New Street (*novo vico*) in Chipping Norton; and that Robert Wale, chaplain, elder brother of the said John, presented at the last vacancy.

341. Institution of Henry Smyth de Bourough, priest, to vicarage of Barford St Michael; patron, P. and C. of Chacombe. Liddington, 12 October 1423.

342. Institution of Nicholas Hunte priest to vicarage of Chesterton, vac. by res. of John Graunger; patron, rector and convent of Ashridge. Liddington, 6 November 1423.

343. Certificate of Thomas Brouns D.C. & Cn.L., canon of Lincoln. In accordance with a commission of vicar-general (dated at Liddington, 7 October 1423), he has instituted Robert Thwaytys to hospital of St James and St John, Aynho; patron, Ralph Frank and Elizabeth his wife. Sealed with the seal of M. John Lynfeld, archdn of Chichester, because he did not have the authentic seal to hand (*quia sigillum authenticum ad manus non habemus*). Old Temple, 26 October 1423.

344. [fo. 143r] Institution of John Dunnyng to vicarage of North Stoke; patron, P. and C. of Broomhall – and of William Mathewe to vicarage of St John in the Isle of Thanet [Margate], dioc. Canterbury; patron, A. and C. of St Augustine, Canterbury. Exchange, by authority of commission of Henry [Chichele], archbp of Canterbury (dated at Lambeth, 28 October 1423). Old Temple, 28 October 1423.

345. [fo. 143v] Institution of Richard Flemyng of *Kyrkeby*, priest, to vicarage of Merton, vac. by res. of Nicholas Blake; patron, A. and C. of Eynsham. Thame, 31 October 1423.

346. Institution of Edward Rede, priest, in person of John Turvey, clerk, his proctor, to church of Ducklington, vac. by death of John Brokhampton; patron, King Henry. Liddington, 28 November 1423. Note that Edward Rede was first presented by Maud, lady Lovel and Holand (the presentation was received at Liddington, 28 April 1423), that subsequently M. Thomas Dunkan was presented by Edmund, earl of March (the presentation was received at Liddington, 30 April 1423), and that the vicar-general issued commissions to M. William Symond, commissary-general, to inquire into these presentations. A royal writ *Ne admittatis* (dated at Westminster, 26 April 1423) was received at Liddington on 1 May 1423 while the dispute between Edmund and Maud was heard in the king's court. The suit having fallen through the death of Maud,[34] the king presented Edward Rede to the living. The vicar-general having then issued similar commissions (dated at Liddington, 15 May 1423) to the said commissary-general to hold similar inquiries, the advowson was disputed in the royal court between the king and the bp of Lincoln. The royal writ (dated at Westminster, 10 November 1423) by which the king recovered the advowson against the bp is given in full. Note that an inquiry was held, by which it was found that the said Maud was true patron as lady of the manor of Ducklington, that the advowson pertained to the said manor, and that Maud presented John Brokhampton at the last vacancy.

347. [fo. 144r] Institution of John Mason, priest, in person of John Payne, literate, his proctor, to perpetual chantry of Holy Cross in church of Standlake, vac. by res. of Richard Wylkyns; patron, John Potter, rector of Standlake. Liddington, 2 February 1423/4.

348. Institution of Robert Colby priest to vicarage of Cowley, vac. by res. of M. Thomas Louthburgh; patron, A. and C. of Osney. Thame, 29 February 1424.

349. Institution of Thomas Benett, priest, in person of Robert Darcy, clerk, his proctor, to church of Bix Gibbewin, vac. by res. of Hugh Jones; patron, John Warfeld, esquire. Thame, 1 March 1423/4. Note that an inquiry was first held by M. William Symond, commissary-general in archdnries of Oxford and Buckingham, by which it was found that the said John was patron in full right for this turn by reason of a feoffment to him of the manor and advowson of Bix Gibbewin, and that he presented at the last vacancy.

350. Institution of John Gully priest to vicarage of King's Sutton; patron, Robert Gylbert, preb. of Sutton cum Buckingham in Lincoln cath. Ind. D. and C. of Lincoln. Liddington, 7 March 1423/4.

351. [fo. 144v] Institution of Thomas Taylur priest to vicarage of Aston Rowant, vac. by death of William Mery; patron, P. and C. of Wallingford. Liddington, 22 March 1423/4.

352. Institution of Thomas Walker, priest, in person of William Betty, clerk, his proctor, to vicarage of Beckley, vac. by death of Roger Pope; patron, P. and C. of Studley. Liddington, 2 April 1424.

353. Institution of M. William Symond priest to vicarage of Ambrosden, vac. by death of M. Walter Blanket; patron, rector and convent of Ashridge. Liddington, 11 April 1424.

354. Institution of John Gerneys, clerk, to church of Launton, vac. by death of John Clerk; patron, A. and C. of Westminster. Liddington, 23 April 1424.

---

[34] Maud died on 7 May 1423: *Complete Peerage* viii. 221.

[fo. 145r]

Duodecimo die mensis Februarii anno domini millesimo CCCC^{mo}
xxiiij^{to} incipit institutiones expedite per honorabilem virum
Magistrum Robertum Leek legum doctorem officialem consistorii
Lincoln' ac commissarium per dominum Cantuarien' in hac parte
sufficienter deputatum ut planius patet in simili rubrica in
Archidiaconatu Lincoln'.

355. Commission to M. William Symond, commissary-general of archbp in
archdnry of Oxford, to inquire into vacancy of church of Begbroke, into the right
of patronage of Thomas Chetewode kt in the same, and into the merits of Henry
Box, presented by the said Thomas to the same; to summon all having an interest
in the vacancy, and in particular William Hawkyng, lately presented by the said
Thomas to the same church. If there is no impediment, he is to institute the said
Henry to the church. Liddington, 6 March 1424/5.

356. Institution of Robert Holewyll priest to church of Cuxham, vac. by death of
Thomas Chilmark; patron, warden and scholars of Merton College, Oxford.
Liddington, 18 March 1424/5.

357. Institution of Thomas William priest to church of Warpsgrove; patron, A.
and C. of Dorchester. Thame, 13 April 1425.

[There is no folio 146.]

[fo. 147r]

Buckynghame (Archdnry of Buckingham institutions. Throughout this section,
it may be assumed that each institution entry includes a mandate to induct
addressed to the archdn of Buckingham or his official, unless otherwise stated. See
introductory note on editorial practice above.)

Quarto kalendas Maii anno domini millesimo quadringentesimo
vicesimo incipit annus primus consecrationis reverendi in Christo
patris et domini domini Ricardi dei gracia Lincolnien' episcopi.

Decimo nono die mensis Maii anno domini millesimo quad-
ringentesimo vicesimo incipiunt institutiones facte per venerabilem
virum magistrum Johannem Southam ecclesie Lincolniensis
canonicum archidiaconum Oxoniensem in eadem reverendi in Christo
patris et domini domini Ricardi dei gracia Lincolniensis episcopi
extra suas civitatem et diocesim in remotis agentis vicarium in
spiritualibus generalem.

358. Institution of John Marton priest, in person of John Hoggesthorp, clerk, his
proctor, to church of Ravenstone, vac. by res. of Adam; patron, P. and C. of
Ravenstone. Lincoln, 15 June 1420.

Johannes Marton presbiter presentatus per priorem et conventum de Ravenston' ad vicariam perpetuam ecclesie parochialis de Ravenston' Lincoln' diocesis per resignationem domini Ade ultimi vicarii eiusdem in manibus dicti vicarii factam et per ipsum admissam vacantem, ad eandem xv⁰ die mensis Junii anno domini supradicto fuit admissus apud Lincoln' et vicarius perpetuus secundum formam constitutionum legatinarum in hoc casu editarum juratus in personam Johannis Hoggesthorp' clerici procuratoris sui sufficienter et legitime in hac parte constituti institutus canonice in eadem, nulla inquisitione previa quia etc. jurata canonica obediencia ut in forma. Scriptum fuit archidiacono Buck' seu ipsius Officiali ad inducendum.

359.   Institution of Robert Tonge M.A. to church of Beaconsfield, vac. by death of M. William Faryngdon; patron, William Rous esquire. Note that an inquiry was carried out by the official of the archdn of Buckingham, by which it was found that the right of patronage belonged to the manor of Undercombe, which the said William Rous, Richard Lovell and George Skydmor held undividedly by hereditary right; that at this vacancy the said William, Richard and George had been unable to present the same person and that therefore the presentation for this turn belonged to William Rous as the senior of the three men. Lincoln, 20 June 1420.

360.   Institution of John Crute priest to vicarage of Turville; patron, A. and C. of St Albans. Lincoln, 15 June 1420.

361.   Institution of John Wylkyn priest to a mediety of church of Walton, vac. by res. of John Bouche; patron, Reynold de Grey, lord Hastings, Wexford and Ruthin. Lincoln, 3 June 1420.

[fo. 147v]

Hic incipiunt institutiones facte per reverendum in Christo patrem et dominum dominum Ricardum dei gracia Lincolnien' episcopum post reditum suum in diocesim Lincoln' anno domini millesimo quadringentesimo vicesimo et consecrationis eiusdem primo.

362.   Institution of Thomas Powtrell priest to vicarage of Tilsworth; patron, P. and C. of St Giles *de Bosco*, Flamstead. London, 2 July 1420.[35]

363.   Institution of Richard Warde priest to church of Maids' Moreton, vac. by death of John Downe; patron, Thomas Wodevyle, John Barton the elder, John Barton the younger, John Olney esquire, Richard Parchemener chaplain and Henry Mauntell. Note that an inquiry was held by Master John Merbury, commissary in archdnries of Oxford and Buckingham, by which it was found that the patrons presented by right of a feoffment to them by Thomas Pever of all his manors tenements and lands, with the advowson of the said church of Maids' Moreton; and that the said Thomas Pever presented at the last vacancy. Langtoft, 28 August 1420.

---

[35] Tilsworth was in fact in the archdnry of Bedford and has been included in the archdnry of Buckingham institutions in error.

364. Institution of M. Robert Ely priest to church of Denham, vac. by death of John Maxfeld; patron, A. and C. of Westminster. Langtoft, 4 September 1420.

365. Institution of William Morys of Turvey priest to vicarage of Lavendon, vac. by death of Henry Boys; patron, A. and C. of Lavendon. Langtoft, 10 September 1420.

366. Institution of William Holbek priest to a mediety of church of Beachampton, vac. by res. of Richard Warde; patron, P. and C. of Luffield. Langtoft, 21 October 1420.

367. Institution of Robert Allerton, in person of M. John Moresburgh, clerk and notary public, his proctor, to church of Amersham; patron, King Henry. Fineshade, 29 October 1420.

368. [fo. 148r] Institution of Thomas Hardyng priest to vicarage of Lavendon, vac. by res. of William Morys; patron, A. and C. of Lavendon. Fineshade, 6 February 1420/1.

369. Institution of William German priest to vicarage of Ivinghoe, newly endowed; patron, rector and convent of Ashridge. Wykeham, 12 March 1420/1.

370. Institution of John Cambus priest to church of Marlow, vac. by death of John Warner; patron, Richard Beauchamp (*Bello Campo*), earl of Worcester and lord Le Despenser. Wykeham, 4 April 1421.

Quarto kalendas Maii anno domini millesimo CCCC^mo vicesimo primo incipit annus secundus consecrationis reverendi in Christo patris et domini domini Ricardi dei gracia Lincolnien' episcopi.

371. [fo. 148v] Institution of William Payne priest, in person of John Turvey clerk his proctor, to vicarage of Linslade, vac. by res. of Henry Haselys; patron, P. and C. of Chicksands. Wykeham, 28 March 1421.

372. Institution of Richard Vynslawe priest to vicarage of West Wycombe alias Haveringdon; patron, P. and C. of Bisham. London, 7 May 1421.

373. Certificate of M. William Duffeld, commissary of John [Kempe], bp of Rochester, *in remotis*. In accordance with a commission of Bp Fleming (dated at Old Temple, 13 May 1421), he has instituted Thomas Wyotte, in person of William Maundevyle his proctor, to church of Eton, vac. by res. of William Gylliotte; patron, William Rous, George Skydmore and Richard Lovell, esquires. By exchange with church of Chislehurst, dioc. Rochester. London, in the chapel of St Mary in the churchyard of St Paul's, 14 May 1421. Received at London, 14 May 1421.

374. Institution of John Colyn priest, in person of John FitzJohn *domicellus* his proctor, to vicarage of Wingrave, vac. by res. of John Smyth; patron, A. and C. of St Albans. London, 14 May 1421.

375.   Institution of Thomas Hogg priest to vicarage of Upton, vac. by res. of Peter Baxster; patron, P. and C. of Merton. London, 27 May 1421.

376.   Institution of John Radcliff to church of Great Horwood; patron, King Henry. London, 29 May 1421.

377.   [fo. 149r] Institution of Richard Burgh priest to church of St Nicholas, Saunderton, vac. by res. of Thomas Madir; patron, Gerard Braybrok kt. Buckden, 2 June 1421.

378.   Institution of Henry Emmot priest, in person of John Hoggesthorp, clerk, his proctor, to vicarage of Westbury, vac. by res. of John Wylyton; patron, A. and C. of Elstow. By exchange with church of Godington. Buckden, 10 June 1421.

379.   Institution of Walter Colswayn priest, in person of John Polreden the younger his proctor, to vicarage of Great Kimble, vac. by res. of Robert Dyer; patron, A. and C. of Missenden. By exchange with church of Britwell Salome. Buckden, 26 June 1421.

380.   Institution of Richard Monke priest, in person of Thomas Petre his proctor, to vicarage of Chesham, vac. by res. of John Garton; patron, A. and C. of Leicester. Buckden, 18 July 1421.

381.   Institution of Richard Patryngton, in person of John Dyer, literate, his proctor, to church of St Nicholas, Saunderton; patron, Richard Haye esquire – and of Richard Burgh to vicarage of Witley, dioc. Winchester; patron, P. and C. of Dartford. Exchange, by authority of a commission of Henry [Beaufort], bp of Winchester (dated at Farnham Castle, 30 July 1421). Buckden, 10 August 1421.

382.   [fo. 149v] Institution of John Hele to church of Moulsoe; patron, P. and C. of Goring – and of John Magot to vicarage of Kemble, dioc. Salisbury; patron, A. and C. of Malmesbury. Exchange, by authority of a commission of John [Chaundler], bp of Salisbury (dated at Ramsbury, 9 August 1421. Buckden, 14 August 1421.

383.   [fo. 150r] Certificate of Walter Eston Lic.C.&Cn.L., vicar general of Thomas [Polton], bp of Hereford *in remotis*. In accordance with a commission of Bp Fleming (dated at Leicester, 12 October 1421), he has instituted Robert Herleston to church of Hedgerley, vac. by res. of John Ludeschelf; patron, Bernard Saunderton esquire, lord of Saunderton. By exchange with church of Pencombe, dioc. Hereford. Hereford, 18 October 1421. Received at Notley, 28 November 1421.

384.   Institution of Robert Burton D.Th. priest, in person of Thomas Hunter clerk his proctor, to church of Drayton Parslow, vac. by death of John Bertram; patron, King Henry. Eynsham, 12 November 1421.

385.   Institution of John Bette priest to vicarage of Swanbourne, vac. by res. of Nicholas Skeret; patron, A. and C. of Woburn. London, 18 December 1421.

386. [fo. 150v] Institution of Aunger Tymberland to church of Radclive; patron, warden and fellows of New College, Oxford – and of William Thode to vicarage of Hughenden; patron, P. and C. of Kenilworth. By exchange. Beaconsfield, 2 December 1421.

387. Institution of Richard Gery to church of Addington; patron, br. Henry Cronhall, lieutenant of br. William Hull, prior of Hospitallers in England – and of John Danyell to church of Tellisford, dioc. Bath and Wells; patron, William Hankeford kt, William Westbury, John Westbury and Roger Trewebody, for this turn by reason of a feoffment made to them by Walter Hungerford kt. Exchange, by authority of a commission of Nicholas [Bubwith], bp of Bath and Wells (dated at London, 5 December 1421). Old Temple, 7 December 1421.

388. Institution of John Tryll priest to chantry of Colney, vac. by res. of Thomas Durnell; patron, John Pulteney kt. London, 8 December 1421.

389. [fo. 151r] Institution of Thomas Roger priest to vicarage of Aylesbury, vac. by res. of William Bode; patron, M. Robert FitzHugh, preb. of Aylesbury in Lincoln cath. By exchange with vicarage of Croxton. London, 9 December 1421.

390. Institution of John Cryps priest to vicarage of East Claydon, newly ordained; patron, P. and C. of Bisham. London, no date.

391. Institution of Thomas Marchall priest, in person of Robert Darcy, clerk, his proctor, to vicarage of Whaddon, vac. by res. of John Mychett; patron, King Henry. St Neots, 21 January 1421/2.

Hic incipiunt institutiones facte per honorabilem virum magistrum Robertum Leek legum doctorem ecclesie Lincoln' canonicum reverendi in Christo patris et domini domini Ricardi Flemmyng dei gracia Lincolnien' episcopi extra suas civitatem et diocesim in remotis agentis vicarium in spiritualibus generalem.

392. Institution of William Monke priest to vicarage of Chesham, vac. by res. of Richard Monke; patron, A. and C. of Leicester. Liddington, 3 March 1421/2.

393. Institution of Thomas Stockyng to vicarage of Everton; patron, P. and C. of St Neots – and of Henry Patews to church of Gayhurst; patron, Robert Nevyll of Prestwold, kt. By exchange. 23 February 1421/2 [no place specified]. Note that an inquiry was held by the official of the archdn of Buckingham, by which it was found that the right of presentation to Gayhurst belonged to the said Robert for this turn only, and that lady Alice Nowers presented at the last vacancy.[36]

394. [fo. 151v] Institution of Peter Gunthorp to church of Loughton Magna with chapel of Loughton Parva annexed; patron, Thomas Dardrys of Turvey – and of William Hawkyn to vicarage of Marden, dioc. Canterbury; patron, A. and

---

[36] Everton was in the archdnry of Huntingdon.

C. of Lesnes. Exchange, by authority of a commission of Henry [Chichele], archbp of Canterbury (dated at Lambeth, 7 February 1421/2). Note that an inquiry was held by the official of the archdn of Buckingham, by which it was found that the right of presentation to Loughton Magna belonged to Thomas Dardrys of Turvey for this turn, and that lady Elizabeth Clynton presented at the last vacancy. Liddington, 11 March 1421/2.

395. Institution of Edward Pepyn priest, in person of M. Robert Somersete, clerk, his proctor, to vicarage of Stoke Poges, vac. by res. of John Cully; patron, P. and C. of St Mary Overy, Southwark. Liddington, 8 June 1422.

396. [fo. 152r] Institution of John Barker priest to church of Beachampton, vac. by res. of William Holbek; patron, P. and C. of Luffield. By exchange with vicarage of Wardley and Belton. Liddington, 17 June 1422.

397. Institution of Thomas Markaunt priest to church of Aston Sandford, vac. by death of John Kyng; patron, Nicholas Thorley esquire and lady Alice his wife. Liddington, 17 July 1422. Note that an inquiry was held by the official of the archdn of Buckingham, by which it was found that the said Nicholas Thorley and lady Alice were true patrons, and that Richard Vere, earl of Oxford, presented the said John Kyng at the last vacancy.

398. Institution of Thomas Laurens priest to vicarage of prebendal church of King's Sutton, vac. by res. of Thomas Ymworth; patron, John Gylberd, proctor of M. Robert Gylberd, preb. of Sutton cum Buckingham in Lincoln cath. Liddington, 30 July 1422. Note that an inquiry was held by the official of the peculiar jurisdiction of the said prebend, by which it was found that the said John Gylberd was true patron for this turn by reason of a sufficient proxy granted to him by the said M. Robert.

Quarto kalendas Maii anno domini millesimo CCCC^mo xxij^do incipit annus tertius consecrationis reverendi in Christo patris et domini domini Ricardi Flemmyng' dei gracia Lincoln' episcopi.

399. Institution of br. John Massy priest to church of Drayton Parslow; patron, King Henry. London, 1422 [day and month blank].

400. [fo. 152v] Institution of William Praunce priest to vicarage of Little Marlow; patron, P. and C. of Marlow. Liddington, 30 July 1422.

401. Institution of John Horle, in person of John Vertjuys, clerk, his proctor, to church of Little Kimble; patron, A. and C. of St Albans – and of William Ayleff, in person of M. Thomas Colstone, clerk, his proctor, to vicarage of Boughton Monchelsea, dioc. Canterbury; patron, P. and C. of Leeds. Exchange, by authority of a commission of Henry [Chichele], archbp of Canterbury (dated at South Malling, 10 August 1422). Liddington, 29 August 1422.

402. Institution of Thomas Smyth priest to vicarage of Thurleigh (*Lega*), newly ordained; patron, P. and C. of Canons Ashby. No date.

403.   Ordination, by Robert Leek LL.D., canon of Lincoln and commissary of Bp Fleming, with the assent of the prior, br. Henry Watteford, and convent of Canons Ashby and of Thomas Smyth, vicar of Thurleigh (*Lega*), of a perpetual vicarage in the church of Thurleigh. The prior and convent are to have all tithes and oblations whatsoever belonging to the said church. They are to pay annually to the said Thomas Smyth, vicar, and his successors, the sum of twelve marks of English money in the church of Thurleigh at four yearly terms, that is, the feasts of the Annunciation, the Nativity of St John the Baptist, Michaelmas and Christmas, or within eight days of the same, by equal portions. They are to pay 100 shillings to the fabric of Lincoln cath. for each term in which the said money is not paid in full. The bp and his successors, his vicar generals and Officials, are to have power to sequestrate the revenues of the said church, both for any part of the said twelve marks that is unpaid, and for the said penalty of 100 shillings. The prior and convent are to bear all the burdens of the church, both ordinary and extraordinary, excepting only the cure of souls which is to be borne by the vicar. The prior and convent are to assign to the vicar within one year following this ordination a suitable house for his dwelling, having a hall, a chamber with pantry and buttery, a kitchen, a stable, another building for storing hay and firewood, and a sufficient garden. The house is to be built in the first instance by the prior and convent at their own expense, and thereafter is to be maintained and repaired at the expense of the vicar and his successors. No date.[37]

404.   [fo. 153r] Institution of John Crypas priest to vicarage of East Claydon, newly ordained; patron, P. and C. of Bisham. Old Temple, 1 February 1421/2.

405.   Ordination of a perpetual vicarage in the church of East Claydon, appropriated to the prior and convent of Bisham. At every vacancy, the prior and convent are to present a suitable candidate to the bp for institution. The vicar is to have all the small tithes, oblations and mortuaries, and a cottage called *Busshes place* for his dwelling. The vicar is to support all the burdens of the church, except the repair of the chancel. The prior and convent are to pay annual pensions of 6s 8d to the bp and of 10s to the archdn of Buckingham. No date.

In dei nomine Amen. Nos Ricardus permissione divina Lincoln' episcopus in infrascripto negotio rite recte et legitime procedentes vicariam perpetuam ecclesie parochialis de Estclaydon' nostre Lincoln' diocesis quam Prior et Conventus de Bustelesham ordinis sancti Augustini Sarum diocesis eis et eorum Prioratui auctoritate apostolica tenent et possident appropriatam de eorundem Prioris et Conventus expressis consensu et assensu et ad eorum instantem petitionem et requisitionem ordinamus dotamus limitamus et assignamus in et de portionibus ac cum oneribus et sub modis et formis infrascriptis. In primis ordinamus limitamus et assignamus quod in dicta ecclesia parochiali de Estclaydon' sit una perpetua vicaria in portionibus et rebus subscriptis dotata ad quam quotiens vacaverit dicti Religiosi viri et eorum successores idoneum virum nobis et successoribus nostris sede plena seu Officiali Lincoln' *sede vacante* canonice presentabunt per nos et successores nostros aut dictum Officialem admittendum. Portionemque congruam

---

[37]   Thurleigh was in the archdnry of Bedford.

ex qua idem vicarius congrue valeat sustentari episcopalia et archidiaconalia iura solvere et alia ordinaria et extraordinaria eidem ecclesie incumbencia subscriptis oneribus dumtaxat exceptis supportare moderatione provida in rebus et proventibus subscriptis dumtaxat et non aliis taxamus et limitamus ac ordinamus.

In primis statuimus et ordinamus quod vicarius huiusmodi qui pro tempore fuerit abhinc semper et imperpetuum habeat omnes et singulas decimas minutas vide-licet lane agnorum [fo. 153v] vitulorum porcellorum ancarum pirorum pomorum et aliorum fructuum et herbarum de arboribus et ortis infra dictam parochiam provenientes ac lini et canabi silue cedue lactis casei cere mellis omniumque molendinorum ovorum columbarum necnon omnimodas oblationes tam ad summum altare quam ad alia loca quecumque infra dictam parochiam qualitercumque provenientes mortuaria eciam tam viva quam mortua: necnon unum Cotagium vocatum Busshes place cum una virgata terre pro manso eiusdem vicarii ab omni seculari servicio et exactione libera et immunia.[38] Item volumus statuimus et ordinamus quod vicarius qui pro tempore fuerit omnia onera episcopalia et archidiaconalia et omnia alia onera ordinaria et extraordinaria eidem ecclesie incumbencia debite supportabit excepto onere reparandi seu reficiendi Cancellum dicte ecclesie quod ad ipsos Religiosos viros quotiens ipsum Cancellum huiusmodi reparatione seu refectione indigeat volumus pertinere. Item excepto onere quarundam pensionum annuarum ratione indempnitatum nobis et successoribus nostris episcopis Lincoln' videlicet sex solidorum et octo denariorum per predecessorem nostrum ratione appropriationis huiusmodi assignatorum ac eciam decem solidorum archidiacono Buckyngham' assignatorum quarum quidem pensionum solutionem dicti Religiosi et eorum successores perpetuo subibunt et agnoscent. Item volumus et ordinamus quod dicti Religiosi viri solvant decimam et omnem partem decime quotiens et quandocumque ipsam domino nostro Regi per Clerum concedi contingat. Item volumus et ordinamus quod dicti Religiosi viri semper sint quieti et liberi ab omni decimatione quarumcumque rerum et proventum Rectorie dicte ecclesie de Estclaydon' qualitercumque spectantium: nec ipse vicarius ad aliqualem solutionem decimarum de rebus quibuscumque in portione vicarie sue superius assignate aliquatenus teneatur nec eciam compellatur sed ab omni huiusmodi solutione liber sit penitus et immunis per presentes. Habebit eciam vicarius huiusmodi omnes putationes vel amputationes anglice Shrydes .i. abscisiones ramorum de arboribus in cimiterio dicte ecclesie crescentibus per eum absque detrimento corporum arborum huiusmodi prestidend' &c.

406. Institution of Thomas Peche to church of Radclive; patron, warden and fellows of New College, Oxford – and collation of vicarage of North Weald, dioc. London, to Aunger Tymberland; patron, bp of London. Exchange, by authority of commission of John [Kempe], bp of London (dated at Fulham, 20 October 1422). Liddington, 2 November 1422.

---

[38] MS 'immuia'.

[fo. 154r]

Hic incipiunt institutiones facte per reverendum in Christo patrem et dominum dominum Ricardum Flemmyng dei gracia Lincolnien' episcopum post reditum suum in diocesim suam Lincoln'.

407. Institution of John Smyth priest to church of Dunton (*Dodyngton*'), vac. by res. of Robert Seman; patron, Simon Wedon and John FitzThomas. London, [blank] March 1422/3. Note that an inquiry was held by M. William Symond, commissary-general in archdnries of Oxford and Buckingham, by which it was found that the patrons presented for this turn by reason of a feoffment to them of the manor and advowson of Dunton, and that they presented at the last vacancy.

408. Institution of John Harpetre to church of St Nicholas, Saunderton; patron, Gerard Braybroke kt – and of Richard de Patryngton to church of Bonnington, dioc. Canterbury; patron, br. Henry Crounehale, preceptor of Buckland and lieutenant of br. William Hulles, prior of Hospitallers in England. Exchange, by authority of commission of Henry [Chichele], archbp of Canterbury (dated at Maidstone, 18 March 1422/3). Old Temple, 23 March 1423 (*recte* 1422/3).

[fo. 154v]

Hic incipiunt institutiones facte per honorabilem virum magistrum Robertum Leek legum doctorem ecclesie Lincoln' canonicum reverendi in Christo patris et domini domini Ricardi Flemmyng' dei gracia Lincoln' episcopi in remotis agentis vicarium in spiritualibus generalem.

409. Certificate of M. William Wynnewyk LL.B. In accordance with commission of vicar-general (dated at Liddington, 27 September 1422), he has carried out an inquiry into the presentation by John Raynes kt of William Hummes to the church of Emberton. It was found that the church was vac. through the death of the last rector, William Whyrler, at Emberton on 24 September 1422; that John Raynes had the right of presentation by reason of a feoffment of certain lands in Emberton with the advowson of the church, made to him by John Tyryngham; that the presentee was of honest life, over thirty years of age and in priest's orders, and that he was rector of Scaldwell in the same diocese. Finding no impediment, he has instituted William Hummes to the church. Emberton, 29 September 1422.

[fo. 155r]

Quarto kalendas Maii anno domini millesimo CCCC^mo vicesimo tertio incipit annus quartus consecrationis reverendi in Christo patris et domini domini Ricardi Flemmyng' dei gracia Lincolnien' episcopi.

410. [fo. 155v] Institution of John Everard priest, in person of William Baker clerk his proctor, to vicarage of Stowe, vac. by res. of M. Thomas Newman; patron, A. and C. of Osney. Liddington, 11 May 1423.

411. Institution of John Ratherby priest to vicarage of Great Kimble, vac. by res. of M. Richard Nayler; patron, A. and C. of Missenden. By exchange with vicarage of Banbury. Liddington, 15 May 1423.

412. Institution of John Hagason of *Sawdeburgh* priest, in person of William Grenelane clerk his proctor, to vicarage of Caversfield; patron, A. and C. of Missenden. Liddington, 1 July 1423.

413. Institution of John Brampton M.A., priest, to church of Taplow, vac. by res. of M. John Bodeman; patron, P. and C. of St Mary, Merton. Liddington, 27 May 1423.

414. Institution of Thomas Wryght priest, in person of M. Robert Somerset clerk his proctor, to vicarage of Medmenham, vac. by res. of Thomas Hythe; patron, A. and C. of Medmenham. Liddington, 3 August 1423.

415. Certificate of M. William Symond, commissary-general and sequestrator in archdnries of Oxford and Buckingham. In accordance with commission of vicar-general (dated at Liddington, 9 July 1423), he has carried out an inquiry into the presentation by John Barton the younger, esquire, of William Tayllour to the church of Thornton. An inquiry was held in full chapter in the said church on Monday after the feast of St James, in the presence of Richard Bek rector of Maids' Moreton, John Tayllour rector of Leckhampstead, John Blanket rector of Akeley, Richard Gery rector of Addington, William Goldryng vicar of Wing, John Prentys vicar of Padbury, Richard Hardyng vicar of Thornborough, and Thomas Marschall vicar of Whaddon. It was found that the church was vac. through the death of William Tillet the last rector, which took place on 23 May 1423; that the said John Barton had the right of presentation for this turn by reason of his lordship of Thornton; that John Chastelton kt, from whom the said John Barton obtained the lordship, presented at the last vacancy. It was also found that the said William Tayllour was free, legitimate, of honest life, in priest's orders, over thirty years of age, and not beneficed elsewhere. Finding no impediment, therefore, he has instituted William Tayllour to the church. Thornton, Monday after the feast of St James, 1423.

416. [fo. 156r] Institution of Thomas Tyngewyk priest, in person of John Gyles his proctor, to church of Wavendon, vac. by death of John Stowe; patron, Mary Talbot, widow of Thomas Grene kt, decd. Liddington, 31 August 1423. Note that an inquiry was held by M. William Symond, commissary-general in archdnries of Oxford and Buckingham, by which it was found that Mary Talbot had the right of presentation by reason of her dowry, which she held by grant of Thomas Grene kt, son and heir of the said Thomas Grene kt, decd.

417. Institution of John Trylle priest, in person of Richard Kyrkeby clerk his proctor, to church of Little Kimble, vac. by res. of John Horele; patron, br. John Blebury, prior of St Albans and commissary of the abbot of the same, *in remotis*. By exchange with perpetual chantry of Colney. Liddington, 7 October 1423.

418.   Institution of John Howell priest, in person of M. Robert Somerset clerk his proctor, to church of Wexham, vac. by death of William Croydon; patron, P. and C. of Southwark. Liddington, 7 October 1423.

419.   [fo. 156v] Certificate of the Official of the Court of Canterbury. In accordance with commission of vicar-general (dated at Liddington, 28 May 1423, and addressed to M. William Alnewyk, keeper of the privy seal; M. William Lyndewode, Official of the Court of Canterbury; and M. John Lynfeld, examiner-general of the said Court), he has collated church of Twyford to Thomas Astell clerk; patron, bp of Lincoln. By exchange with wardenship of perpetual altar of Goldes in collegiate church of Maidstone, in the collation of the archbp of Canterbury. Abingdon, 9 September 1423.

420.   Certificate of institution, by Andrew Sondres LL.B., vicar-general of John [Langdon], bp of Rochester, of Thomas Bromsale to church of Radnage, vac. by res. of John Palmer; patron, br. Henry Crounhale, preceptor of Eagle and lieutenant of br. William Hulles, prior of Hospitallers in England, *in remotis*. Exchange, by authority of commission of vicar-general (dated at Liddington, 18 August 1423), with vicarage of Eltham, dioc. Rochester. Dartford, 21 August 1423. Received at Liddington, 7 October 1423.

421.   [fo. 157r] Institution of Richard Man priest to vicarage of Datchet, vac. by death of John Gloucestre; patron, warden and chapter of royal free chapel of St George, Windsor. Liddington, 2 November 1423.

422.   Institution of Walter Laurence clerk to church of Farnham Royal, vac. by res. of John Stokes; patron, John, lord Talbot and Furnivale. Old Temple, 6 December 1423.[39]

423.   Institution of Richard Petteworth clerk, in person of Richard Ab his proctor, to church of Quainton, vac. by death of last rector; patron, John Cheyne esquire and lady Isabel his wife. Old Temple, 5 October 1423.[40]

424.   Institution of Robert Seman priest to church of Great Hampden, vac. by res. of John Sterlyng; patron, Thomas Durem and Nicholas Bagenhale. Old Temple, 19 November 1423.[41]

425.   Institution of Walter Kynghen priest, in person of M. Robert Somersete clerk his proctor, to vicarage of Wendover, vac. by death of John Pakker; patron, P. and C. of St Mary, Southwark. Liddington, 13 November 1423.

426.   Institution of br. Theobald Wynchestre, canon of St Frideswide, Oxford, priest, to vicarage of Oakley; patron, P. and C. of St Frideswide, Oxford. Liddington, 7 December 1423.

---

[39] MS gives year as 1422.
[40] MS gives year as 1422.
[41] MS gives year as 1422.

427. [fo. 157v] Institution of John Carbrok priest to portion of church of Waddesdon, vac. by res. of M. John Castell; patron, King Henry. Liddington, 14 December 1423.

428. Institution of William Aylyff priest, in person of M. Richard Kyrkeby clerk his proctor, to vicarage of Great Kimble; patron, A. and C. of Missenden. Liddington, 7 February 1423/4.

429. Institution of M. John Duffeld of *Scarle*, in person of Robert Darcy his proctor, to vicarage of Wing; patron, Queen Joan – and collation of church of Halton in jurisdiction of Canterbury to William Goldryng, in person of M. William Symond his proctor; patron, archbp of Canterbury. Exchange, by authority of commission of Henry [Chichele], archbp of Canterbury (dated at Lambeth, 11 January 1423/4). Thame, 29 February 1423/4.

[Most of fo. 158r is blank.]

[fo. 158v]

Quarto kalendas Maii anno domini millesimo CCCC^{mo} xxiiij^{to} incipit annus quintus consecrationis reverendi in Christo patris et domini domini Ricardi dei gracia Lincolnien' episcopi.

430. Institution of Adam Babyngton priest, in person of M. Thomas Colstone, clerk and notary public, his proctor, to church of Milton Keynes, vac. by death of John Megin; patron, Thomas Chaworth kt and Isabel his wife, Humfrey Stafford esquire and Eleanor his wife. Liddington, 30 April 1424. Note that an inquiry was held by M. William Symond, commissary-general in archdnries of Oxford and Buckingham, by which it was found that the patrons presented by hereditary right of the said Isabel and Eleanor, daughters and heiresses of Thomas Aylesbury kt decd, late lord of the manor of Milton Keynes to which the advowson appertained; and that John Aylesbury kt decd, father of the said Thomas Aylesbury, presented John Megin at the last vacancy.

431. Institution of John Wenge priest, in person of John Turvey clerk his proctor, to chaplaincy in church of Newport Pagnell, vac. by death of John Matheu; patron, John Barton the younger. Liddington, 2 May 1424. Note that an inquiry was held by the official of the archdn of Buckingham, by which it was found that the said John Barton was true patron by reason of a charter of feoffment made to him for life; and that at the last vacancy John, late bp of Lincoln, collated the benefice to the said John Matheu by lapse, through the negligence of Thomas Harecourt kt, patron at that time.

432. Institution of Nicholas Thornerton priest to vicarage of Whaddon, vac. by res. of Thomas Marschall; patron, King Henry. Old Temple, 15 May 1424.

433. Institution of Geoffrey Barge priest to church of Creslow, vac. by res. of Walter; patron, br. Henry Crounehale, lieutenant of br. William Hulles, prior of Hospitallers in England. Old Temple, 19 May 1424. Note that an inquiry was held by M. William Symond, commissary-general in archdnries of Oxford and Buckingham, by which it was found that the said br. Henry presented for this turn as lieutenant, and that the prior of Hospitallers presented the said Walter at the last vacancy.

[fo. 159r]

Duodecimo die mensis Februarii anno domini millesimo CCCC^mo xxiiij^to incipit institutiones expedite per honorabilem virum magistrum Robertum Leek legum doctorem officialem et commissarium in hac parte per dominum Cantuar' sufficienter deputatum prout planius patet in simili rubrica in quaterno archidiaconatus Lincoln'.

434. Certificate of institution, by John [Wheathampstead], abbot of St Albans, of Peter Braunch to vicarage of Steeple Claydon, vac. by res. of M. William Gordcote; patron, A. and C. of Osney. Exchange, by authority of commission of M. Robert Leek (dated at Liddington, 21 March 1424/5), with vicarage of Winslow, dioc. Lincoln and jurisdiction of St Albans. St Albans, 23 March 1424/5. Received at Liddington, 25 March 1424/5.

435. Institution of Laurence Stafford clerk to church of Grendon Underwood, vac. by res. of Walter Chyton; patron, Eleanor, lady St Amand. Thame, 15 April 1425.

436. Institution of John Fuller priest to chantry of St Mary the Virgin in church of Newport Pagnell, vac. by death of John Wenge; patron, John Barton the younger, lord of Thornton. Northampton, 19 April 1425.

[fo. 159v is blank. Fos 160–162 have been excised.]

[fo. 163r]

Collationes prebendarum
(Collations of prebends and dignities. Throughout this section, it may be assumed that each entry includes a mandate to install addressed to the dean and chapter of Lincoln, unless otherwise stated. See introductory note on editorial practice.)

Quarto kalendas Maii anno domini millesimo CCCC^mo vicesimo incipit annus primus consecrationis reverendi in Christo patris et domini domini Ricardi Flemmyng' dei gracia Lincoln' episcopi.

437. Collation of prebend of Liddington, vac. by death of M. Robert Wyntryngham, to M. Richard Burnham priest. Grantham, 7 July 1420.

Vacantibus canonicatu ecclesie Lincoln' et prebenda de Lidyngton' in eadem per mortem magistri Roberti Wyntryngham ultimi canonici et prebendarii eorundem, reverendus in Christo pater et dominus dominus Ricardus dei gracia Lincoln' episcopus eosdem canonicatum et prebendam sic vacantes et ad collationem suam pleno jure spectantes dilecto sibi in Christo magistro Ricardo Burnham presbitero contulit intuitu caritatis et ipsum canonicum et prebendarium eorundem investivit et instituit canonice in eisdem apud Grantham vij die mensis Julii anno domini millesimo CCCC^{mo} xx^o, nulla inquisitione previa quia etc. jurata canonica obediencia etc. ut in forma. Scriptum fuit decano et capitulo ecclesie Lincoln' predicte seu ipso decano absente cuicumque presidenti et capitulo eiusdem ad faciendum quod etc.

438. Collation of precentorship of Lincoln, with prebend of Kilsby annexed, vac. by res. of M. Robert Gilbert, to M. William Burton priest. Same day and place.

439. Collation of prebend of Sanctae Crucis, vac. by res. of M. William Burton, to M. Robert Gilbard priest, in person of M. Richard Heth, archdn of Huntingdon, his proctor. Same day and place.

440. Collation of prebend of Dunham, vac. by death of John Everdon, to William Bothe clerk. Langtoft, 10 October 1420.

441. Collation of prebend of Sutton cum Buckingham, vac. by death of M. Henry Rumworth, to M. Robert Gilbert D.Th., in person of Thomas Yonge clerk, his proctor. Fotheringhay, 31 October 1420.

442. Collation of prebend of Sanctae Crucis to M. John Southam priest. Same place, 1 November 1420.

443. Collation of prebend of Welton Beckhall to M. John Haversham priest. Fineshade, 3 November 1420.

444. Collation of prebend of Nassington, vac. by death of M. Nicholas Colnet, to M. Robert Leek. Royston, 28 November 1420.

445. [fo. 163v] Collation of prebend of Decem Librarum to Walter Shiryngton, in person of M. William Freman clerk, his proctor – and of Richard Rycheman to prebend of Minor Pars Altaris in Salisbury cath. Exchange, by authority of commission of John [Chaundler], bp of Salisbury (dated at his hospice in Fleet Street, London, 8 December 1420). Westminster, 14 December 1420.

446. Collation of prebend of Luda, vac. by death of M. John Waynflete, to Alan Humbrestone priest. Old Temple, 11 February 1420/1.

447. Collation of prebend of Stoke, vac. by res. of Alan Humbreston, to M. Richard Burnham. Same day and place.

448. Collation of prebend of Liddington, vac. by res. of Richard Burnham, to Robert Iwardeby priest. Same day and place.

[fo. 164r] **Quarto kalendas Maii anno domini millesimo quadringentesimo vicesimo primo incipit annus secundus consecrationis reverendi in Christo patris et domini domini Ricardi dei gracia Lincolniensis episcopi.**

449. Collation of prebend of Dunham, vac. by res. of William Bothe, to William Malberthorp priest. Old Temple, 27 May 1421.

450. Collation of prebend of Corringham, vac. by death of John Thorp, to M. Simon de Teramo LL.D. Osney, 16 November 1421.

451. Collation of prebend of Welton Ryval, vac. by res. of Thomas Nassh, to John Hayworth priest, in person of M. Thomas Hill, his proctor. Old Temple, 14 December 1421.

452. Collation of archdnry of Huntingdon, vac. by res. of M. Richard Hethe, to M. William Lassels priest. Old Temple, 15 December 1421.

453. [fo. 164v] Collation of prebend of Leicester St Margaret, vac. by death of Thomas More, to M. Thomas Barnesley priest. Buckden, 1421 [day and month blank in MS].

Quarto kalendas Maii anno domini millesimo quadringentesimo vicesimo secundo incipit annus tertius consecrationis reverendi in Christo patris et domini domini Ricardi Flemmyng' dei gracia Lincoln' episcopi.

454. Collation of office of verger (one of four serving in Lincoln cath.), vac. by dimission of Robert Stokes, to Stephen Parkehouse. Liddington, 11 October 1422.

455. Collation of prebend of Welton Painshall, vac. by death of John Parke, to M. Thomas Whyston priest. Liddington, 12 October 1422.

456. Collation of prebend of Thame, vac. by death of William Kynwolmersh, to M. Robert Leek priest. Billinghay, 16 December 1422.

457. Collation of prebend of Nassington, vac. by res. of M. Robert Leke, to John Macworth priest. Same day and place.

458. Collation of prebend of Empingham to Thomas Belton chaplain. Same day and place.

459. [fo. 165r] Collation of prebend of Norton Episcopi, vac. by res. of M. John Thorneton, to Thomas Wykersley priest. Boston, 23 January 1422/3.

460. Collation of prebend of Marston St Lawrence, vac. by res. of M. Thomas Stretton, to M. William Berford D.Th., priest. Old Temple, 26 November 1422.

Hic incipiunt collationes facte per venerabilem virum magistrum Robertum Leek legum doctorem canonicum ecclesie Lincoln' reverendi in Christo patris et domini domini Ricardi dei gracia Lincoln' episcopi in remotis agentis vicarium in spiritualibus generalem et in hac parte commissarium sufficienter deputatum.

461. Collation of archdnry of Bedford, vac. by death of William Aghton, to M. Richard Caudray priest. Liddington, 17 April 1423.

462. Institution of M. John Forster, in person of John Bridlyngton, clerk, his proctor, to prebend of Biggleswade; patron, King Henry. The royal letters patent of presentation (dated at Westminster, 26 January 1423) and the royal writ notifying that the king had recovered his presentation to the prebend against Bp Repingdon and M. John Ixworth (dated at Westminster, 14 May 1423) are given in full. Liddington, 19 May 1423.

463. Collation of prebend of Langford Manor, vac. by the institution of M. John Forster to the prebend of Biggleswade, to M. Thomas Brouns LL.D., priest. Liddington, 20 May 1423.

[fo. 165v]

464. Collation of chancellorship of Lincoln, with the prebend of Sutton in Marisco and church of Nettleham annexed to the same, vac. by death of M. Thomas Duffeld, to M. John Castell D.Th., priest. Liddington, 15 November 1423.

465. Collation of prebend of Asgarby to M. Thomas Rosell, in person of Robert Iwardeby his proctor. Liddington, 13 September 1423.

466. Collation of prebend of St Botolph to Thomas Wodeford, clerk. Liddington, 6 October 1423.

467. Collation of prebend of Milton Ecclesia, vac. by death of M. Walter Coke, to Robert Nevyll, clerk. Liddington, 3 January 1423/4.

468. Collation of precentorship of Lincoln, with the prebend of Kilsby annexed, vac. by death of M. William Burton, to M. William Clynt D.Th., priest. Liddington, 8 January 1423/4.

469. Collation of prebend of North Kelsey, vac. by death of John Wade, to M. Thomas Whyston D.Dec., priest. Liddington, 12 February 1423/4.

470. Collation of prebend of Welton Painshall to M. Thomas Chapman LL.B., in person of Thomas Colstone, clerk, his proctor. Liddington, 13 February 1423/4.

[fos 166–168 are missing]

[fo. 169r]

471.   Ordination celebrated by John, bp *Ancoraden'*, in conventual church of priory of St Katherine outside Lincoln, 1 June 1420.

Ordines generales celebrati in ecclesia conventuali prioratus sancte Katerine extra Lincoln' die sabbati quatuor temporum in vigilia sancte Trinitatis videlicet kalendas Junii anno domini millesimo CCCC^mo vicesimo per venerabilem patrem dominum Johannem Ancoraden' episcopum de mandato et ex commissione venerabilis viri magistri Johannis Southam archidiaconi Oxonie canonici ecclesie Lincoln' reverendi in christo patris et domini domini Ricardi dei gracia Lincoln' episcopi in remotis agentis vica[r]ii in spiritualibus generalis anno consecrationis dicti reverendi patris primo.

Ralph Benyngton, of York dioc., by letters dimissory, to the first tonsure.

Beneficed acolytes. John Proketour, rector of St Peter, Yarburgh (*Yerburgh Petri*).[42] Robert Frende, rector of Waltham.[43] John Balderston and William Stonle, choristers in Lincoln cath.

Acolytes in religious orders. Philip de Melton, Richard de Barton, William de Barton, canons of Newhouse. Thomas Fery, Austin friar of Lincoln. Peter Fulneby, Hugh Fryskeney, Dominican friars of Lincoln. John de Candelsby, William de Wrangyll, monks of Louth Park (*Parco Lude*). William Kyrkeby, canon of Launde. Thomas Gretham, William Kele, monks of Humberston. William Spayne, canon of St Katherine outside Lincoln.

Unbeneficed acolytes. Robert Tevelby. Robert Stevenson. Henry Bradley. Roger Creke. John Clareley. William Caton. Thomas Parkour. John Kesteven. Simon Whytyng. Thomas Spencer. John James. John Clement. Robert Gybbys. Thomas Helett. John Gunnore. William Redysdale. Robert Plungeon. John Lodyngton. John Wright. John Mawer. William Gremoncestre. John Nowell. John Russell. Thomas de Lee. John Wryght. Gerard Spayn. John Heyden of Northill. William Rychedale. William Claxby. John atte Hall. William Draper. Richard Acton. William Blawhorn. William Basset. John Salman. Henry Gercoke. John Berveyle. Richard Ingoldmels. John Potter. [fo. 169v] John Peretre. Thomas Fyssher. John Stalyngburgh. William Spaldyng. James Holbeche. John Sergeant. John Copper.

Beneficed subdeacons. John Proketour, rector of Yarburgh. Robert Frende, rector of Waltham. John de Depyng, rector of Market Overton.[44] John Trassh, minister of Lincoln cath.

---

[42] John Proktour, having the first tonsure, was instituted to Yarburgh on 30 July 1419 [Reg. 14, fo. 100r].
[43] Robert Frende was instituted to Waltham on 18 November 1419 [Reg. 14, fo. 102r].
[44] Master John de Depyng was instituted to Market Overton on 2 August 1419 [Reg. 14, fo. 278r].

Subdeacons in religious orders. John de Melton,[45] Richard de Barton, William de Barton, canons of Newhouse. Robert Sudbury, canon of Croxton. Albert, friar minor of Lincoln. John de Candelesby, William de Wrangyll, monks of Louth Park. William Kyrkeby, canon of Launde. Robert Cokeryngton, William Foulestowe, canons of Ormsby. Thomas Gretham, William Kele, monks of Humberston. William Spayne, canon of St Katherine outside Lincoln.

Unbeneficed subdeacons. Thomas Milner of *Langeport*, t. Hospital of St John, Northampton (subdeacon). Thomas Baron of Hanslope, t. Ravenstone (*Ravnston*) Priory. William Coventre of Oakham, t. Launde Priory. Simon Luffenham of *Melton*, t. Burton Lazars. Hugh Burton of Lincoln, t. Priory of St Katherine outside Lincoln. Adam Sylk, t. Croxton Abbey. Henry Grantham of *Irby*, t. Nun Cotham (*Nuncotom*) Priory. William Boys of *Goudeby*, t. Tupholme Abbey. Robert Laverok of Elsham, t. Louth Park Abbey. John Code of West Keal, t. Kirkstead Abbey. John Aleyn, t. Cotterstock (*Cotherstoke*) College. Hugh Worliby of *Worliby*, t. Thornton. Robert Cokys of *Marom*, t. Bullington. Richard Caleflet of Burgh le Marsh, t. Legbourne. John Faukes of *Rothebury*, t. Barlings. Robert s. Walter Est of Brigsley, t. Nun Cotham. John Skynner of *Coryngham*, t. Heynings. John Hudson of Wrangle, t. Revesby. John Wastell of Oakham, t. St Katherine outside Lincoln. Richard Marneham. William Basset of Oundle, t. Cotterstock chantry. Gerard Spayn, t. Vaudey (*Valle Dei*). Robert Heryng of Sloothby, t. Markby. John Asgardeby of Welton le Wold, t. Louth Park. William Thornton of Kirton in Holland, t. Swineshead. John Heryot of Cotterstock, t. Cotterstock chantry. William Dunston of Elstow, t. Elstow. Robert Stepyngley of *Dalby*, t. Thurgarton. William Stene of *Russhenden*, t. Harrold. John atte Oke of *Haldenby*, t. Garendon. Henry Symon, t. Harrold. Roger House, t. Kirkstead. Richard Caltoft of Orby, t. Alvingham. Richard Pippewell of *Wermyngton*, t. Fineshade. Robert Atterton of *Croft*, t. Nun Cotham. Laurence Purley of Melton Mowbray, t. St Katherine outside Lincoln. John Roke of *Badyngton*, t. Newstead (*Novo Loco*) by Stamford. William Howet of Leicester, t. Ulverscroft. Richard Hert of Gumley, t. Sulby. Edmund Serle of *Thurleby*, t. Bourne. Thomas Leveryk of *Irby*, t. Louth Park.

Beneficed deacon. Simon Melburn, rector of Caythorpe.[46]

Deacons in religious orders. John Ludburgh, William Esterton, Austin friars of Lincoln. Thomas Forster, John Hunte, Robert de Malton, canons of Bullington. Thomas Harwode, canon of St Katherine outside Lincoln. John Astwatt, Roger Colman, Dominican friars of Lincoln. [fo. 170r] Thomas Gretham, monk of Louth Park. John Morecroft, canon of Barlings.

Unbeneficed deacons. Thomas Reve of *Molyngton*, t. Heynings. William Caton, t. Heynings. Thomas Fyssher of Huttoft, t. Hagnaby. William Burton of Market Rasen (*Estrasen*), t. Sixhills. Thomas Kyng s. John Kyng of *Multon*, t. (subdeacon and deacon) hospital of St John, Northampton. Richard Litster of Kimbolton, t. Stonely. Robert Gylmyn of *Multon*, t. St Mary Delapré by Northampton. John

---

[45] He is described as Philip de Melton among the acolytes above. See also no 485 below.
[46] Simon Melburne was instituted to Caythorpe on 28 October 1419 [Reg. 14, fo. 102r].

Meskyn of *Ulceby*, t. Thornton. John Barston of Banbury, t. Barlings. Robert Dey, t. Bullington. Henry Bayns, t. St Katherine by Lincoln. John Erle of *Driby*, t. Kirkstead. Robert Melton of Ailsworth (*Eylysworth*), t. Newstead by Stamford. Thomas Hevy of Middle Rasen, t. Sixhills. John s. Richard Walker of Horncastle, t. Revesby. John Baron, t. St Michael by Stamford. William Segbroke of Grantham, t. Croxton. William Peck of *Russhenden*, t. Harrold. Richard Wright of Leicester, t. Burton Lazars. Thomas Wragge, t. Revesby. John Irner of Byfield, t. Catesby. Stephen Ferrour of *Twyford*, t. Hospital of St John, Northampton. Thomas Wright of *Worliby*, t. St Katherine by Lincoln. John Fraunceys of Stamford, t. Newstead by Stamford. John Grene of Belchford, t. Louth Park. Richard Dorley of Hanslope, t. Ravenstone. William Faryngton of Olney, t. Lavendon. Richard Gybson of Boston, t. Kyme. Robert Coucher of Saltfleet Haven, t. Alvingham. Nicholas Tapurto of *Barewell*, t. Nuneaton. John Coventre s. William Coventre of *Rothewell*, t. (deacon) Hospital of St John, Northampton. John Botiler of *Depyng*, t. Bourne. John Philipp of Boston, t. Markby. Thomas Plungeon of Leicester, t. Ulverscroft. William North of Partney, t. Revesby.

Beneficed priests. William Couper, rector of Kenardington, dioc. Canterbury, by letters dimissory.[47] William Waynflete, rector of Binbrook St Mary.[48]

Priests in religious orders. John Gaytes, Austin friar of Lincoln. Richard Neusom, friar minor of Lincoln. John Tamworth, canon of Ulverscroft. Nicholas Holbeche, canon of Launde. Peter Scarthowe, canon of Barlings. Walter Freskeney, Dominican friar of Lincoln. Hugh de Bourne, Robert de Edenham, canons of Bourne. John Waynflet, monk of Bardney. John Donkaster, Carmelite friar of Lincoln. William Lincoln, John Thorp, canons of Thornholm.

Unbeneficed priests. Richard Barbour of *Barton*, t. Humberston. John Burdon of Stickford, t. Revesby. John Gryndyll of Wymington, t. Harrold. William Andrewe, t. Ulverscroft. John Fouler, t. Bradley. William Bulbek of Ravenstone, t. Ravenstone. Thomas Grendon of *Eketon*, t. (priest) Daventry. William Bogge, t. Osney. William Bagot of Great Grimsby, t. Alvingham. John Marschall, t. St Katherine outside Lincoln. John Midulton of Melton Mowbray, t. Burton Lazars. Robert Lety, t. St Frideswide, Oxford. Thomas Clement of *Diryngton*, t. Kyme. John Bouer of *Belton*, t. Bradley. Richard Roke s. Thomas Roke of Kettering, t. (priest) hospital of St John, Northampton. William Hede of Spalding, t. St Michael by Stamford. William Curteys, t. Crowland. [fo. 170v] John Kyng s. Thomas Kyng of *Multon*, t. (priest) Sulby. Thomas Parson of Huntingdon, t. Royston. Robert Blessot of Tilbrook, t. Ravenstone. Thomas Barett of Rippingale, t. Spalding. Robert Colby of *Somerby*, t. Bourne. John Salteby of Grantham, t. Catesby. Walter Rowle, t. Crowland. Richard Wryght, t. Sewardsley. John Walker s. Richard Walker of Horncastle, t. Revesby.

---

[47] Couper, who was instituted to Kenardington on 30 May 1419, was of Lincoln diocese [*Reg. Chichele* i. 187–8].
[48] William Waynflete was instituted to Binbrook St Mary on 28 January 1415/6 [Reg. 14, fo. 77v].

472. Ordination celebrated by Bp Fleming in the parish church of Deeping St James, 21 September 1420.

Ordines generales celebrati in ecclesia parochiali sancti Jacobi de Depyng Lincolnien' diocesis die sabbati quatuor temporum proximo post festum exaltationis sancte Crucis videlicet xj^mo kalendas Octobris anno domini millesimo quadringentesimo vicesimo per reverendum in Christo patrem et dominum dominum Ricardum dei gracia Lincolnien' episcopum anno consecrationis sue primo.

Beneficed acolytes. Richard Frysby, canon of Lincoln and prebendary of Milton Manor. Robert Monter, rector of Puttenham.[49] John Bukden, rector of Bawdeswell, dioc. Norwich, by letters dimissory.

Acolytes in religious orders. William Anderby, canon of Hagnaby. John Botheby, Dominican friar of Stamford. William Awnsell, William Oundell, Thomas Stanierus, Carmelite friars of Stamford. John Bescolby, Robert de Sproxton, canons of Croxton. Thomas Iwardeby, Thomas de Boston, monks of Swineshead. William Bottesford, canon of Newbo.

Unbeneficed acolytes. John Brygg. Godfrey Graunt. John Trotter. John Clerk. Richard Dighton. John Rote. William Gudehed. William Wynwyk. John Dere. Henry Gode. Thomas Eynysbury. William Grocok. William Fraunceys. Thomas Trotter. William Athurston. Richard Bloston. John Knotte. William Roseson. John Beke. John Huby of [blank] dioc., by letters dimissory. Henry Colles. Robert Godelake. Stephen Sergeant. Thomas Barton. William Gyrsby. John Phyppys. John Cokk. [fo. 171r] Robert Hoper. Thomas Greneley.

Beneficed subdeacons. Robert Monter, rector of Puttenham. Thomas More, rector of Northmoor.[50] John Bukden, rector of Bawdeswell dioc. Norwich, by letters dimissory.

Subdeacons in religious orders. William Bykeleswade, William Wolaston, John Rothewell, Richard Sonewell, canons of Newnham. Peter de Dordraco, friar minor of Boston. John de Broghton, [blank] de Horke, canons of Ulverscroft. William Awnsell, William Oundell, Carmelite friars of Stamford. Thomas Depyng, monk of Peterborough. Thomas Iwardeby, Thomas Boston, monks of Swineshead. John Bescolby, Robert de Sproxton, canons of Croxton. William Anderby, canon of Hagnaby. William Bottesford, canon of Newbo.

Unbeneficed subdeacons. John Elmyn of Boston, t. Tupholme. Ralph London of Little Harrowden (*Harewedon Parva*), t. hospital of St John, Northampton. William Draper of Stamford, t. Newstead by Stamford. Simon Hareby, t. Markby. John Salmondus of Crowland, t. Crowland. Thomas Walton of Leicester, t. hospital of

---

[49] Monter was instituted to Puttenham on 2 March 1419/20 [*Reg. Chichele* i. 177].
[50] Thomas s. Thomas de la More was instituted to Northmoor on 10 January 1419/20 [Reg. 14, fo. 423v].

St John, Leicester. John Rote of Crowland, t. Crowland. Richard Colne of Bourne, t. Bourne. Thomas William, t. Beaulieu. Robert Gybbe, t. Launde. Simon Whytyng of Bratoft, t. St Katherine outside Lincoln. William Gromonchestre of Peterborough, t. St Michael outside Stamford. John Clareley of *Weldon*, t. Launde. John Odam of Tydd St Mary, t. St Michael outside Stamford. Roger Wauwen, t. Alvingham. John James, t. Cotterstock. Henry Bradley, t. Stixwould. John Heydone of Northill (*Northyevell*), t. Elstow. Robert Hoper, t. Bruern. William Quenyne of Godmanchester, t. Sawtry. Roger Creke of Leicester, t. Charley. William Croft of Orby, t. Hagnaby. Godfrey Graunt of *Pykworth*, t. Newstead by Stamford. John Kesteven of *Rothewell*, t. Sulby. John Wykynby of *Houton*, t. Tupholme. William Redysdale of Kirkby Laythorpe, t. Haverholme. Henry Jercok of Oundle, t. Cotterstock. William Dene of *Keston*, t. St Katherine outside Lincoln. Robert Raulynson of *Ratheby*, t. Fosse. John Beford of Grimsby, t. Revesby.

Beneficed deacons. John Trassh, minister of Lincoln cath., t. chapter of Lincoln. M. John de Depyng, rector of Market Overton, t. his benefice *de quo reput' se contentum*.

Deacons in religious orders. John Bredon, Roger Stanley, Robert Staunton, canons of Leicester. John Friday, Dominican friar of Stamford. John de Wodethorp, John de Well, canons of Hagnaby. Robert Cokeryngton, canon of Ormsby. [fo. 171v] William Chevesby, canon of Chacombe. William de Kele, monk of Humberston. Peter Kyme, John Sautre, Robert Brampton, Robert Alwalton, monks of Sawtry. Richard de Gouxhill, Thomas de Thurleby, canons of Markby. Nicholas Dudyngton, canon of Fineshade.

Unbeneficed deacons. John Cod of West Keal (*Westerkele*), t. Kirkstead. Edmund Serle of *Thurleby*, t. Bourne. Adam Silk, t. Croxton. John Hudson of Wrangle, t. Revesby. Henry Grantham of *Irby*, t. Nun Cotham. John Skynner of Corringham, t. Heynings. Richard Caltoft of Orby, t. Alvingham. Thomas Leveryk of *Irby*, t. Louth Park. Richard Caleflete of Burgh le Marsh (*Burgh iuxta Waynflete*), t. Legbourne. Robert Stepyngley of *Dalby*, t. Thurgarton. Robert Cokys of *Marum*, t. Bullington. William Boys of *Goudeby*, t. Tupholme. Robert Atterton of *Croft*, t. Nun Cotham. Henry Symon, t. Harrold. John Faukes of *Rothebury*, t. Barlings. Thomas Baron of Hanslope, t. Ravenstone. Hugh Burton of Lincoln, t. St Katherine outside Lincoln. William Thornton of Kirton in Holland, t. Swineshead. Roger House, t. Kirkstead. John Aleyn of Tansor, t. Cotterstock. John Wastell of Oakham, t. St Katherine outside Lincoln. John atte Oke of *Haldenby*, t. Garendon. Thomas Milner of *Langeport*, t. (deacon and priest) Sulby. Richard Hert of Gumley, t. Sulby. Laurence Purley, t. St Katherine outside Lincoln. John Heryot of Cotterstock, t. Cotterstock. Robert Heryng of Sloothby, t. Markby. Richard Pippewell of *Wermyngton*, t. Fineshade. William Coventre of Oakham, t. Launde. William Steyne of *Russhenden*, t. Harrold. William Bele of Leicester, t. Ulverscroft. Simon Luffenham of *Meelton*, t. Burton Lazars. William Howet of Leicester, t. Ulverscroft. William Duston of Elstow, t. Elstow.

Beneficed priest. Simon Melburn, rector of Caythorpe.

Priests in religious orders. John Cornewale, canon of Alvingham. John Kyldesby, monk of Pipewell. Robert Stowe, monk of Biddlesden. Roger Colman, Dominican friar of Leicester. Richard Fosdyk, canon of Newbo. John Waynflet, canon of Markby. Richard Champeden, canon of Chacombe. John Rysle, Thomas Legger, canons of Dunstable. Henry Gretham, Austin friar of Stamford. John Eton, monk of St Neots.

Unbeneficed priests. John Baron, t. St Michael outside Stamford. Richard s. William Roper of *Benyngton*, t. Revesby. John Nicoll of Peterborough, t. Fineshade. John Fraunceys of Stamford, t. Newstead by Stamford. William Faryngdon of Olney, t. Lavendon. Robert Gylmyn of *Multon*, t. St Mary Delapré, Northampton. John Barston of Banbury, t. Barlings. John Philipp of Boston, t. Markby. John Boteler of *Depyng*, t. Bourne. William Caton, t. Heynings. Richard Wryght of Leicester, t. Burton Lazars. Thomas Fyssher of Huttoft, t. Hagnaby. John Grave of Stickford, t. Markby. John Irner of Byfield, t. Catesby. John Erle of *Driby*, t. Kirkstead. Henry Bayns, t. St Katherine outside Lincoln. [fo. 172r] Nicholas Tapyrto of *Barwell*, t. Nuneaton. Robert Melton of Ailsworth, t. Newstead by Stamford. Robert Dey, t. Bullington. Richard Litster of Kimbolton, t. Stonely. Robert Coucher of Saltfleet Haven, t. Alvingham. John Coventre s. William Coventre of *Rothewell*, t. (priest) Hospital of St John, Northampton. William Pekk of *Russheden*, t. Harrold. Stephen Ferrour of *Twyford*, t. Hospital of St John Baptist, Northampton. John Grene of Belchford, t. Louth Park. Thomas Kyng s. John Kyng of *Multon*, t. Hospital of St John Baptist, Northampton. Thomas Fynemour, t. Rewley (*Regali Loco iuxta Oxon*). William North of Partney, t. Revesby.

473. Ordination celebrated by Bp Fleming in conventual church of Dominican Friary, Dunstable, 21 December 1420.

Ordines generales celebrati in ecclesia conventuali fratrum predicatorum ville de Dunstaple Lincolnien' diocesis die sabbati quatuor temporum in festo sancti Thome apostoli xij^{mo} videlicet kalendas Januarii anno domini millesimo CCCC^{mo} vicesimo per reverendum in Christo patrem et dominum dominum Ricardum dei gracia Lincolnien' episcopum anno consecrationis primo.

Beneficed acolytes. Henry Syreston, rector of Marston Moretaine.[51]

Acolytes in religious orders. John Godfray, Thomas Bedford, friars minor of Bedford. William Bylyngdon, Robert Lawles, William Waneford, John Edwyn, Richard Nettelden, Robert Burneham, Dominican friars of Dunstable. John Hungarford, John Abyndon, canons of St Frideswide, Oxford. John Bolyngton, canon of Chicksands.

---

[51] Syreston was instituted on 3 November 1420 [no 213 above].

Unbeneficed acolytes. Thomas Amys. Stephen Roberam. Oliver Mille. Gilbert Bacsmale. William Conquest. Richard Trezyn of Exeter dioc., by letters dimissory. Michael Trenorth of Exeter dioc., by letters dimissory. Thomas Holand. Thomas Gyseld. William Bredon. John Smyth. Thomas Symon. John Philipp. Robert Cole. William Hopkyns. Robert Colby. William Lofthouse. William Dalton. Stephen Gardener. William Graan. William Prentys. John Carpenter. Reginald Pecok. Richard Whapelod. Thomas Lughtburgh. John Rosecastell. Thomas Chapman. John Fletcher. John Parke. [fo. 172v] John Hanney. John Porter.

Beneficed subdeacons. William Prentys, John Carpenter, Reginald Pecok, fellows of Oriel College, Oxford. Richard Wapelode, fellow of New College, Oxford. Henry Syreston, rector of Marston Moretaine. Robert Genne, rector of Nether Broughton.[52]

Subdeacons in religious orders. Richard Berenveyle, friar minor of Bedford. John Merydyth, William Stelyng, Franco de Bosco Ducis, Dominican friars of Dunstable. Thomas Rede, Patrick Denrose, Dominican friars of Northampton. Stephen London, monk of St Albans. Thomas Bynham, canon of Wymondley. John Hungarford, John Abyndon, canons of St Frideswide, Oxford. John Bolyngton, canon of Chicksands.

Unbeneficed subdeacons. Thomas Enesbury, t. Sawtry. William s. Robert Rosson of *Halton*, t. Revesby. Henry Gode, t. St Mary, Leicester. John Gunnore of *Ryngested*, t. (subdeacon) Harrold. Henry Colle of Cold Ashby, t. Daventry. Thomas Flowres of Irchester, t. (subdeacon) Harrold. William Taillour, t. Launde. Thomas Fyssher, t. Pipewell. William Yvus of Bicester, t. Bicester. John Welles of *Marston*, t. Caldwell. John Piers of Exeter dioc., by letters dimissory, t. Launceston. William Oldham of Coventry and Lichfield dioc., by letters dimissory, t. Chicksands. Thomas Aylewyn, t. Markyate. John Bregon of Hereford dioc., by letters dimissory, scholar of Oriel College, Oxford, t. his college. Robert Toryton of Salisbury dioc., by letters dimissory, t. Vaux College, Salisbury (*domus scolarum de Valle Sarum*). Richard Grymmok of Salisbury dioc., by letters dimissory, t. Bradenstoke. John Hurneman of Bath and Wells dioc., by letters dimissory, t. hospital of St John, Oxford. William Wormewode of York dioc., by letters dimissory, t. St Frideswide, Oxford. William Wynwyk of Biggleswade, t. Elstow. William Messyngham, t. Tupholme. John Gody of Exeter dioc., by letters dimissory, t. St Gregory, Canterbury. William Waynflete of Spalding, t. Spalding. William Pye of St Neots, t. Caldwell. Robert Colby, t. Gokewell. John Rosecastell, t. Rewley. Richard Homme of Hereford dioc., by letters dimissory, t. Osney.

Beneficed deacons. Robert Genne, rector of Nether Broughton. Robert Monter, rector of Puttenham. Peter Hayford, fellow of New College, Oxford, t. his college *de quo r' se contentum.* John Eburton, rector of Wigginton (*Wygyngton'*). John Bukdene, rector of Old (*Wolde*). John Lee, rector of Miserden, dioc. Worcester, by letters dimissory.

---

[52] Genne was instituted on 3 November 1420 [no 18 above].

Deacons in religious orders. Thomas Darby, friar minor of Bedford. Simon Bever, Austin friar of Oxford. William Bykeleswade, William Wolaston, John Rothewell, Richard Swynwell, canons of Newnham. John Baron, Richard Everdon, canons of St James, Northampton. John Aston, Richard Russell, monks of St Albans.

Unbeneficed deacons. Roger Creke of Leicester, t. Charley. John Kesteven of *Rothewell*, t. Sulby. [fo. 173r] John Wykenby of *Houton*, t. Tupholme. Ralph London, t. hospital of St John, Northampton. William Dene of *Keston*, t. St Katherine outside Lincoln. Simon Hareby, t. Markby. Robert s. Walter Est of Brigsley, t. Nun Cotham. Robert Rawlynson of *Ratheby*, t. Fosse. John Clarby of *Weldon*, t. Launde. William Quenyne of Godmanchester, t. Sawtry. Richard Marnham of Boston, t. Stixwould. William Croft of Orby, t. Hagnaby. John Emlyn of Boston, t. Tupholme. Gerard Spayn of Utrecht (*Traiecten'*) dioc., by letters dimissory, t. Vaudey (*Walle Dei*). Robert Gybbe, t. Launde. John James, t. Cotterstock. Roger Wauwen, t. Alvingham. John Bramfeld of *Newenham*, t. Daventry. William Redysdale of Kirkby Laythorpe, t. Haverholme. Richard Coln of Bourne, t. Bourne. Thomas Willyam, t. Beaulieu (*Bello Loco*). John Plear of Worcester dioc., by letters dimissory, t. St Mary de Pré (*de prato*) by St Albans. John Salmond of Crowland, t. Crowland. Robert Hoper, t. Bruern. Richard Credy of Exeter dioc., by letters dimissory, t. Rewley. Robert Rote of Crowland, t. Crowland. Godfrey Graunt of *Pykworth*, t. Newstead by Stamford. William Draper of Stamford, t. Newstead by Stamford. Thomas Davy of Bath and Wells dioc., by letters dimissory, t. Cleeve (*Clyva*).

Beneficed priests. John Rysby, rector of St Petroc, Exeter, by letters dimissory. Hawell ap Jen[or]n ap Lli, rector of Dinas, dioc. St David's, by letters dimissory, t. his benefice *de quo ut asseruit reputavit se contentum*.

Priests in religious orders. William Chevesby, canon of Chacombe. John Walyngford, Stephen Langley, canons of Notley. John Astwell, Dominican friar of Dunstable. William Smale, friar minor of Oxford. Thomas Barowe, Austin friar of Northampton.

Unbeneficed priests. Richard Hert of Gumley, t. Sulby. Henry Symon, t. Harrold. Thomas Baron of Hanslope, t. Ravenstone. Robert Atterton of *Croft*, t. Nuneaton. John Skynner of *Coryngham*, t. Heynings. Henry Grantham of *Irby*, t. Nun Cotham. Robert Stepyngley of *Dalby*, t. Thurgarton. Thomas Milner of *Langeport*, t. Sulby. John Cod of West Keal, t. Kirkstead. Thomas Plungeon of Leicester, t. Ulverscroft. William Duston of Elstow, t. Elstow. William Steyne of *Russhenden*, t. Harrold. John Huwell, dioc. Exeter, by letters dimissory, t. Rewley. Roger House, t. Kirkstead. John Cokys of *Marom*, t. Bullington. John Faukys of *Rothebury*, t. Barlings. Richard Caleflet of Burgh le Marsh (*Burgh iuxta Waynflete*), t. Legbourne. Robert Heryng of Sloothby, t. Markby. William Thornton of Kirton in Holland, t. Swineshead. Simon Lufnam of *Melton*, t. Burton Lazars. Adam Sylk, t. Croxton. Thomas Horspole of Litchborough, t. Chacombe. John Rygman, t. Royston. Edmund Serle of *Thurleby*, t. Bourne. William Helyng, t. Catley. Thomas Stokton of Salisbury dioc., by letters dimissory, t. Ivychurch (*Ederosi*). Richard Pyppewell of *Warmyngton*, t. Fineshade. John Dagben of Norwich dioc., by letters dimissory, t. St Mary, Ixworth.

[fo. 173v]

474. Ordination celebrated by Bp Fleming in the parish church of Hatfield, 15 February 1421.

Ordines generales celebrati in ecclesia parochiali de Hatfeld' episcopi Lincolnien' diocesis per reverendum in Christo patrem et dominum dominum Ricardum dei gracia Lincolnien' episcopum die sabbati quatuor temporum in prima septimana quadragesime videlicet xv kalendas Marcii anno domini millesimo CCCC^{mo} xx^{mo} et consecrationis sue anno primo.

Unbeneficed acolytes. Robert Cory. John Copgray. William Basset. John Wykys. John Glover. Thomas Gerard. John Ingryth. John Baldewyn. Richard Dalby. William Lorde. William Edwarde. Thomas Norton. William Inster. William Thomas. Richard Lloid, dioc. St David's, by letters dimissory. Maurice ap Phelip of St David's dioc., by letters dimissory.

Beneficed subdeacons. John Redesdale, minister of Lincoln cath.. Gervase Amery, rector of Todenham, dioc. Worcester, by letters dimissory.

Subdeacons in religious orders. John Godfray, friar minor of Bedford. Thomas Wold, Robert Jakesley, canons of St Mary, Huntingdon.

Unbeneficed subdeacons. John Spencer, t. Waltham. John Wykes, t. Swineshead. William Breton de Creton, t. Sulby. John Copgray of Godmanchester, t. Merton. Richard Harpeswell of Harpswell, t. Newhouse. John Copper of *Belton*, t. Legbourne. William Denyas of Blunham, t. Caldwell. Roger Betson of Coningsby, t. Markby. John Lodyngton of Old (*Wold*), t. Lavendon. John Clement, t. Holy Trinity Repton. John Maynard, t. Eynsham. William Sleford, t. St Katherine outside Lincoln. Thomas Norton, t. Cold Norton. Michael Trenerth of Exeter dioc., by letters dimissory, t. Osney. Richard Lloid of St David's dioc., by letters dimissory, t. Strata Florida. William Thomas of Exeter dioc., by letters dimissory, t. Bodmin. John Sare of Exeter dioc., by letters dimissory, t. Bodmin. Maurice ap Phelip of St David's dioc., by letters dimissory, t. Rewley.

Beneficed deacons. Robert Genne, rector of Nether Broughton. Henry Syreston, rector of Marston Moretaine, t. his benefice *de quo reputavit se &c.*

Deacons in religious orders. Richard Barnevyll, friar minor of Bedford. John Bulyngton, canon of Chicksands. Thomas Rede, Patrick Denerose, Dominican friars of Northampton. Thomas Bynham, canon of Wymondley.

Unbeneficed deacons. William Waynflete of Spalding, t. Spalding. [fo. 174r] Henry Gode, t. Leicester. Thomas Enesbury, t. Sawtry. Stephen Gardyner, t. (deacon and priest) Woburn. Robert Hilton, dioc. Bangor, by letters dimissory, t. Royston. William Yvus of Bicester, t. Bicester. Simon Whytyng, t. St Katherine outside Lincoln. William Pye of St Neots, t. Caldwell. Henry Colle of Cold Ashby, t. Daventry. Henry Jercok of Oundle, t. Cotterstock. William Taylour, t. Launde.

William Wynwyk of Biggleswade, t. Elstow. John Gunnore of *Ryngested*, t. Harrold. Robert Colby, t. Gokewell. John Perys of Exeter dioc., by letters dimissory, t. Launceston. William Prentys, fellow of University College, Oxford, t. his college *de quo reputavit se contentum*. John Brecon, perpetual scholar of Oriel College, Oxford, t. his college *de quo reputavit se contentum*. John Carpenter, perpetual scholar of the same college, t. his college *de quo reputavit se contentum*. Reginald Pecok, perpetual scholar of the same college, t. his college *de quo reputavit se contentum*. John Mark of Exeter dioc., by letters dimissory, t. Rewley. Richard Homme of Hereford dioc., by letters dimissory, t. Osney. Thomas Marom, t. St Katherine outside Lincoln.

Beneficed priests. John Bukden, rector of Old. Thomas Caterall, rector of Toynton St Peter (*Toynton inferior*).[53]

Priests in religious orders. Thomas Shepeshed, canon of St Mary, Leicester.

Unbeneficed priests. Ralph London of Little Harrowden (*Harwdon Parva*), t. hospital of St John, Northampton. John Clareby of *Weldon*, t. Launde. William Dene of *Keston*, t. St Katherine outside Lincoln. William Draper of Stamford, t. Newstead by Stamford. Gerard Spayne of Utrecht (*Traiecten'*) dioc., by letters dimissory, t. Vaudey. John Jamys, t. Cotterstock. Richard Coln of Bourne, t. Bourne. John Salmond of Crowland, t. Crowland. Robert Hoper, t. Bruern. Thomas Wryght of *Wolryby*, t. St Katherine outside Lincoln. John Heyden of Northill, t. Elstow. John Kesteven of *Rothewell*, t. Sulby. John Hudson of Wrangle, t. Revesby. William Redysdale of Kirkby Laythorpe, t. Haverholme. Roger Crek of Leicester, t. Charley. Robert s. Walter Est of Brigsley, t. Nun Cotham. William Howet of Leicester, t. Ulverscroft. John Wykynby of *Houton*, t. Tupholme. John Plear of Worcester dioc., by letters dimissory, t. St Mary de Pré (*de prato*) by St Albans. John atte Oke of *Haldenby*, t. Garendon. Robert Gybbe, t. Launde. John Bramfeld of *Newenham*, t. Daventry. Roger Waweyn, t. Alvingham. Richard Crody of Exeter dioc., by letters dimissory, t. Rewley by Oxford. Thomas Davy of Bath and Wells dioc., by letters dimissory, t. Cleeve (*Clyva*).

475.   Memorandum that on 16 February 1420/1, celebrating high mass in the chapel within his hospice of the Old Temple, Bp Fleming by force of a certain special privilege promoted Robert Allerton, rector of Amersham (*Agmundesham*), having the first clerical tonsure, to all four minor orders and then to the subdiaconate, to the title of his benefice *de quo ut asseruit reputavit se contentum*. Present: Robert Iwardeby canon of Lincoln, John Redburn clerk and me, Thomas Colston, notary public and bp's registrar.

[fo. 174v]

476.   Ordination celebrated by Bp Fleming in conventual church of Spalding Priory, 8 March 1421.

Ordines celebrati in ecclesia conventuali prioratus de Spaldyng Lincoln' diocesis per reverendum in Christo patrem et dominum

[53] Caterall was instituted on 13 December 1420 [*Reg. Fleming* i. 17].

dominum Ricardum dei gracia Lincolnien' episcopum die sabbati qua cantabatur in ecclesia dei officium Sitientes viij° videlicet idus Marcii anno domini millesimo CCCC^{mo} xx^{mo} et consecrationis sue primo.

Unbeneficed acolytes. Nicholas Lessy. Thomas Smyth. Robert Toft. William Warner. John Sybsey. Thomas Champneys. John Schort. John Totell. Richard Strykard. Philip Sqwyer. Henry Wryght. William Herynger. Robert Burton. Richard Gybson. William Wryght. Walter Botyler. John Walker. John Awbrey. Thomas Ryder. John Willyamson. John Bukkes. Stephen Watkynson. William Stokton. Simon Walker. Roger Hunne. Thomas Alford. William Wryght. John Deken. Thomas Bony. Richard Brace. Robert Whytebred. Ralph Goose. Robert Frank. Thomas Northampton. Matthew Janyn. Simon Scarlet. Thomas Flete. Simon Smith. Richard Brooun. Thomas Stekylthorn. Simon Robertson.

Beneficed subdeacons. Thomas Farford, vicar of Lincoln cath.

Subdeacons in religious orders. John Lesyngham, John More, John Spaldyng, monks of Peterborough. John Botheby, Dominican friar of Stamford.

Unbeneficed subdeacons. John Clerk of Grantham, t. Croxton. Thomas Helot of Ropsley, t. Vaudey. William s. John Grave of *Leke*, t. Revesby. Roger Munc, t. Owston. John Coke of Tydd St Mary, t. Chatteris. William Barnewell of Ryhall, t. St Michael by Stamford. Thomas Nunton s. Ralph Nunton of *Oseby*, t. Thurgarton. William Saddyng of Spalding, t. Spalding. Thomas Gerard, t. Barnwell. Richard Markeby, t. Kirkstead. Stephen Sargeant of Maxey, t. St Michael by Stamford. [fo. 175r] Walter Trowe of Ingoldmells, t. Louth Park. Thomas Geesle, t. Sawtry. William Irford of North Thoresby, t. Louth Park. John Reppele of Bedford, t. Caldwell. William Godehede, t. Crowland. Thomas de Luthburgh, t. Ulverscroft. John Glover of *Morton*, t. Vaudey. Walter Boteler of Edenham, t. Bourne. Thomas Bony, t. Osney.

Beneficed deacons. William Stevenot, vicar of Lincoln cath. John Redysdale, vicar of Lincoln cath.

Deacons in religious orders. Thomas Depyng, monk of Peterborough. Thomas Wold, Robert Yakesley, canons of Huntingdon. William Aunsell, Carmelite friar of Stamford.

Unbeneficed deacons. William s. Robert Rosson of *Halton*, t. Revesby. John Beford of Grimsby, t. Revesby. John Asgardeby of Welton le Wold (*Welton iuxta Ludam*), t. Louth Park. John Maynard, t. Eynsham. John Copgray of Godmanchester, t. Merton. Richard Herpeswell of Harpswell, t. Newhouse. John Copper of *Belton*, t. Legbourne. William Sleford, t. St Katherine outside Lincoln. William Denyas of Blunham, t. Caldwell. John Spencer, t. Waltham. Richard Lloid of St David's dioc., by letters dimissory, t. Strata Florida. Thomas Norton, t. Cold Norton. William Messyngham, t. Tupholme.

Beneficed priests. Richard Belgrave, vicar of Lincoln cath. John Breton, perpetual scholar of Oriel College, Oxford, t. his college *de quo reputavit se contentum.* John Carpenter, perpetual scholar of the same college, t. his college *de quo reputavit se contentum.* Robert Genne, rector of Nether Broughton, t. his benefice *de quo reputavit se contentum.* John Parker, rector of Laverstoke, dioc. Winchester, by letters dimissory. Robert Monter, rector of Puttenham.

Priests in religious orders. Thomas Dorham, canon of Kyme. Thomas Bynham, canon of Wymondley. John Fryday, Dominican friar of Stamford.

Unbeneficed priests. Simon Hareby, t. Markby. William Bele of Leicester, t. Ulverscroft. Robert Raulynson of *Ratheby*, t. Fosse. Thomas Leveryk of *Irby*, t. Louth Park. Stephen Gardyner, t. Woburn. William Craft of Orby, t. Hagnaby. Richard Caltoft of Orby, t. Alvingham. Reginald Pecok, perpetual scholar of Oriel College, Oxford, t. his college *de quo &c.* John Rote of Crowland, t. Crowland. Robert Hilton of Bangor dioc., by letters dimissory, t. Royston. John Meskyn of *Ulceby*, t. Thornton. William Burton of Market Rasen (*Estrasen*), t. Sixhills. John Snell, t. Bourne. John Elmyn of Boston, t. Tupholme. Robert Colby, t. Gokewell. John Rosecastell of Exeter dioc., by letters dimissory, t. Rewley by Oxford. Richard Homme of Hereford dioc., by letters dimissory, t. Osney. John Gody of Exeter dioc., by letters dimissory, t. St Gregory, Canterbury. John Mark of Exeter dioc., by letters dimissory, t. Rewley. John Wastell of Oakham, t. St Katherine outside Lincoln. Simon Whytyng, t. St Katherine outside Lincoln. Richard Marnham of Boston, t. Stixwould. John Perys of Exeter dioc., by letters dimissory, t. Launceston.

[fo. 175v]

477. Ordination celebrated by Bp Fleming in the parish church of Spalding, 22 March 1421.

Ordines celebrati in ecclesia parochiali de Spaldyng Lincolnien' diocesis in sabbato sancto pasche xj^{mo} videlicet kalendas Aprilis anno domini millesimo CCCC^{mo} vicesimo per reverendum in Christo patrem et dominum dominum Ricardum dei gracia Lincolnien' episcopum anno consecrationis sue primo.

Unbeneficed acolytes. William Barbour. Robert Gilbert. Richard Stalker. William Neve. William Kyrkeby. Thomas Watton. Robert Lightfote. John Mychell. Thomas Fayrford.

Unbeneficed subdeacons. Philip Squyer of Donington in Holland, t. Swineshead. Thomas Champneys, t. Sempringham. John s. John Totell of Alford, t. Revesby. William Neve, t. St Katherine outside Lincoln. Roger Hun of Peterborough, t. St Michael outside Stamford. William Kyrkeby, t. Osney. Thomas Watton, t. Snelshall.

Unbeneficed deacons. William Saddyng of Spalding, t. Spalding. Thomas Helot of Ropsley, t. Vaudey. Richard Markeby, t. Kirkstead. William Irford of North

Thoresby, t. Louth Park. William s. John Grave of *Leek*, t. Revesby. Thomas Nunton s. Ralph Nunton of *Oseby*, t. Thurgarton. William Godehed, t. Crowland. Thomas de Luthburgh, t. Ulverscroft. Stephen Sergeant of Maxey, t. St Michael by Stamford. Walter Trowe of Ingoldmells, t. Louth Park.

Unbeneficed priests. John Maynard, t. Eynsham. John Spencer, t. Waltham. Thomas Norton, t. Cold Norton. John Asgardeby of Welton le Wold (*Welton iuxta Ludam*), t. Louth Park. William Sleford, t. St Katherine outside Lincoln. William s. Robert Rosson of *Halton*, t. Revesby.

478. Ordination celebrated by Bp Fleming in chapel of Totteridge by Barnet, 17 May 1421.

Ordines generales celebrati in capella de Tatterygge Lincolnien' diocesis iuxta Barnett die sabbati quatuor temporum in vigilia sancte Trinitatis videlicet xvj° kalendas Junii anno domini millesimo CCCC^{mo} xxj^{mo} per reverendum in Christo patrem et dominum dominum Ricardum dei gracia Lincolnien' episcopum anno consecrationis sue secundo.

Unbeneficed acolytes. Thomas Parson. John Bate. Thomas Thorp. Thomas Garlyk. Simon B[ra]mpton of Mentmore. John Taunt. William Creke. Thomas Rysley. William Permereth. John atte Kyrk of South Scarle of York dioc., by letters dimissory.

[fo. 176r]

Beneficed subdeacons. Walter Proctor, vicar choral in Lincoln cath.

Unbeneficed subdeacons. Thomas Swan of West Keal, t. Louth Park. William Dalton of Ashby St Ledgers, t. (subdeacon) Daventry. William Hanney of *Foleby*, t. Revesby. Robert Tevelby of *Castre*, t. Thornton. John Smyth of *Wotton*, t. (subdeacon) Hospital of St John Baptist, Northampton. William Rychedale of Gainsborough, t. Heynings. William Dawson of *Westburgh*, t. Shelford. Thomas Chapman of Dunstable, t. Dunstable. John Gamige of *Bukby*, t. Daventry. John Parteney of Horncastle, t. St Michael outside Stamford. John Mawer of *Overton*, t. Repton. William Gilmote, t. Luffield. Thomas Amys of Wymington, t. Harrold. Thomas Person of *Fenton*, t. Alvingham. John Garton of York dioc., by letters dimissory, t. St John outside Eastgate, Oxford. John Taunt of Ingoldmells, t. Markby. John atte Kyrk of South Scarle, of York dioc., by letters dimissory, t. Newstead by Stamford. William Penreth of *Coryngham*, t. Heynings. Simon Bampton of Mentmore, t. Snelshall. Thomas Thorp of Noseley, t. Launde. William Creek, t. Luffield.

Beneficed deacons. James Beek, vicar choral of Lincoln cath.

Deacons in religious orders. William Foulestowe, canon of Ormsby. Alan Wrangle, canon of Clattercote.

Unbeneficed deacons. Walter Jones of Salisbury dioc., by letters dimissory, t. Bradenstoke. John Clement, t. Repton. Robert Laverok of Elsham, t. Thornton. Roger Betson of Coningsby, t. Markby. William Breton of *Creton*, t. Sulby. Thomas Gerard, t. Barnwell. Hugh Wolrykby, t. Thornton. John Cokle of Tydd St Mary, t. Chatteris. Philip Squyer of Donington in Holland, t. Swineshead.

479. Ordination celebrated by Bp Fleming in chapel of Totteridge by Barnet, 17 May 1421.

Ordines generales celebrati in capella de Taterige iuxta Barnet Lincoln' diocesis die sabbati quatuor temporum in vigilia sancte Trinitatis videlicet xvj° kalendas Junii anno domini millesimo CCCC^{mo} xxj^{mo} per reverendum in Christo patrem et dominum dominum Ricardum dei gracia Lincoln' episcopum anno consecrationis sue secundo.

Unbeneficed acolytes. Thomas Person. John Bate. Thomas Thorp. Thomas Garlyk. John Taunt. William Creke. Thomas Rysley. William Penreth. Simon Brampton of Mentmore. John at Kyrke of South Scarle, of York dioc., by letters dimissory.

Beneficed subdeacons. Walter Proktour, vicar choral of Lincoln cath.

Unbeneficed subdeacons. Thomas Swan of West Keal, t. Louth Park. William Dalton of Ashby St Ledgers (*Assheby Lyger*), t. (subdeacon) Daventry. William Hannay of *Foleby*, t. Revesby. Robert Telby of *Castre*, t. Thornton. John Smyth of *Wotton*, t. (subdeacon) Hospital of St John Baptist, Northampton. [fo. 176v] William Rychedale of Gainsborough, t. Heynings. William Daweson of *Westburgh*, t. Shelford. Thomas Chapman of Dunstable, t. Dunstable. John Gamage of *Buckeby*, t. Daventry. John Parteney of Horncastle, t. St Michael outside Stamford. John Mower of *Overton*, t. Repton. William Gylmote, t. Luffield. Thomas Amys of Wymington, t. Harrold. Thomas Person of *Fenton*, t. Alvingham. John Garton of York dioc., by letters dimissory, t. St John outside Eastgate, Oxford. John Taunt of Ingoldmells, t. Markby. John at Kyrke of South Scarle, of York dioc., by letters dimissory, t. Newstead by Stamford. William Penereth of *Coryngham*, t. Heynings. Simon Brampton of Mentmore, t. Snelshall. Thomas Thorp of Noseley, t. Launde. William Creek, t. Luffield.

Beneficed deacons. James Beke, vicar choral of Lincoln cath.

Deacons in religious orders. William Foulestowe, canon of North Ormsby (*Nunormesby*). Alan Wrangle, canon of Clattercote.

Unbeneficed deacons. Walter Jones of Salisbury dioc., by letters dimissory, t. Bradenstoke. John Clement, t. Repton. John Laverok of Elsham, t. Thornton. Roger Betson of Coningsby, t. Markby. William Breton of *Gretton*, t. Sulby. Thomas Gerard, t. Barnwell. Hugh Wolrykby, t. Thornton. John Cokke of Tydd St Mary (*Tydde beate Marie*), t. Chatteris. Philip Sqwyer of Donington in Holland, t. Swineshead. Roger Munk, t. Owston. Thomas Fyssher, t. Pipewell. John Glover of *Morton*, t. Vaudey. Thomas Geesley, t. Sawtry. John Lodyngton of Old (*Wold*), t.

Lavendon. John Respele of Bedford, t. Caldwell. John Welles of *Merston*, t. Caldwell. William Kyrkeby, t. Osney. Thomas Whatton, t. Snelshall. Thomas Flowrys of Irchester, t. Harrold. William Neve, t. St Katherine outside Lincoln. John Roke of *Badyngton*, t. Newstead by Stamford.

Beneficed priests. Thomas Belton, vicar choral of Lincoln cath. John Trassh, minister of Lincoln cath.

Priests in religious orders. Thomas Rede, Patrick Denerose, Dominican friars of Northampton. John Baron, canon of St James outside Northampton.

Unbeneficed priests. William Irford of North Thoresby, t. Louth Park. William Boys of *Goudeby*, t. Tupholme. William Saddyyng of Spalding, t. Spalding. Walter Trowe of Ingoldmells, t. Louth Park. John Copgray of Godmanchester, t. Merton. Henry Colle of Cold Ashby, t. Daventry. John Gunnore of *Ryngstede*, t. Harrold. William Yvus of Bicester, t. Bicester. William Denyas of Blunham, t. Caldwell. John Heryot of Cotterstock, t. Cotterstock. Henry Jercok of Oundle, t. Cotterstock. Thomas Eynesbury, t. Sawtry. William Prentys, fellow of University College, Oxford, t. his college. Thomas de Loughburgh, t. Ulverscroft. William Pye of St Neots, t. Caldwell. Wiliam Messyngham, t. Tupholme. William Taylour, t. Launde. William Coventre of Oakham, t. Launde.

Facta collatione concordat cum rotulis: Colstone.

480.   Ordination celebrated by Bp Fleming in prebendal church of Sleaford, 20 September 1421.

Ordines generales celebrati in ecclesia prebendali de Sleford Lincoln' dioc' die sabbati quatuor temporum in vigilia sancti Mathei apostoli videlicet xij° kalendas Octobris anno domini millesimo CCCC^mo xxj^mo per reverendum in Christo patrem et dominum dominum Ricardum dei gracia Lincoln' episcopum anno consecrationis sue secundo.

Acolytes in religious orders. Richard Grendon, canon of Kirby Bellars. Thomas Langarth, canon of Croxton. Thomas Feltewell, canon of Kyme. Thomas Holand, James Boston, Richard Bardeney, monks of Bardney.

Unbeneficed acolytes. [fo. 177r] John Belle of Oakham. Thomas Colstone. William Bampton. John Hubbard. John Averey. John Babley. Henry Hardy. Robert Luminer. Richard Mathewe. Robert Dughty. Richard Tapy of Elsham. Thomas be the Broke. William Breton. John othe Hill. Walter Munke. William Baker. Thomas Pacell. Thomas Newham. John Glade. Thomas Clerke. Thomas Smyth. Robert Blythe. John Nundy. Guy Wilham. John Bartelmewe. John Ketelthorp. John Esteby of Tealby. Martin Symon. Stephen Dunyngton. Thomas Clerke. Robert Limmer.

Beneficed subdeacons. Richard Frysseby, canon of Lincoln and prebendary of Milton Manor, t. his prebend. William Shipton, vicar choral of Lincoln cath., t. chapter of Lincoln. Robert Forster, rector of Hougham.[54]

Subdeacons in religious orders. Thomas Holand, James Boston, Richard Bardeney, monks of Bardney. Christopher Freston, Thomas Feltwell, canons of Kyme. Richard Grendon, canon of Kirby Bellars. Thomas Mumby, canon of Barlings. Thomas Langarth, canon of Croxton. John Tanfeld, friar minor of Boston.

Unbeneficed subdeacons. Thomas Dale of *Stonesby*, t. Launde. Simon Scarlet of Whaplode, t. Heynings. William Bampton, t. Kirkstead. John Hubberd of *Langham*, t. Owston. Robert Lonysdale of Durham dioc., by letters dimissory, t. (subdeacon and deacon) hospital of St John Baptist, Northampton. John Russell of *Wytheryngton*, t. St Michael by Stamford. John s. William de Swaton, t. Sempringham. Richard Tapy of Elsham, t. Launde. Thomas be the Broke, t. Chacombe. William Breton, t. Chacombe. John at Kyrke of *Malteby*, t. Sixhills. William Saunderson of Leasingham, t. Vaudey. Robert Lelley, t. Thornton. John at Hall of Ingoldmells, t. Markby. Thomas Cook of Maltby le Marsh, t. Sempringham. Henry Bell of *Merston*, t. St Katherine outside Lincoln. William Wryght of *Gouxhill*, t. Thornton. Walter Whyte of East Kirkby (*Kyrkeby iuxta Bulyngbroke*), t. Revesby. John Esteby of Tealby, t. Louth Park. Martin Symon, t. Crowland. Robert Limmer, t. Kirkstead. John Averey, t. St James outside Northampton.

Beneficed deacons. John Marshall, vicar choral of Lincoln cath. John Clerk s. Nicholas Clerk of Grantham, rector of Little Ponton.[55]

Deacons in religious orders. John Bescolby, Robert de Sproxton, canons of Croxton. Robert Swabury, canon of Wroxton. Philip Melton, Richard Barton, William Barton, canons of Newhouse. John Broughton, John Yorke, canons of Ulverscroft. William Anderby, canon of Hagnaby. Conrad Scale, Dominican friar of Boston. Peter de Dordraco, friar minor of Boston. John Draghton, friar minor of Stamford. William Scarburgh, canon of St Katherine outside Lincoln.

Unbeneficed deacons. William Greek, t. Luffield. William Bernewell of Ryhall, t. St Michael outside Stamford. Walter Botyler of Edenham, t. Bourne. John Gamage of *Buckeby*, t. Daventry. John s. John Totell of Alford, t. Revesby. William Bryggeford, t. St Michael outside Stamford. William Dalton of Ashby St Ledgers (*Assheby Lyger*), t. Daventry. William Gilmot, t. Luffield. Roger Hun of Peterborough, t. St Michael outside Stamford. Thomas Thorp of Noseley, t. Launde. Thomas Swan of West Keal, t. Louth Park. John Taunt of Ingoldmells, t. Markby. William Rychedale of Gainsborough, t. Heynings. John Wykes, t. Swineshead. Simon Brampton of Mentmore, t. Snelshall. William Hannay of *Foleby*, t. Revesby. John Mower of *Overton*, t. Repton. Henry Bradeley, t. Stixwould. John Parteney of Horncastle, t. St Michael outside Stamford. John Telby of *Castre*, t. Thornton.

---

[54] Forster was instituted on 18 September 1420 [*Reg. Fleming* i. 14].
[55] Clerk was instituted on 2 May 1421 [*Reg. Fleming* i. 19].

William Penereth of *Coryngham*, t. Heynings. William Daweson of *Westburgh*, t. Shelford. John at Kyrke of South Scarle, of York dioc., by letters dimissory, t. Newstead by Stamford. Thomas Person of *Fenton*, t. Alvingham. Thomas Champeneys, t. Sempringham. John Garton of York dioc., by letters dimissory, t. St John outside the East Gate, Oxford.

Beneficed priests. Robert Boston, vicar choral of Lincoln cath.

[fo. 177v] *Priests in religious orders.* Adam de Wyllyngham, canon of Croxton. William Clyfton, canon of Wellow. Richard Gouxhill, Thomas Thurleby, canons of Markby. John Boston, John Morecrofte, canons of Barlings. Gilbert Multon, monk of Crowland. Nicholas Dodyngton, canon of Fineshade. Alan Wrangle, canon of Clattercote. William Besthorp, Dominican friar of Lincoln. John Tannesover, friar minor of Stamford.

Unbeneficed priests. William Segbroke of Grantham, t. Croxton. Roger Munke, t. Owston. Stephen Sargeaunt of Maxey, t. St Michael outside Stamford. William Wynwyk of Biggleswade, t. Elstow. William s. John Grave of *Leek*, t. Revesby. Thomas Helot of Ropsley, t. Vaudey. John Cokke of Tydd St Mary, t. Chatteris. Thomas Gerard, t. Barnwell. John Reppeley of Bedford, t. Caldwell. William Breton of *Greton*, t. Sulby. Robert Laverok of Elsham, t. Thornton. Thomas Nunton s. Ralph Nunton of *Oseby*, t. Thurgarton. William Neve, t. St Katherine outside Lincoln. Richard Harpeswell of Harpswell, t. Newhouse. Thomas Geesley, t. Sawtry. Thomas Hoby of Middle Rasen, t. Sixhills. Thomas Whatton, t. Snelshall. Richard Gybson of Boston, t. Kyme. John Clement, t. Repton. Hugh Wolrygby, t. Thornton. Thomas Marum, t. St Katherine outside Lincoln. Roger Betson of Coningsby, t. Markby. William Wodehede, t. Crowland. John Lodyngton of Old, t. Lavendon. Hugh Burton of Lincoln, t. St Katherine outside Lincoln. John Sqwyer of Donington in Holland, t. Swineshead. Godfrey Graunt of *Pykworth*, t. Newstead by Stamford.

Facta collatione concordat cum rotulis. Colstone.

481. Ordination celebrated by Bp Fleming in the parish church of All Saints, Hertford, 20 December 1421.

Ordines generales celebrati in ecclesia parochiali omnium sanctorum Hertford' Lincoln' dioc' die sabbati quatuor temporum in vigilia sancti Thome apostoli videlicet xiij° kalendas Januarij anno domini millesimo CCCC^{mo} xxj^{mo} per reverendum in Christo patrem et dominum dominum Ricardum dei gracia Lincoln' episcopum anno consecrationis sue secundo.

Beneficed acolytes. John Abburbury, rector of Passenham.[56] M. Henry Kayle, provost of Oriel College, Oxford.

---

[56] Abburbury was instituted on 17 February 1421 [*Reg. Fleming* i. 67].

Acolytes in religious orders. William Podyngton, Robert Wodehull, canons of Bushmead. Thomas Sondey, monk of Wardon.

Unbeneficed acolytes. John Paulyn. William atte Welles. John Taylour. John Crouche. John Froste. John Graunt. Richard Croxton. John Shelton. John Marshall. Richard Bedeford. William atte Welle. John Andrewe. Thomas Webbe. William Merwyn. Adam Roberde. John Wetherfeld. Simon Lovelyche. Richard Edows. William Gregory. Adam Roberde. William Brytteby.

Beneficed subdeacons. John Abburbury, rector of Passenham. M. Thomas Bekyngton, rector of Sutton Courtenay, dioc. Salisbury, by letters dimissory. M. Henry Kayle, provost of Oriel College, Oxford. M. William Byrteby, fellow of Queen's College, Oxford.

Subdeacons in religious orders. William Podyngton, Robert Wodehull, canons of Bushmead. Thomas Sondey, monk of Wardon.

Unbeneficed subdeacons. John Nowell, t. Sawtry. John Dekyn of Kirton in Holland, t. Swineshead. John s. John Dekyn of Kirton in Holland, t. Swineshead. [fo. 178r] William Burton, t. Vaudey. John Baldewyn of Collingtree, t. (subdeacon) hospital of St John Baptist, Northampton. John Ingryth of Hanslope, t. Lavendon. Richard s. William atte Well of Marston Trussell, t. Sulby. William Stokton of Bratoft, t. Tupholme. John Wetheresfeld of Great Gransden (*Grauntesden Magna*), t. Bushmead. Richard Edowe of Offord Cluny, t. Bushmead. Guy Wyllam of Pinchbeck, t. Newstead by Stamford. Thomas Bevyle, t. Hinchingbrooke. John Bell of Oakham, t. Owston. William Bramenanger, t. St Giles by Flamstead. Robert Blythe of Thoresway, t. Louth Park. John Nundy of Brocklesby, t. Newhouse. John Paulyn, t. Chacombe. William atte Well, t. Chacombe. Adam Roberde, t. Kyme. Simon Walker, t. Legbourne. Oliver Mille, t. Tickford.

Beneficed deacons. Thomas Fraunceys, rector of Blaby.

Unbeneficed deacons. Thomas be the Broke, t. Chacombe. Thomas Chapman of Dunstable, t. Dunstable. Walter Whyte of East Kirkby, t. Revesby. John Russell of *Wytheryngton*, t. St Michael by Stamford. William Saunderson of Leasingham, t. Vaudey. William Breton, t. Chacombe. Robert Lonysdale of Durham dioc., by letters dimissory, t. (subdeacon and deacon) hospital of St John Baptist, Northampton. John s. William de Swaton, t. Sempringham. John atte Hall of Ingoldmells, t. Markby. Thomas Dale of *Stonesby*, t. Launde. John Smyth of *Wotton*, t. (deacon) hospital of St John Baptist, Northampton. John Hubberd of *Langham*, t. Owston. Henry Belle of *Merston*, t. St Katherine outside Lincoln. Robert Lelley, t. Thornton. William Wryght of *Gouxhill*, t. Thornton. John Esteby of Tealby, t. Louth Park. John Averey of Litchborough, t. St James outside Northampton. William Hamball of Wilton, by letters dimissory, t. Stoke, dioc. Norwich.

Beneficed priests. John Clerk s. Nicholas Clerk of Grantham, rector of Little Ponton. Robert s. Henry, Lord Fitzhugh, archdn of Northampton.

Priests in religious orders. William Bykeleswade, William Wolaston, John Rothewell, canons of Newnham. Richard Everdon, canon of St James outside Northampton. Thomas Pountfreit, monk of Durham.

Unbeneficed priests. William Creek, t. Luffield. John Taunt of Ingoldmells, t. Markby. John s. John Totell of Alford, t. Revesby. Thomas Swan of West Keal, t. Louth Park. William Anable of Spalding, t. Newstead by Stamford. John Wykes, t. Swineshead. William Gylmot, t. Luffield. William Brygeford, t. St Michael outside Stamford. William Dalton of Ashby St Ledgers, t. Daventry. Thomas Fyssher, t. Pipewell. John Welles of *Merston*, t. Caldwell. William Bernewell of Ryhall, t. St Michael outside Stamford. Walter Boteler of Edenham, t. Bourne. John Gamage of *Buckeby*, t. Daventry. William Dawson of *Westburgh*, t. Shelford. Thomas Person of *Fenton*, t. Alvingham. John at Kyrke of South Scarle, of York dioc., by letters dimissory, t. Newstead by Stamford. William Rychedale of Gainsborough, t. Heynings. Simon Brampton of Mentmore, t. Snelshall. Thomas Wyllyam, t. Beaulieu. John Russell of Norwich dioc., by letters dimissory, t. [blank]. William Kyrkeby, t. Osney. John Mower of *Overton*, t. Repton. Thomas Flowrys of Irchester, t. Harrold. Robert Telby of *Castre*, t. Thornton. John Garton of York dioc., by letters dimissory, t. hospital of St John outside the East Gate, Oxford. William Penreth of *Coryngham*, t. Heynings.

Facta collatione concordat cum rotulis. Colstone.

[fo. 178v]

482.   Ordination celebrated by John, bp *Ancoraden'*, in prebendal church of Liddington, 7 March 1422.

Ordines generales celebrati in ecclesia prebendali de Lidyngton' Lincoln' dioc' die sabbati quatuor temporum in prima septimana quadragesime videlicet nonas Marcii anno domini millesimo CCCC^{mo} xxj^{mo} per venerabilem patrem dominum Johannem Ancoraden' episcopum vice et auctoritate Reverendi in Christo patris et domini domini Ricardi dei gracia Lincoln' episcopi et de mandato honorabilis viri magistri Roberti Leek legum doctoris canonici ecclesie Lincoln' eiusdem reverendi patris in remotis agentis vicarii in spiritualibus generalis anno consecrationis dicti reverendi patris secundo.

Acolytes in religious orders. John Daventree, Richard Daventree, monks of Daventry. Richard Beaver,[57] canon of Kirby Bellars. Thomas Iudkyn, monk of St Andrew, Northampton. William Yarum, canon of Launde. William Barnewell, John Swafham, John Tychemersh, John Cambrige, monks of Ramsey. Richard Welford, John Hampslap, John London, canons of Sulby.

---

[57] MS 'Richard Richard'.

Unbeneficed acolytes. Thomas Sollay. John Gardyner. Henry Burley. John Puttenham. John Taylour. Thomas Bryght. Richard Newman. William Chaterys. John Jacob. Thomas Bette. William Thorp. Walter Bekyngham. John Bolton. William Barton. William Motte. John Sausthorp. Thomas Denet. John Wace. Richard Whitesyde. Robert Barton. Thomas Bayly. Thomas Ferman. Henry Rukbar, dioc. Bath and Wells, by letters dimissory. John Mussenden. William Pope. Thomas Bampton. Thomas Sclatyer. Geoffrey German. Robert Howes. Thomas Lynde of Castleford, of York dioc., by letters dimissory. William Mold of Bath and Wells dioc., by letters dimissory. William Helmesley of York dioc., by letters dimissory. William Smyth. Henry Garbera. Richard Seman of Sempringham. Geoffrey Dode.

Beneficed subdeacons. John Bate, rector of a mediety of Sheepy. John Morell, rector of a mediety of Sheepy. Thomas Sovreby, rector of Market Overton. John Ferley, rector of Broughton.[58]

Subdeacons in religious orders. John Wyttelesey, William Bernewell, John Swafham, John Tychemersh, monks of Ramsey. John Daventre, Richard Daventre, monks of Daventry. Richard Beaver, canon of Kirby Bellars. Thomas Iudkyn, monk of St Andrew, Northampton. Thomas Asshelyn, br. of hospital of St John Baptist, Northampton. Theodoric Simonis, Dominican friar of Stamford.

Unbeneficed subdeacons. Hugh Cokulday of Tilton, t. Launde. William Warner of Boston, t. Swineshead. John Sybsey, t. Kirkstead. William Wryght of Friskney, t. Revesby. William Crawe, t. Kyme. Robert Franke of Morcott, t. Launde. Richard Desford, t. Ulverscroft. Richard Croxton of *Brokesby*, t. Launde. Thomas Pacyll, t. Kyme. Thomas s. John Spenser of Theddlethorpe, t. Revesby. Walter s. Gilbert Monk of Mablethorpe, t. Markby. John Bate of Guilsborough, t. Sulby. William Merewyn, t. Owston. John Browne, t. Sawtry. William Basset, t. Cotterstock. William Catton of *Foston*, t. Ulverscroft. John Cok of *Wottan*, t. hospital of St John Baptist, Northampton. Thomas Smyth of Brant Broughton, t. Louth Park. Robert Cory of Harpole, t. Canons Ashby. John Castelton of Bassingham, t. Thornton. John othe Hyll of Ropsley, t. Bourne. Thomas Sawagge of Stallingborough, t. Newhouse. John Shelton of *Chelston*, t. Stonely. Robert Barton of Swineshead, t. Swineshead. Stephen Cuton of Swineshead, t. Swineshead. Thomas Bett of Algarkirk, t. Swineshead. Henry Rukbar of Bath and Wells dioc., by letters dimissory, t. hospital of St John Baptist, Bridgwater. William s. Walter of Claxby (*Claxby iuxta Wylugby*), t. Revesby. John Bek, t. Kirkstead. Thomas Sollay of *Toft*, t. Kirkstead. William Pope of Morcott, t. Launde. Richard Seman of Sempringham, t. Sempringham. Thomas Stykilthorn, t. Crowland. Robert Howe of Lolham, t. Newstead by Stamford. William Helmesley of York dioc., by letters dimissory, t. Guisborough (*Gysburn*). William Molde of Bath and Wells dioc., by letters dimissory, t. Longleat. [fo. 179r] Richard Stirkhird of Low Toynton, t. Revesby. John Wace of Freiston (*Freston in Holand*), t. Fineshade.

---

[58] Ferley was instituted on 24 November 1421 and 7 March 1422 [*Reg. Fleming* i. 59].

Beneficed deacons. Thomas Southam, rector of Tattershall.[59]

Deacons in religious orders. Richard Grendon, canon of Kirby Bellars. Thomas Mumby, canon of Barlings. John Yerdeburgh, monk of Pipewell. John Panton, John Candelesby, William Wrangle, monks of Louth Park. William Bottesford, canon of Newbo. John Red, Dominican friar of Stamford. John Tanfeld, friar minor of Boston. Robert Wodehull, William Podyngton, canons of Bushmead. William Kyrkeby, canon of Launde. John Lesyngham, monk of Peterborough.

Unbeneficed deacons. John Bell of Oakham, t. Owston. William Bampton, t. Kirkstead. John s. John Dekyn of Kirton in Holland, t. Swineshead. John Pawlyn, t. Chacombe. William Stokton of Bratoft, t. Tupholme. John Ingryth of Hanslope, t. Lavendon. John Baldewyn of Collingtree, t. (deacon and priest) Ravenstone. Robert Limmer, t. Kirkstead. Martin Symon, t. Crowland. John Dekyn of Kirton in Holland, t. Swineshead. William at Well, t. Chacombe. Richard s. William atte Well of Marston Trussell, t. Sulby. John Nundy of Brocklesby, t. Newhouse. John at Kyrke of *Malteby*, t. Sixhills. Thomas Bramenanger, t. St Giles by Flamstead. John Nowell, t. Sawtry. Thomas Coke of Maltby le Marsh, t. Sempringham. Simon Scharlet of Whaplode, t. Heynings. John Wetheresfeld of Great Gransden, t. Bushmead. William Burton, t. Vaudey. Simon Walker, t. Legbourne. Richard Edows of Offord Cluny, t. Bushmead.

Beneficed priests. John Redesdale, minister in the choir of Lincoln cath., t. chapter of Lincoln.

Priests in religious orders. John Broughton, John Yorke, canons of Ulverscroft. Robert Cokerygton, William Luthburgh, canons of Ormsby. John Howden, canon of Sulby. William Midelburgh, friar minor of Boston. John Pavy, William Aunsell, Carmelite friars of Stamford. John Grene, monk of Pipewell. Thomas Depyng, monk of Peterborough.

Unbeneficed priests. Robert Lonysdale of Durham dioc., by letters dimissory, t. (priest) hospital of St John Baptist, Northampton. John Smyth, t. hospital of St John Baptist, Northampton. Thomas Thorp of Noseley, t. Launde. John Roke of *Badyngton*, t. Newstead by Stamford. Thomas bethe Broke, t. Chacombe. William Breton, t. Chacombe. Thomas Dale of *Stonesby*, t. Launde. William Saunderson of Leasingham, t. Vaudey. William Wade of *Screlby*, t. Kirkstead. Robert Lollay, t. Thornton. William Rychedale of Gainsborough, t. Heynings. Roger Hun of Peterborough, t. St Michael by Stamford. John Esteby of Tealby, t. Louth Park. Henry Bell of *Merston*, t. St Katherine outside Lincoln. William Hannay of *Foleby*, t. Revesby. John Hubberd of *Langham*, t. Owston. William Wryght of *Gouxhill*, t. Thornton. John Parteney of Horncastle, t. St Michael by Stamford. John atte Halle of Ingoldmells, t. Markby. William Hambald of Wilton, of Norwich dioc., by letters dimissory, t. college of Stoke, dioc. Norwich. John Averey of Litchborough, t. St James by Northampton. John s. William de Swaton, t. Sempringham. Thomas Champeneys, t. Sempringham.

---

[59] Southam was instituted on 30 January 1419/20 [Reg. 14, fo. 102v].

Facta collatione concordat cum rotulis. Colstone.

[fo. 179v]

483. Ordination celebrated by John, bp *Ancoraden'*, in prebendal church of Liddington, 28 March 1422.

Ordines celebrati in ecclesia prebendali de Lidyngton' Lincoln' dioc' die sabbati qua cantatur officium Sitientes videlicet v^{to} kalendas Aprilis anno domini millesimo CCCC^{mo} xxij^o per reverendum patrem dominum Johannem Ancoraden' episcopum vice et auctoritate Reverendi in Christo patris et domini domini Ricardi dei gracia Lincoln' episcopi et de mandato honorabilis viri magistri Roberti Leek legum doctoris canonici ecclesie Lincoln' eiusdem reverendi patris in remotis agentis vicarii in spiritualibus generalis anno consecrationis eiusdem reverendi patris secundo.

Beneficed acolytes. John Wrauby, vicar choral of Lincoln.

Unbeneficed acolytes. John Rote. John Peke. William Bugden. John Burton. John Armestronge. Henry Harper. Thomas Fermour. Richard Dey of Constance dioc., by papal letters dimissory. Henry Sherman. John Gerbeys.

Beneficed subdeacons. John Wrauby, vicar choral of Lincoln. William Wawen, minister in the choir of Lincoln cath.

Unbeneficed[60] *subdeacons.* John Trotter of Leicester, t. hospital of St John Evangelist, Leicester. Richard Whitehorne of Bath and Wells dioc., by letters dimissory, t. Muchelney. Robert Plonioun of Old Dalby (*Dalby super le Wolde*), t. Launde. John Martyn, t. Chatteris. John Bolton of *Melton*, t. Croxton. John Gardyner of Guilden Morden (*Gylden Moreton*), t. hospital of St John Evangelist, Leicester. William Carswell, t. Cold Norton. John s. Thomas of Sausthorpe, t. Louth Park. Richard Dey of Constance dioc., by papal letters dimissory, t. Rewley by Oxford.

Beneficed deacons. Thomas Sobreby, rector of Market Overton. Walter Proctour, vicar choral of Lincoln cath. John Ferley, rector of Broughton.

Deacons in religious orders. William Yarum, canon of Launde. Simon de Boston, Reginald de Dunyngton, William de Osolveston, canons of Owston.

Unbeneficed deacons. Robert Blythe of Thoresway, t. Louth Park. Robert Franke of Morcott, t. Launde. William Wryght of Friskney, t. Revesby. Thomas Smyth of Brant Broughton, t. Louth Park. Hugh Cokulday of Tilton, t. Launde. Thomas s. John Spenser of Theddlethorpe, t. Revesby. John Bate of Guilsborough, t. Sulby. Richard Desford, t. Ulverscroft. Thomas Sawagge of Stallingborough, t. New-house. John othe Hill of Ropsley, t. Bourne. William Pope of Morcott, t. Launde.

---

[60] MS 'benefic'.

John Sybsey, t. Kirkstead.[61] Thomas Bette of Algarkirk, t. Swineshead. Richard Croxton of *Brokesby*, t. Launde. William Catton of *Foston*, t. Ulverscroft. Robert Cory of Harpole (*Horpoll*), t. Canons Ashby. William Merwyn, t. Owston. John Browne, t. Sawtry. Henry Rukbar of Bath and Wells dioc., by letters dimissory, t. hospital of St John Baptist, Bridgwater. Thomas Sollay of *Toft*, t. Kirkstead. William Crawe, t. Kyme. Robert Hows of Lolham, t. Newstead by Stamford. John Wace of Freiston (*Freston in Holand*), t. Fineshade. William Basset, t. Cotterstock. Thomas Crosse of Blyth, of York dioc., by letters dimissory, t. hospital of St John Evangelist, Cambridge. John Tykton of Beverley, of York dioc., by letters dimissory, t. Barnwell. John Cok of *Watton*, t. hospital of St John Baptist, Northampton. John Castelton of Bassingham, t. Thornton. Thomas Stykylthorne, t. Crowland. William s. Walter of Claxby (*Claxby iuxta Wylugby*), t. Revesby. Robert Barton of Swineshead, t. Swineshead. William Helmesley of York dioc., by letters dimissory, t. Guisborough. William Molde of Bath and Wells dioc., by letters dimissory, t. Longleat. Richard Seman of Sempringham, t. Sempringham. Edmund Brange of Clare, of Norwich dioc., by letters dimissory, t. Walden.

Beneficed priests. John Marshall, vicar choral of Lincoln cath.

Priests in religious orders. John Candelesby, monk of Louth Park. William Podyngton, Robert Wodehull, canons of Bushmead.

Unbeneficed priests. William Bampton, t. Kirkstead. John Newell, t. Sawtry. William Burton, t. Vaudey. John atte Kyrke of *Malteby*, t. Sixhills. Robert Limmer, t. Kirkstead. Richard s. William Well of Marston Trussell, t. Sulby. [fo. 180r] William Stokton of Bratoft, t. Tupholme. John Paulyn, t. Chacombe. John Wethersfeld of Great Gransden, t. Bushmead. Simon Scarlet of Whaplode, t. Heynings. John Dekyn of Kirton in Holland, t. Swineshead. Martin Symon, t. Crowland. John Ingrith of Hanslope, t. Lavendon. Richard Edows of Offord Cluny, t. Bushmead.

Facta collatione concordat cum rotulis. Colstone.

484. Ordination celebrated by John, bp *Ancoraden'*, in conventual church of Sempringham, 11 April 1422.

Ordines celebrati in ecclesia conventuali de Sempyngham Lincoln' dioc' in sancto sabbato pasche videlicet tertio Idus Aprilis Anno Domini Millesimo CCCC^{mo} xxij° per venerabilem patrem dominum Johannem Ancoraden' Episcopum vice et auctoritate Reverendi in Christo patris et domini domini Ricardi dei gracia Lincoln' episcopi et de mandato honorabilis viri magistri Roberti Leek legum doctoris canonici ecclesie Lincoln' eiusdem reverendi patris in remotis agentis vicarii in spiritualibus generalis anno consecrationis eiusdem reverendi patris secundo.

---

[61] MS 'Kyrkeby'.

Unbeneficed priests. Robert Barton of Swineshead, t. Swineshead. Richard Seman of Sempringham, t. Sempringham.

485.   Ordination celebrated by John, bp *Ancoraden'*, in prebendal church of Liddington, 6 June 1422.

Ordines celebrati in ecclesia prebendali de Lidyngton' Lincoln' dioc' die sabbati quatuor temporum in vigilia sancte Trinitatis videlicet viij° Idus Junii Anno Domini Millesimo CCCC^{mo} xxij° per venerabilem patrem dominum Johannem Ancoraden' Episcopum vice et auctoritate Reverendi in Christo patris et domini domini Ricardi dei gracia Lincoln' episcopi et de mandato honorabilis viri magistri Roberti Leek legum doctoris canonici ecclesie Lincoln' eiusdem reverendi patris in remotis agentis vicarii in spiritualibus generalis anno consecrationis eiusdem reverendi patris tertio.

Acolytes in religious orders. Jacob of Ghent (*Gandavo*), Austin friar of Northampton. John Trekman, Carmelite friar of Stamford. William Buckyngham, William Culworth, Thomas Sutton, canons of Canons Ashby. [fo. 180v] Thomas Moreys, Henry Gyseley, Robert Leycestre, canons of St Mary Leicester. John Holand, John Haltoft, Thomas Lynne, monks of Crowland.

Unbeneficed acolytes. Richard Josson. Richard Wyllyamson. Richard Dymmok. Thomas Waryn. William Chaumberleyn. Thomas Herte. John Well. Thomas Jekyn. William Fyncher. John Fyndern. William Wytherogg. William Hankyn. John Kemp. William Smyth. Robert Skynner. John Kynge. Richard Brynkhill. Robert Waryn. John atte Hall of Frisby. Richard Gaunt. John Gallard. Robert Archare. John Copuldyke. John Smyth. M. John Croxby. William Carlele.

Subdeacons in religious orders. William Buckyngham, William Culworth, Thomas Sutton, canons of Canons Ashby. William Fryday, Thomas Moreys, Henry Gyseley, Robert Leycestre, canons of St Mary Leicester. John Holand, John Haltoft, Thomas Lynne, monks of Crowland.

Unbeneficed subdeacons. William Randis of Whaplode, t. St Michael outside Stamford. Thomas Rysle of Bedford, t. Caldwell. Nicholas Robert, t. St Frideswide Oxford. Richard Newman, t. Luffield. William Hobkyns of Farthingstone, t. Daventry. Richard Brynkyll, t. Osney. William Whasshyngburgh, t. Godstow. John Mussenden, t. Osney. John Manton, t. Owston. Richard Whiteside of *Holt*, t. Bradley. Richard Dymmok, t. St Katherine outside Lincoln. Richard Josson of *Freston*, t. Kyme. John Rote of *Frampton*, t. Kirkstead. William Blawehorne, t. St Katherine outside Lincoln. Robert Waryn of Bedford, t. Caldwell. Thomas Waryn of Banbury, t. Bicester. John at Hall of Frisby on the Wreake, t. Launde. John Croxby of Croxby, t. Newhouse.

Beneficed deacons. Robert Forster, rector of Hougham. John Malberthorp, rector of Denton.[62]

---

[62] Instituted on 6 November 1421 [see no 146 above].

Deacons in religious orders. Roger Sceybell, Simon de Byllyngburgh, monks of Spalding. Richard Beaver, canon of Kirby Bellars. George de Columba, Austin friar of Northampton. Hermanus de Nussia, friar minor of Boston. Thomas Asshyn, Hospital of St John Baptist, Northampton.

Unbeneficed deacons. William Warner of Boston, t. Swineshead. Thomas Pacill, t. Kyme. Walter s. Gilbert Monk of Mablethorpe, t. Markby. Oliver Mille, t. Tickford. John Ireby, dioc. Carlisle, by letters dimissory, t. Osney. John Bek, t. Kirkstead. John Bolton of *Melton*, t. Croxton. John s. Thomas of Sausthorpe, t. Louth Park. John Martyn, t. Chatteris. William Carswell, t. Cold Norton. Richard Styrkhird of Low Toynton, t. Revesby. Adam Roberd, t. Kyme. John Shelton of *Chelston*, t. Stonely. John Baker, dioc. Canterbury, by letters dimissory, t. nuns of West Malling. Stephen Cuton of Swineshead, t. Swineshead.

Beneficed priests. John Eburton, rector of Wigginton. Robert Wade, rector of Spettisbury, dioc. Salisbury, by letters dimissory. John Ledes, fellow of St Peter's College, Cambridge. John Farley, rector of Broughton, dioc. Lincoln.

Priests in religious orders. Robert Sudbury, canon of Wroxton. John Panton, William Wrangle, monks of Louth Park. Thomas Mumby, canon of Barlings. Philip de Melton, Richard de Barton, William de Barton, canons of Newhouse. Richard Grendon, canon of Kirby Bellars. Thomas Malborowe, Carmelite friar of Stamford. John Burgh, Dominican friar of Stamford. John Brumley, friar minor of Stamford. John de Colonia, friar minor of Boston. William de Lincoln, canon of Sempringham.

Unbeneficed priests. John Sybsey, t. Kirkstead. Walter Whyte of Kirkby by Bolingbroke, t. Revesby. John Baldewyn of Collingtree, t. Ravenstone. William Wryght of Friskney, t. Revesby. John s. John Dekyn of Kirton in Holland, t. Swineshead. Thomas s. John Spenser of Theddlethorpe, t. Revesby. John Bate of Guilsborough, t. Sulby. John othe Hill of Ropsley, t. Bourne. [fo. 181r] William Merwyn, t. Owston. William Crawe, t. Kyme. Thomas Sawagge of Stallingborough, t. Newhouse. John Copper of *Belton*, t. Legbourne. Thomas Bete of Algarkirk, t. Swineshead. John Browne, t. Sawtry. Robert Cory of Harpole, t. Canons Ashby. William atte Welle, t. Chacombe. William s. Walter of Claxby (*Claxby iuxta Wylugby*), t. Revesby. Robert Blythe of Thoresway, t. Louth Park. John Cok of *Wotton*, t. hospital of St John Baptist, Northampton. Robert Hows of Lolham, t. Newstead by Stamford. Simon Walker, t. Legbourne. Thomas Stykelthorn, t. Crowland. William Catton of *Foston*, t. Ulverscroft.

Facta collatione concordat cum rotulis. Colstone.

486. Ordination celebrated by John, bp *Ancoraden'*, in conventual church of Spalding, 19 September 1422.

Ordines generales celebrati in ecclesia conventuali de Spaldyng' Lincoln' dioc' die sabbati quatuor temporum proximo post festum Exaltationis sancte Crucis videlicet xiij° kalendas Octobris Anno

Domini Millesimo CCCC^{mo} xxij° per venerabilem patrem dominum Johannem Ancoraden' Episcopum vice et auctoritate Reverendi in Christo patris et domini domini Ricardi dei gracia Lincoln' episcopi et de mandato honorabilis viri magistri Roberti Leek legum doctoris canonici ecclesie Lincoln' eiusdem reverendi patris in remotis agentis vicarii in spiritualibus generalis anno consecrationis ipsius reverendi patris tertio.

Beneficed acolytes. Henry Fenton, rector of Waltham on the Wolds.

Acolytes in religious orders. John Gulle, Dominican friar of Boston. John Goldesmyth, Thomas Aylesby, Robert Somercotes, John Tolson, canons of Wellow. Thomas Hesell, Robert Hyldeston, canons of Thornton.

Unbeneficed acolytes. John Slory. John Byngham. Simon Tomlynson. John Ruston. Robert Goldesmyth. Thomas Wylde. William Date. John Fryday. John Gare. William Patefyn. Thomas Hull. John Mortymer. John Bede. Robert Mody. Richard Michell. Augustine Qwassh. William Bowdon. Nicholas Welles. William Brymley. Augustine Freknam. Thomas Smyth. John Filhous. John Powton. Henry Wyles. John Cooke. John Thurleby.

Beneficed subdeacons. Henry Fenton, rector of Waltham on the Wolds. Robert Galbart, vicar choral of Lincoln cath.

Subdeacons in religious orders. John Bachiler, John Goldesmyth, John Aylesby, Robert Somercotes, canons of Wellow. Thomas Hesyll, Robert Hildeston, canons of Thornton.

Unbeneficed subdeacons. John Slory, t. Haverholme. William Fynche of Sutton in the Marsh, t. Markby. John Swyneshede of Stamford, t. Spalding. John Polle of *Kybbeworth*, t. St Mary, Leicester. Walter s. Stephen de Croft, t. Kyme. Robert Archer of Lincoln, t. Kirkstead. Thomas Bampton of *Thorneton*, t. Hinchingbrooke. Richard Dykelun of *Northburgh*, t. Newstead by Stamford. Augustine Qwassh, t. Stonely. William Chaumberleyn of Shepshed, t. Garendon. John Jakson of Strubby, t. Markby. William Hawkyn, t. (subdeacon) Daventry. Robert Gilbert, t. Crowland. Thomas Hert of Yelden (*Yevelden*), t. Stonely. Geoffrey German, t. nuns of Huntingdon. John Roger of Eynesbury, t. Stonely. Thomas Bryzte, t. Catesby.

Beneficed deacons. Thomas Farforth, vicar choral of Lincoln cath.

[fo. 181v] *Deacons in religious orders.* Thomas Ewardeby, Thomas de Boston, monks of Swineshead. William Leverton, monk of Kirkstead. John Holand, John Haltoft, Thomas Lynne, monks of Crowland. John Wytlesey, William Bernewell, John Swafham, John Tychemersh, monks of Ramsey. John More, John Spaldyng, monks of Peterborough. James Boston, Richard Browne, monks of Bardney.

Unbeneficed deacons. John atte Hall of Frisby, t. Launde. John Trotter of Leicester, t. hospital of St John Evangelist, Leicester. John Gardyner of Guilden Morden, t. hospital of St John Evangelist, Leicester. Thomas Rysley of Bedford, t. Caldwell.

Richard Newman, t. Luffield. Richard Jasson of *Freston*, t. Kyme. John Mussenden, t. Osney. William Randis of Whaplode, t. St Michael, Stamford. Robert Plunioun of Old Dalby, t. Launde. Nicholas Robert, t. St Frideswide, Oxford. William Hobkyns of Farthingstone, t. Daventry. John Manton, t. Owston. Richard Dymmoke, t. St Katherine outside Lincoln. William Walben, minister in the choir of Lincoln cath., t. chapter of Lincoln. Richard Whytesyde of *Holt*, t. Bradley. William Whassyngburgh, t. Godstow. Guy Wyllam of Pinchbeck, t. New[stead] by Stamford. John Croxby of Croxby, t. Newhouse. Richard Brynkyll, t. Osney. John Rote of *Frampton*, t. Kirkstead.

Beneficed priests. James Beke, vicar choral of Lincoln. Thomas Fraunceys, rector of Blaby. John Malberthorp, rector of Denton. Robert Forster, rector of Hougham.

Priests in religious orders. Thomas Elmyt, Dominican friar of Boston. Robert Alwalton, monk of Sawtry. John Thorp, monk of Kirkstead.

Unbeneficed priests. John Wace of Freiston (*Freston in Holand*), t. Fineshade. Richard Croxton of *Brokesby*, t. Launde. John Belle of Oakham, t. Owston. John s. Thomas of Sausthorpe, t. Louth Park. Hugh Cokulday of Tilton, t. Launde. John Martyn, t. Chatteris. Thomas Sollay of *Toft*, t. Kirkstead. Oliver Mille, t. Tickford. Thomas Pacill, t. Kyme. John Castelton of Bassingham, t. Thornton. Thomas Chapman of Dunstable, t. Dunstable. Richard Markeby, t. Kirkstead. Henry Goode, t. Leicester. John Beke, t. Kirkstead. Richard Styrkhird of Low Toynton, t. Revesby. John Russell of *Wytheryngton*, t. St Michael by Stamford. William Carsevell, t. Cold Norton. Walter s. Gilbert Monk of Mablethorpe, t. Markby. Thomas Cook of Maltby in the Marsh, t. Sempringham. Thomas Smyth of Brant Broughton, t. Louth Park. John Ireby of Carlisle dioc., by letters dimissory, t. Osney. John Baker of Canterbury dioc., by letters dimissory, t. nuns of West Malling.

Facta collatione concordat cum rotulis. Colstone.

487. Ordination celebrated by Bp Fleming in conventual church of Bardney, 19 December 1422.

Ordines generales celebrati in ecclesia conventuali monasterii de Bardeney Lincoln' dioc' die sabbati quatuor temporum proximo post festum sancte Lucie virginis videlicet xiiij° kalendas Januarii Anno Domini Millesimo CCCC^mo xxij° per Reverendum in Christo patris et domini domini Ricardi dei gracia Lincoln' episcopum anno consecrationis sue tertio.

[fo. 182r is blank]

[fo. 182v]

488. Ordination celebrated by John, bp *Solton'*, in prebendal church of Liddington, 27 February 1423.

Ordines generales celebrati in ecclesia prebendali de Lidyngton' Lincoln' dioc' sabbato quatuor temporum in prima septimana quadragesime videlicet tertio kalendas Marcii Anno Domini Millesimo CCCC^mo xxij° per venerabilem patrem dominum Johannem Solton' Episcopum vice et auctoritate Reverendi in Christo patris et domini domini Ricardi dei gracia Lincoln' episcopi anno consecrationis sue tertio.

Beneficed acolytes. Richard Hobkyn, rector of Wyke Dyve.

Acolytes in religious orders. William Cosyngton, canon of Kirby Bellars. John Brandon, Austin friar of Northampton.

Unbeneficed acolytes. William Bryghteve. Richard Fokes. Thomas Tyler. John Avys. Thomas Talbon of *Bynyngton*. Thomas Porter. Robert Randolfe. John Baxster. Ralph Pratte. Michael Adam. Robert Godechep. Roger Baker of Kirby Bellars. John Pecok. John Aleyn.

Beneficed subdeacons. Richard Hobkyn, rector of Wyke Dyve.

Subdeacons in religious orders. William Cosyngton, canon of Kirby Bellars. John Claydon, friar minor of Leicester. Richard Welford, John Hampslap, canons of Sulby. Odo Heythe, friar minor of Northampton. John Brandon, Austin friar of Northampton.

Unbeneficed subdeacons. Robert s. Robert Stepy of Huttoft, t. Markby. John Armestronge of *Botheby*, t. Bourne. John Pelreden of Exeter dioc., by letters dimissory, t. Bedminster. John Marshall of *Wynwyk*, t. Sawtry. Thomas de Smythy of Bourne, t. Swineshead. John Brygg of *Gretham*, t. St Michael outside Stamford.

Deacons in religious orders. Hermannus Truper, friar minor of Northampton. Thomas Judkyn, monk of St Andrew, Northampton. John Daventre, Richard Daventre, monks of Daventry.

Unbeneficed deacons. Thomas Farman, t. Catesby. William Baker of *Malteby*, t. Sixhills. William Hawkyn, t. (deacon) Daventry. John Wylmot, t. St James, Huntingdon. John Gerveys, t. Crowland.

Beneficed priests. Henry Sireston, rector of Marston Moretaine. Henry Fenton, rector of Waltham on the Wolds.

Priests in religious orders. [fo. 183r] William Agmer, friar minor of Leicester. William Burton, canon of Kirby Bellars. Roger Karoll, friar minor of Northampton. John of Ghent (*Gandavo*), Austin friar of Northampton.

Unbeneficed priests. John Gardyner of Guilden Morden, t. [hospital of] St John Evangelist, Leicester. Richard Desford, t. Ulverscroft. William Randys of Whaplode, t. St Michael outside Stamford. Thomas Bryghte, t. Catesby. John Jakson of Strubby, t. Markby. William Habkyns of Farthingstone, t. Daventry. John Bolton of *Melton*, t. Croxton. Robert Waryn of Bedford, t. Caldwell. Thomas Bampton of *Thorneton*, t. Hinchingbrooke. John Roger of Eynesbury, t. Stonely. Thomas Herte of Yelden (*Yevelden*), t. Stonely. William Chaumberleyn of Shepshed, t. Garendon.

Facta collatione concordat cum rotulis. Colstone.

489. Ordination celebrated by John, bp *Solton'*, in prebendal church of Liddington, 20 March 1423.

Ordines celebrati in ecclesia prebendali de Lidyngton' Lincoln' dioc' die sabbati qua cantatur officium Sitientes videlicet xiij kalendas Aprilis Anno Domini Millesimo CCCC^{mo} xxij° per venerabilem patrem dominum Johannem Solton' Episcopum vice et auctoritate Reverendi in Christo patris et domini domini Ricardi dei gracia Lincoln' episcopi anno consecrationis sue tertio.

Unbeneficed acolytes. John Hornlee. William Fermour. William Blogwyn. William Coke. Thomas Wylford.

Unbeneficed subdeacons. William Bryghteve of Kirton in Holland, t. Swineshead. John Avys of Beeby, t. hospital of St John Evangelist, Leicester. John Pecok of *Wyvelyngham*, t. Heynings. Richard Fox of *Kyrketon*, t. Swineshead. John Hornlee, t. Wroxton. Thomas Tyler, t. Dunstable. William Fermour, t. Hinchingbrooke. Thomas Porter, t. Harrold. John Crouche of Adstock, t. (subdeacon) Luffield. Thomas Talbon of *Bynyngton*, t. Newbo.

Beneficed deacons. Richard Hobkyn, rector of Wyke Dyve.

Unbeneficed deacons. John Marshall of *Wynwyk*, t. Sawtry. Robert s. Robert Stepy of Huttoft, t. Markby. John Brygg of *Gretham*, t. St Michael outside Stamford. John Hamond of Waddington, t. St Katherine outside Lincoln.

Priests in religious orders. Rayner de Halesfeld, friar minor of Leicester.

Unbeneficed priests. John Powle of *Kybbeworth*, t. St Mary de Pratis, Leicester. Thomas Langton of *Langton*, dioc. York, by letters dimissory, t. Kyme. John Gerveys, t. Crowland. William Hawkyn, t. (priest) Daventry.

Facta collatione concordat cum rotulis. Colstone.

490.   Ordines celebrati in monasterio de Ramesey sancto sabbato Pasche Anno Domini M° CCCC^{mo} xxiij°.
Letters of John, abbot of Ramsey, to Bp Fleming. In accordance with the bp's licence (dated at Ramsey, 3 February 1422/3), John bp *Stephanen'*, suffragan in the archdnries of Bedford and Huntingdon, has held an ordination in the conventual church of Ramsey on Saturday 3 April 1423, at which the following monks were ordained: John Wytlesey and John Swafham to the priesthood, and John Cantibrigge to the diaconate. Dated at Ramsey, 5 April 1423.

[fo. 183v]

491. Ordination celebrated by John, bp *Solton'*, in prebendal church of Liddington, 29 May 1423.

Ordines generales celebrati in ecclesia prebendali de Lidyngton' Lincoln' dioc' die sabbati quatuor temporum in vigilia sancte Trinitatis videlicet iiij^to kalendas Junii Anno Domini Millesimo CCCC^mo xxiij° per venerabilem patrem dominum Johannem Solton' Episcopum vice et auctoritate Reverendi in Christo patris et domini domini Ricardi dei gracia Lincoln' Episcopi et de mandato honorabilis viri magistri Roberti Leek legum doctoris canonici ecclesie Lincoln' eiusdem Reverendi patris in remotis agentis vicarii in spiritualibus generalis anno consecrationis ipsius Reverendi patris quarto.

Beneficed acolytes. Thomas Marton, minister in choir, Lincoln cath. Robert Thwaytes, rector of Terrington (*Tiryngton'*), dioc. York, by letters dimissory.

Acolytes in religious orders. Richard Litlyngton, William Thornham, John Stachesden, canons of Newnham. John Whitewyk, Thomas Boseworth, canons of Ulverscroft. Thomas Preston, monk of Eynsham. Richard Durham, Alan Qwaplode, monks of Pipewell. John Bryd, Richard Sulhull, William Brystowe, Carmelite friars of Northampton. John Lutkyn, Thomas Assh, John Freston, Thomas Somerby, Austin friars of Boston.

Unbeneficed acolytes. Rowland Barker. Hugh Beveryge. William Godewyn. Robert Clerk. Robert Ratheby. Robert Merston. John Toutheby. Thomas Wynturton of Coventry and Lichfield dioc., by letters dimissory. Ambrose Felawe. John Chaumbre. Robert Weste. William Sygge. William Lyson. William Bek. William Louth.

Beneficed subdeacons. Thomas Benteley, Thomas Marton, ministers in choir, Lincoln cath. Robert Twaytes, rector of Terrington, dioc. York, by letters dimissory. John Chace, rector of Langton, dioc. York, by letters dimissory.[63] Thomas de Greveley, rector of Stibbington.

Subdeacons in religious orders. Richard Litlyngton, William Thorneham, John Stachesden, canons of Newnham. John Whitewyk, Thomas Boseworth, canons of Ulverscroft. Robert Scaldeford, John Shepeshed, monks of Garendon. Thomas Preston, monk of Eynsham. John Bryd, Carmelite friar of Northampton. Richard Durham, Alan Qwaplode, monks of Pipewell. John Lutkyn, Thomas Asshe, John Freston, Thomas Somerby, Austin friars of Boston.

Unbeneficed subdeacons. Thomas Garlek of Thorpe by Daventry, t. Catesby. Thomas Barker of Carlisle dioc., by letters dimissory, t. Launde. John None, t. St Katherine

---

63 Instituted to Langton on 18 September 1422 (*Fasti Parochiales* v. 27).

outside Lincoln. Richard Chaumberlayn of *Folkyngham*, of York dioc., by letters dimissory, t. Sempringham. John Boleyn of Stickford, t. Revesby. John Browne of Kettlethorpe, t. St Katherine outside Lincoln. Gilbert Hacksmall, t. Caldwell. Robert Thornsby of *Hogham*, t. Shelford. William Bowdon of Stamford, t. hospital of St John, Northampton. William atte Townende of *Gretton*, of York dioc., by letters dimissory, t. St Katherine outside Lincoln.

Beneficed deacons. John Bate, rector of a mediety of Sheepy. John Morell, rector of a mediety of Sheepy.

Deacons in religious orders. Thomas Sondey, monk of Wardon. John Bacheler, John Goldesmyth, canons of Wellow. William Buckyngham, William Coldworth, canons of Canons Ashby. Richard Welford, John Hampslap, canons of Sulby. William Fryday, Thomas Moreys, Henry Gyseley, Robert Leycestre, canons of St Mary of the Meadows (*de Pratis*), Leicester.

Unbeneficed deacons. William Bryghteve of Kirton in Holland, t. Swineshead. John Armestronge of *Botheby*, t. Bourne. Thomas Porter, t. Harrold. John Avys of Beeby, t. hospital of St John, Leicester. Thomas de Smythy of Bourne, t. Swineshead. Robert Lyghtfote of Moulton in Holland, t. Swineshead. John Hornlee, t. Wroxton. William Fermour, t. Hinchingbrooke. Thomas Tyler, t. Dunstable. Robert Ampylford of York dioc., by letters dimissory, t. hospital of St John, Oxford.[64] William Sakerlegh of Exeter dioc., by letters dimissory, t. St Frideswide, Oxford. [fo. 184r] John Pecok of *Wyvelyngham*, t. Heynings. Richard Dykelun of *Northburgh*, t. Newstead by Stamford. Richard Rasyn, t. Tupholme. John Crouche of Adstock, t. Luffield. John Slory, t. Haverholme. Thomas Talbon of *Bynyngton*, t. Newbo. Robert Hampton, t. St Katherine outside Lincoln.

Beneficed priests. William Wawne, minister in choir, Lincoln cath. William Hoper, rector or portionary of Waddesdon. William Spenser, dioc. York, fellow of Balliol Hall, Oxford, by letters dimissory.

Priests in religious orders. John Yerdeburgh, monk of Pipewell. Roger Bulder, canon of St Mary *de Pratis*, Leicester.

Unbeneficed priests. Thomas Farman, t. Catesby. John Swyneshede of Stamford, t. Spalding. William Fynche of Sutton in the Marsh, t. Markby. Robert s. Stephen de Croft, t. Kyme. John Rote of *Frampton*, t. Kirkstead. John Marshall of *Wynnewyk*, t. Sawtry. Robert s. Robert Stepy of Huttoft, t. Markby. John Brygg of *Gretham*, t. St Michael by Stamford. William Baker of *Malteby*, t. Sixhills. John Wylmot, t. nuns by Huntingdon.

Facta collatione concordat cum rotulis. Colstone.

492. Ordination celebrated by John, bp *Solton'*, in prebendal church of Liddington, 18 September 1423.

---

[64] For his ordination as acolyte and subdeacon, see *BRUO*, p. 32.

Ordines generales celebrati in ecclesia prebendali de Lidyngton' Lincoln' dioc' die sabbati quatuor temporum proximo post festum Exaltationis sancte Crucis videlicet xiiij° kalendas Octobris Anno Domini Millesimo CCCC^{mo} xxiij° per venerabilem patrem dominum Johannem Solton' Episcopum vice et auctoritate Reverendi in Christo patris et domini domini Ricardi dei gracia Lincoln' Episcopi et de mandato honorabilis viri magistri Roberti Leek legum doctoris canonici ecclesie Lincoln' eiusdem Reverendi patris in remotis agentis vicarii in spiritualibus generalis anno consecrationis ipsius Reverendi patris quarto.

Beneficed acolytes. Hugh Bozon, rector of Beckingham.[65] Robert Morton, rector of Thenford.

Acolytes in religious orders. Simon Holbech, monk of Spalding. Nicholas Berewell, canon of Notley. Richard Dorhand, Nicholas Barnak, Robert Botheby, Carmelite friars of Stamford. John Newenton, John Islep, canons of [Cold] Norton. William Bredon, monk of Tickford. Richard Abyndon, monk of Eynsham. Simon Olyver, John Pety, canons of St James by Northampton. William Depyng, Austin friar of Stamford.

Unbeneficed acolytes. John Cade. Nicholas Melton. Robert Smyth. John Wawen. John Wardon. John Justyce. William Reve. Robert Kyrkeby. Peter Langton.

Beneficed subdeacons. Hugh Bozon, rector of Beckingham. Robert Moreton, rector of Thenford. John Nedham, minister in choir of Lincoln cath, t. Chapter.

Subdeacons in religious orders. Simon Holbech, Richard Spaldyng, John Boston, Richard Boston, monks of Spalding. William Kyrtlyngton, John Wynchestre, canons of Notley. Thomas Thorp, Carmelite friar of Lincoln. William Depyng, Austin friar of Stamford. Richard Dorhand, Carmelite friar of Stamford. John Newenton, John Islep, canons of [Cold] Norton. William Bredon, monk of Tickford. Richard Abendon, monk of Eynsham. Simon Olyver, John Pety, canons of St James by Northampton. Thomas Hedon, canon of Newhouse. Nicholas Berwell, canon of Notley.

Unbeneficed subdeacons. [fo. 184v] William Chaterys of Nassington, t. St Michael by Stamford. Thomas Tyler of Daventry, t. (subdeacon) Daventry. Robert Goldesmyth of Knipton, t. Harrold. Hugh Benerech of Abbotsley, t. Bushmead. John s. Richard Baxster of Great Bowden, t. Sulby. John Maryot, s. John Maryot of *Merston*, t. Haverholme. Robert Merston, t. Sempringham. John Ganvill, t. Ulverscroft. William Louth, t. Gokewell. Thomas Alford of Gosberton, t. Crowland. Roger Baker of Kirby Bellars, t. Shelford. Thomas Clerk of *Gouxhill*, t. Tupholme. Augustine Frecnam, t. Newstead by Stamford. William Bekke of *Carleton*, t. St Katherine by Lincoln. John Mason of Swaby, t. Louth Park. Simon Tomlynson of Clee, t. Pipewell.

---

[65] Instituted *c.* April 1423 [*Reg. Fleming* i. 31].

Beneficed deacons. William Shipton, vicar choral of Lincoln cath., t. Chapter. Thomas Marton, minister in choir of Lincoln cath., t. Chapter. Thomas More, rector of Northmoor. Thomas Greveley, rector of Stibbington.

Deacons in religious orders. William Thorneham, John Stachesden, canons of Newnham. Thomas Walyngford, canon of Notley. Richard Durham, Alan Quaplode, monks of Pipewell. Thomas Boseworth, John Whitewyk, canons of Ulverscroft. Robert Shelford, John Shepeshede, monks of Garendon. Thomas Somerby, Austin friar of Boston. Thomas Preston, monk of Eynsham.

Unbeneficed deacons. Thomas Garlek of Thorpe by Daventry, t. Catesby. Richard s. John Turpyn of Withern, t. Markby. William Bowdon of Stamford, t. hospital of St John Baptist, Northampton. Richard Fox of *Kyrketon*, t. Swineshead. William atte Townende of *Gretton*, of York dioc., by letters dimissory, t. St Katherine outside Lincoln. Richard Chaumberleyn of *Folkyngham*, of York dioc., by letters dimissory, t. Sempringham. Thomas Barker of Carlisle dioc., by letters dimissory from York (see of Carlisle being vacant), t. Launde. John None, t. St Katherine outside Lincoln. Gilbert Hacksmall, t. Caldwell. John Browne of Kettlethorpe, t. St Katherine outside Lincoln. John Smyth of Thornton by Horncastle, t. Kirkstead. Robert Galbard, t. Elsham. Robert Thoresby de Hogham, t. Shelford.

Beneficed priest. William Stevenot, vicar choral of Lincoln cath., t. Chapter.

Priests in religious orders. Thomas Appley, canon of Newstead on Ancholme. Thomas Belesby, John Sutton, Carmelite friars of Lincoln. Thomas Derby, John Elford, friars minor of Stamford. Thomas Iwardeby, Thomas Boston, monks of Swineshead. Simon Boston, canon of Owston.

Unbeneficed priests. John Trotter of Leicester, t. hospital of St John Evangelist, Leicester. William Bryghteve of Kirton in Holland, t. Swineshead. John Avys of Beeby, t. hospital of St John Evangelist, Leicester. William Basset, t. Cotterstock. Thomas Porter, t. Harrold. John Armestrong of *Botheby*, t. Bourne. Augustine Qwassh, t. Stonely. William Fermour, t. Hinchingbrooke. Robert Plunioun of Old Dalby, t. Launde. John Hornlee, t. Wroxton. William Pope of Morcott, t. Launde. Richard Rasyn, t. Tupholme. Thomas Tyler, t. Dunstable. Robert Lyghtfote of Moulton in Holland, t. Swineshead. John Crouche of Adstock, t. Luffield. Thomas Talbon of *Bynyngton*, t. Newbo. Robert Hampton, t. St Katherine outside Lincoln.

Facta collatione concordat cum rotulis. Colstone.

[fo. 185r]

493. Ordination celebrated by John, bp *Solton'*, in prebendal church of Liddington, 18 December 1423.

Ordines generales celebrati in ecclesia prebendali de Lidyngton' Lincoln' dioc' die sabbati quatuor temporum proximo post festum Sancte Lucie Virginis videlicet xv^mo kalendas Januarii Anno Domini Millesimo CCCC^mo xxiij° per venerabilem patrem dominum

Johannem Solton' Episcopum vice et auctoritate Reverendi in Christo patris et domini domini Ricardi dei gracia Lincoln' Episcopi et de mandato honorabilis viri magistri Roberti Leek legum doctoris canonici ecclesie Lincoln' eiusdem Reverendi patris in remotis agentis vicarii in spiritualibus generalis anno consecrationis ipsius Reverendi patris quarto.

Beneficed acolytes. John Homme, rector of South Molton, dioc. Exeter, by letters dimissory. William Stokes, rector of Garsington.

Acolytes in religious orders. Thomas Gloucestre, William Stoke, Thomas Halcote, Carmelite friars of Northampton. Richard Holme, friar minor of Stamford. John Bedeford, Richard Barry, friars minor of Bedford. John Holand, Austin friar of Northampton.

Unbeneficed acolytes. Robert Echard. Richard Toplas. Thomas Palfray. John Frere. Robert West. William Forsiens. Thomas Robertson. John Eton. William Carlele. William Pacye. William Henrys. Thomas Stales. John Gygar. Thomas Wryght. Thomas Alynson. John Perkyn. Richard Trayk of Durham dioc., by letters dimissory. John Burgh of Carlisle dioc., by letters dimissory.

Beneficed subdeacons. John Homme, rector of South Molton, dioc. Exeter, by letters dimissory. William Stokes, rector of Garsington.

Subdeacons in religious orders. Richard Sulhull, William Brystowe, William Stoke, Thomas Holcote, Carmelite friars of Northampton. Roger Teversham, Dominican friar of Stamford. Godfrey Romeskyrk, Richard Holme, friars minor of Stamford. John Bedeford, Richard Barry, friars minor of Bedford. Robert Walsyngham, canon of Canons Ashby. William Dalyngton, Austin friar of Northampton.

Unbeneficed subdeacons. Robert Hawkyn of Bourne, t. Bourne. Richard s. William de Benyngton, t. Swineshead. Simon Smyth of Whaplode, t. Crowland. Thomas Jekyn of *Denford*, t. (subdeacon) Stonely. John Shyrreve, t. Arbury. William Mote, t. Sawtry. William Goodewyn, t. Hinchingbrooke. William Reve of *Ravensthorp*, t. St Mary Delapré, Northampton. John Strangman of Great Coates, t. Kirkstead. John Galbard of Howyrton, t. (subdeacon) Stonely. William Paytefyn of *Cokeryngton*, t. Louth Park. William Carlele, t. Newstead by Stamford. Robert Echard, t. St Michael by Stamford. Thomas Forster of Metheringham (*Metryngham*), t. Kyme. John Kempe of *Rolleston*, t. Burton Lazars. Michael s. Adam of *Bynyngton*, t. Shelford. John Thorp of *Willugby*, t. Kyme. John Burgh of Carlisle dioc., by letters dimissory, t. Shap (*Hepp'*).

Beneficed deacon. Hugh Bozon, rector of Beckingham.

Deacons in religious orders. William Bredon, monk of Tickford. William Cosyngton, canon of Kirby Bellars. Richard Durant, Carmelite friar of Stamford. William Crendon, canon of Notley. Richard Abendon, monk of Eynsham. John Brandon, Austin friar of Northampton. John Freston, Austin friar of Boston.

Unbeneficed deacons. Thomas Tyler of Daventry, t. Daventry. John Mason of Swaby, t. Louth Park. Hugh Beverech of Abbotsley, t. Bushmead. William Louth, t. Gokewell. Simon Tomlynson of Clee, t. Pipewell. William Chateris of Nassington, t. St Michael by Stamford. William Beek of *Carleton*, t. St Katherine by Lincoln. Robert Merston, t. Sempringham. John s. Richard Baxster of Great Bowden, t. Sulby. John Ganvill, t. Ulverscroft. Augustine Frecnam, t. Newstead by Stamford. Robert Goldesmyth of Knipton, t. Harrold. John Mariot, s. John Mariot of *Merston*, t. Haverholme. Thomas Alford of Gosberton, t. Crowland.

Beneficed priests. [fo. 185v] John Marton of Messingham, minister in choir of Lincoln cath., t. chapter. John Bate, rector of mediety of Sheepy.

Priests in religious orders. William Kele, monk of Humberston. Gilbert Harlam, Dominican friar of Stamford. William Coleworth, canon of Canons Ashby. William Enderby, Thomas Multon, monks of Crowland.

Unbeneficed priests. Stephen Garbode of Coventry and Lichfield dioc., by letters dimissory, t. Daventry. John Pecok of *Wyvelyngham*, t. Heynings. Thomas Garlek of Thorpe by Daventry, t. Catesby. William Bowden of Stamford, t. St Michael by Stamford. Richard Chaumberleyn of *Folkyngham*, of York dioc., by letters dimissory, t. Sempringham. John Browne of Kettlethorpe, t. St Katherine outside Lincoln. John None, t. St Katherine outside Lincoln. Thomas Barker of Carlisle dioc., by letters dimissory, t. Launde. William atte Tounende of *Gretton*, t. St Katherine outside Lincoln. John Smyth of Thornton by Horncastle, t. Leicester. Robert Galberd, t. Elsham. Stephen Cuton, t. Swineshead. Robert Thornsby of *Hogh*, t. Shelford.

Facta collatione concordat cum rotulis. Colstone.

494. *Inspeximus* and confirmation by Robert Leek, vicar-general, of the letters of orders of John Herby, dioc. Lincoln, chaplain. His orders were conferred by John, archbp of Corinth, as follows: subdeacon on 23 February 1415 in the church of the Friars Minor, Constance; deacon on 16 March 1415 in the parish church of St Mary, Tettnang; priest on 30 March 1415 in the same parish church.[66] Liddington, 24 February 1423/4.

Universis sancte matris ecclesie filiis presentes litteras inspecturis Robertus Leek' legum doctor, canonicus ecclesie Lincoln' Reverendi in Christo patris et domini domini Ricardi dei gracia Lincoln' episcopi in remotis agentis vicarius in spiritualibus generalis salutem in domino sempiternam et certam presentibus dare fidem. Noverit universitas vestra quod nos litteras ordinum sacrorum dilecti nobis in Christo domini Johannis Herby Lincoln' diocesis capellani nobis per partem eiusdem domini Johannis presentatas inspeximus in hec verba UNIVERSIS Christi fidelibus presentes litteras inspecturis Johannes miseratione divina Archiepiscopus Corinth' salutem in domino sempiternam. Noverit universitas vestra quod nos die sabbati quatuor temporum in prima septimana quadragesime videlicet xxiij⁰ die mensis Februarii anno a nativitate domini millesimo CCCC^mo

---

[66] The dates all refer to the calendar year 1415.

xv⁰ in ecclesia conventuali fratrum minorum Civitatis Constancien' auctoritate domini nostri pape sacros ordines celebrantes dilectum nobis in Christo Johannem Herby Lincoln' diocesis in subdiaconum, Die eciam sabbati qua cantatur officium Sitientes die videlicet xvj mensis Marcii proximo tunc sequente in ecclesia parochiali beate Marie de Tetnang' Constancien' diocesis auctoritate qua supra sacros ordines celebrantes prefatum Johannem Herby in diaconum, Deinde vero in vigilia pasche proxima extunc sequente in dicta ecclesia parochiali beate Marie de Tetnang' auctoritate superius expressata supradictum Johannem Herby iuxta stilum et consuetudinem Romane Curie in presbiterum canonice ordinavimus ut est moris. In quorum omnium testimonium atque fidem presentes litteras nostras exinde fieri nostrique sigilli appensione fecimus communiri. Dat' apud Tetnang' dicte Constancien' diocesis sub anno mensibus diebus et locis superius expressatis. Indictione vero viijᵃ Pontificatus sanctissimi in Christo patris et domini nostri domini Johannis divina providencia pape xxiij anno quinto. Nos igitur litteras predictas ac predicti domini Johannis ordinationem prefatorumque sacrorum ordinum collationem ratas habentes atque gratas eas auctoritate dicti Reverendi patris atque nostra acceptamus ratificamus approbamus et tenore presentium confirmamus. In cuius rei testimonium sigillum dicti Reverendi patris ad causas quo de ipsius voluntate utimur in hoc officio presentibus est appensum. Dat' apud Lidyngton' xxiiij die mensis Februarii anno domini millesimo quadringentesimo vicesimo tertio.

495. Ordination celebrated by John, bp *Solton'*, in prebendal church of Liddington, 18 March 1424.

Ordines generales celebrati in ecclesia prebendali de Lidyngton' Lincoln' dioc' die sabbati quatuor temporum in prima septimana quadragesime videlicet xvᵐᵒ kalendas Marcii[67] Anno Domini Millesimo CCCCᵐᵒ xxiij⁰ per venerabilem patrem dominum Johannem Solton' Episcopum vice et auctoritate Reverendi in Christo patris et domini domini Ricardi dei gracia Lincoln' Episcopi et de mandato honorabilis viri magistri Roberti Leek legum doctoris canonici ecclesie Lincoln' eiusdem Reverendi patris in remotis agentis vicarii in spiritualibus generalis anno consecrationis eiusdem Reverendi patris quarto.

Beneficed acolyte. Thomas Astell, rector of Twyford.

Acolytes in religious orders. William Irby, William Conyngeston, canons of Thornton. William Lincoln, canon of Newhouse. Simon Elkyngton, canon of Barlings. John Wyrton, John Forman, canons of Croxton. John Markeby, canon of Nocton Park. John Pape, Dominican friar of Boston.

Unbeneficed acolytes. Thomas Kyrkegate. Thomas Vele. Thomas Dygby. William Wygott. William Fermor. John Overton. Henry Crosse. William Sautree. William Mylle. John Grene. William Kyseby. William Coston. William Bowre. John

---

[67] An error for 'Aprilis'.

Cadeby. Richard Bayly. William Rouceby. Thomas Wryght. John Kyrkeby.
Robert Manton. John Barrot. William Hawkyn. [fo. 186r] John Manypeny.
Robert Glatton. John Lyndesey. Henry Hopkyns. John Walker. Richard Curtys.
Robert Thetelthorp. Robert Curtys. Thomas Blake. Thomas Brygge. William
Weston. William Goslyn.

Beneficed subdeacon. Thomas Astell, rector of Twyford.

Subdeacons in religious orders. William Irby, William Conyngeston, canons of
Thornton. Simon Elkyngton, canon of Barlings. John Wyrton, John Forman,
canons of Croxton. John Markeby, canon of Nocton Park. John Pape, Dominican
friar of Boston. John Myssenden, monk of Thame.

Unbeneficed subdeacons. William Fraunceys, t. St Michael by Stamford. John Cade of
Sutton, t. Tupholme. William Sygge of Conisholme, t. Alvingham. John Eton of
Stretton Parva, t. hospital of St John Evangelist, Leicester. John s. John Walker of
High Toynton, t. Revesby. John Dousyng of Hagnaby by Bolingbroke, t. Revesby.
John de Crayk of Durham dioc., by letters dimissory, t. Newbo. John Grene, t.
hospital of St John Evangelist, Leicester. William Lyson of *Thoresby,* t.
Humberston. Nicholas Welles, t. St Michael by Stamford. Hugh Non, t. Gokewell.
William Herry of Galby, t. Launde. Thomas Wryght, t. Croxton. William
Atherston, t. hospital of St John Evangelist, Leicester. Robert Brygge, t. St Kath-
erine by Lincoln. Richard Curtys, t. (subdeacon) Owston. Robert Thetelthorp, t.
Sempringham. Henry Burley, t. St Michael by Stamford. Robert Kyrkeby of
Kirby Bellars, t. Launde. John Sargeaunt, t. St Katherine by Lincoln. John Taylor
of *Deen,* t. Fineshade. John Smyth of *Wardon,* t. Lavendon. John s. John Sadyler of
Harborough (*Hauerbryge*), t. Sulby. James de Halghton of Coventry and Lichfield
dioc., by letters dimissory, t. Rewley by Oxford. John Cateby, t. St Katherine by
Lincoln. William Welton, t. Osney. Thomas Alanson of Heydour, t. Haverholme.
William Jewster of *Bereford,* t. Chacombe. John Brace, t. Fineshade.

Beneficed deacons. Thomas Benteley, minister in choir of Lincoln cath., t. chapter.
William Stokes, rector of Garsington. John Proctor, rector of Yarburgh. Robert
Twaytes, rector of Terrington, dioc. York, by letters dimissory.

Deacons in religious orders. Robert Walsyngham, canon of Canons Ashby. Thomas
Langar, canon of Croxton. John Bedeford, Richard Barry, friars minor of Bedford.
Thomas Hedon, canon of Newhouse. William Daylyngton, Austin friar of
Northampton. Simon Holbech, Richard Boston, monks of Spalding. John
Wynchestre, canon of Notley. Thomas Wyldebore, canon of Barlings. Everard
Spycar, friar minor of Leicester.

Unbeneficed deacons. Thomas Clerk of *Gouxhill,* t. Tupholme. John Gallard of *Overton,*
t. (deacon and priest) Stonely. Thomas Jekyn of *Thenford,* t. (deacon and priest)
Stonely. John Kempe of *Rolleston,* t. Burton Lazars. Simon Smyth of Whaplode, t.
Crowland. John Strangman of Great Coates, t. Kirkstead. Robert Hawkyn of
Bourne, t. Bourne. William Wylughby of York dioc., by letters dimissory, t.
Hagnaby. Roger Baker of Kirby Bellars, t. Shelford. John Sherreve, t. Arbury.
Robert Gylbard of West Haddon, t. Daventry. William Mote, t. Sawtry. William

Reve of *Ravensthorp*, t. St Mary Delapré, Northampton. William Carlele, t. St Michael by Stamford. Thomas Forster of Metheringham, t. Kyme. William Godewyn, t. Hinchingbrooke. John Thorp of *Wylugby*, t. Kyme. William Paytfyn of *Cokeryngton*, t. Louth Park. Michael s. Adam of *Benyngton*, t. Shelford. John Burgh of Carlisle dioc., by letters dimissory, t. Shap.

Beneficed priests. Hugh Bozon, rector of Beckingham. Thomas More, rector of Northmoor.

Priests in religious orders. John Daventree, Richard Daventree, monks of Daventry. William Buckyngham, canon of Canons Ashby. John Bescoby, Robert Sprouston, canons of Croxton. Thomas Waltham, John Doncastre, friars minor of Lincoln. Thomas Hesill, canon of Thornton. John Brandon, Austin friar of Northampton. Roger Seyvyll, Simon Byllyngburgh, monks of Spalding. William Crendon, Thomas Walyngford, canons of Notley.

Unbeneficed priests. [fo. 186v] Thomas Tyler of Daventry, t. (priest) Daventry. John Mason of Swaby, t. Louth Park. William Beke of *Carleton*, t. St Katherine outside Lincoln. Robert s. John Turpyn of Withern, t. Markby. William Louth, t. Gokewell. Robert Franke of Morcott, t. Launde. Gilbert Hackesmall, t. Caldwell. Simon Tomlynson of Clee, t. Pipewell. William Chaterys of Nassington, t. St Michael by Stamford. John s. Richard Baxster of Great Bowden, t. Sulby. John Ganvill, t. Ulverscroft. Augustine Freknam, t. Newstead by Stamford. John Mariot s. John Mariot of *Merston*, t. Haverholme. Thomas Alford, t. Crowland. Robert Goldesmyth of Knipton, t. Harrold. Robert Archer, t. Kirkstead. John Bevereche of Abbotsley, t. Bushmead. William Blawhorne, t. St Katherine outside Lincoln.

Facta collatione concordat cum rotulis. Colstone.

496.   Ordination celebrated by John, bp *Ancoraden'*, in prebendal church of Liddington, 8 April 1424.

Ordines celebrati in ecclesia prebendali de Lidyngton' Lincoln' dioc' die sabbati qua cantatur officium Sitientes videlicet vj^{to} Idus Aprilis anno domini millesimo CCCC^{mo} xxiiij^{to} per venerabilem patrem dominum Johannem Ancoraden' episcopum vice et auctoritate reverendi in Christo patris et domini domini Ricardi dei gracia Lincoln' episcopi et de mandato honorabilis viri magistri Roberti Leek' legum doctoris canonici ecclesie Lincoln' eiusdem reverendi patris in remotis agentis vicarii in spiritualibus generalis anno consecrationis eiusdem reverendi patris quarto.

Unbeneficed acolytes. Thomas Wedon. Robert Luffe. Roger Herry. William Syston. John Waryn. Thomas Taylor. John Burbache.

Unbeneficed subdeacons. William Langham, t. Ulverscroft. William Bugden, t. Ulverscroft. John Waryn, t. hospital of St John Evangelist, Canterbury. Robert Curtys, t. (subdeacon) Owston. Robert Smyth, t. Thornholm. John Burbache, fellow of Merton College, Oxford, t. his college.

Unbeneficed deacons. John Grene, t. hospital of St John Evangelist, Leicester. William Fraunceys, t. St Michael by Stamford. Robert Echard, t. St Michael by Stamford. Robert Thetelthorp, t. Sempringham. Henry Burley, t. St Michael by Stamford. Robert Kyrkeby of Kirby Bellars, t. Launde. John s. John Sadyler of Harborough, t. Sulby. John Bolyn of Stickford, t. Revesby. John Eton of Stretton Parva, t. hospital of St John Evangelist, Leicester. John Taylor of *Deen*, t. Fineshade. John Smyth of *Wardon*, t. Lavendon. Richard Curtys, t. (deacon and priest) Pipewell. Richard Brace, t. Fineshade. Thomas Alanson of Heydour, t. Haverholme. William Welton, t. Osney.

Priest in religious orders. William Bredon, monk of Tickford.

Unbeneficed priests. John Gallard of *Overton*, t. Stonely. Simon Smyth of Whaplode, t. Crowland. William Mote, t. Sawtry. Richard Foxe of *Kyrketon*, t. Swineshead. John Sherreve, t. Arbury. William Carlele, t. St Michael by Stamford. Robert Gylbard of West Haddon, t. Daventry. John Strangman of Great Coates, t. Kirkstead. John Kempe of *Rolleston*, t. Burton Lazars. William Wylugby of York dioc., by letters dimissory from chapter of York, *sede vacante*, t. Hagnaby. William Paytfyn of *Cokeryngton*, t. Louth Park. Robert Hawkyn of Bourne, t. Bourne.

Facta collatione concordat cum rotulis. Colstone.

[fo. 187r]

497. Ordination celebrated by John, bp *Ancoraden'*, in conventual church of Sempringham Priory, 22 April 1424.

Ordines celebrati in ecclesia conventuali prioratus de Sempyngham Lincoln' dioc' in sancto sabbato pasche videlicet x^mo kalendas Maii anno domini millesimo CCCC^mo xxiiij^to per venerabilem patrem dominum Johannem Ancoraden' episcopum vice et auctoritate reverendi in Christo patris et domini domini Ricardi dei gracia Lincoln' episcopi et de mandato honorabilis viri magistri Roberti Leek' legum doctoris canonici ecclesie Lincoln' eiusdem reverendi patris in remotis agentis vicarii in spiritualibus generalis anno consecrationis dicti reverendi patris domini Lincoln' quarto.

Unbeneficed priests. Robert Thetelthorp, t. Sempringham. John Smyth of *Wardon*, t. Lavendon.

Facta collatione concordat cum rotulis. Colstone.

498. Ordination celebrated by John, bp *Ancoraden'*, in prebendal church of Liddington, 17 June 1424.

Ordines generales celebrati in ecclesia prebendali de Lidyngton' Lincoln' dioc' die sabbati quatuor temporum in vigilia sancte

Trinitatis videlicet xv kalendas Junii[68] **anno domini millesimo CCCC^mo xxiiij^to per venerabilem patrem dominum Johannem Ancoraden' episcopum vice et auctoritate reverendi in Christo patris et domini domini Henrici dei gracia Cantuar' archiepiscopi totius Anglie primatis et apostolice sedis legati ad quem omnis et omnimoda iurisdictio ecclesiastica infra civitatem et diocesim Lincoln' ratio visitationis sue metropolitice hac vice dinoscitur pertinere.**

Acolytes in religious orders. John Gurmuncestre, John Crawlee, monks of Woburn. John Lynn, Austin friar of Lincoln.

Unbeneficed acolytes. John Kyrke. Richard Hare. John Mell. John Paryssh. Richard Kemsall. Walter Muchawnt. John Waynflete. Thomas Gilbert. John Coke. William Smyth. William Cusson. Thomas Tank. John Syvely of Stamford. John Evedon of Evedon. William Morys. Nicholas Rycheman. Thomas Ireland. John Norwode. Roger Dewesbury. William Templer.

Beneficed subdeacon. Richard Beche, minister in Lincoln cath., t. chapter.

Subdeacons in religious orders. John Gurmuncestre, John Crawlee, monks of Woburn. John Assheby, Austin friar of Stamford. John Lynn, Austin friar of Lincoln. Henry Weston, canon of Launde.

Unbeneficed subdeacons. Nicholas Melton of Wigston Magna (*Wykyngeston*), t. Ulverscroft. Robert Clerke of *Somercotes*, t. Alvingham. John Toutheby of Thoresthorpe, t. Markby. Robert West of Conisholme, t. Sempringham. William Goslyn of Thornton by Horncastle, t. Tupholme. Henry Cros of Melchbourne, t. Bushmead. John Syvely of Stamford, t. St Michael by Stamford. John s. Robert Wryght of Clee, t. Wellow by Grimsby. John Evedon of Evedon, t. Kyme. John Copuldyke of *Kyrketon*, t. St Michael by Stamford. Robert Ratheby of *Luthburgh*, t. Kyme. Thomas Wylford of *Burlee*, t. Newstead by Stamford. John Manypeny of Godmanchester, t. Hinchingbrooke. Thomas Barton of Cadney, t. Fineshade. John Clerk of *Stanton*, of Coventry and Lichfield dioc., by letters dimissory, t. Dale. John Dere s. Thomas Dere of Hughenden, t. Luffield. Richard Gaunt, t. (subdeacon) Launde. William Kyseby of Alwalton, t. St Michael by Stamford.

Beneficed deacon. John Nedeham, minister in Lincoln cath., t. chapter.

[fo. 187v] *Deacons in religious orders.* Robert Somercotes, canon of Grimsby. Simon Elkyngton,[69] canon of Barlings. John Lutkyn, Austin friar of Stamford. John Mussenden, monk of Thame. Roger Taversham, John Mendham, Dominican friars of Stamford. John Whyte, Austin friar of Lincoln. John Tiryngton, John Moubray, canons of Sempringham.

---

68 An error for 'Julii'.
69 MS 'Ellyngton'.

Unbeneficed deacons. William Atherston, t. hospital of St John Evangelist, Leicester. John Cade of *Sutton*, t. Tupholme. William Langham, t. Ulverscroft. William Sygge of Conisholme, t. Alvingham. Richard s. William de Benyngton, t. Swineshead. William Bugden, t. Ulverscroft. Nicholas Welles, t. St Michael by Stamford. John s. John Walker of High Toynton, t. Revesby. John Dowsyng of Hagnaby by Bolingbroke, t. Revesby. Hugh None, t. Gokewell. Robert Curteys, t. (deacon and priest) Bradley. James de Halghton of Coventry and Lichfield dioc., by letters dimissory, t. Rewley by Oxford. William Herry of Galby, t. Launde. Thomas Wryght, t. Croxton. William Lyson of *Thoresby*, t. Humberston. William Jewster of *Berford*, t. Chacombe.

Beneficed priests. William Stokes, rector of Garsington, t. his benefice *de quo reputavit se contentum.* Thomas Benteley, minister in Lincoln cath., t. chapter.

Priests in religious orders. Richard Tynwell, William Thornham, canons of Newnham. William Woburn, John London, monks of Woburn. Thomas Blyton, canon of Kyme. Simon Holbech, Richard Boston, monks of Spalding. William Cossyngton, canon of Kirby Bellars. William Yarum, canon of Launde. John Haltoft, monk of Crowland.

Unbeneficed priests. John Grene, t. hospital of St John Evangelist, Leicester. John Eton of Little Stretton, t. hospital of St John Evangelist, Leicester. Thomas Clerk of *Gouxhill*, t. Tupholme. William Reve of *Ravensthorp*, t. St Mary Delapré, Northampton. Thomas Jekyn of *Denford*, t. Stonely. John s. John Sadyler of Harborough, t. Sulby. William Fraunceys, t. St Michael by Stamford. John Bolyn of Stickford, t. Revesby. Richard Dykelun of *Northburgh*, t. Newstead by Stamford. Robert Kyrkeby of Kirby Bellars, t. Launde. Richard Curteys, t. Pipewell. Robert Gilbert of Crowland, t. Crowland.

Facta collatione concordat cum rotulis. Colstone.

499.   Note that on Saturday following the feast of St Matthew, viz. 23 September 1424, in the parish church of Higham Ferrers, Henry [Chichele], archbp of Canterbury, by reason of his metropolitical visitation of the city and diocese of Lincoln then being unfinished, caused a general ordination to be celebrated by John, bp *Ancoraden'*, but that no ordination was celebrated in December.

500.   Ordination celebrated by John, bp *Ancoraden'*, in prebendal church of Liddington, 3 March 1425.

Ordines generales celebrati in ecclesia prebendali de Lidyngton' Lincoln' dioc' die sabbati quatuor temporum in prima septimana quadragesime videlicet v^to idus[70] Marcii anno domini millesimo CCCC^mo xxiiij^to per venerabilem patrem dominum Johannem Ancoraden' episcopum de mandato et auctoritate honorabilis viri magistri Roberti Leek' legum doctoris officialis consistorii Lincoln'

[70] An error for 'nonas'.

**ac commissarii ad exercendum omnem et omnimodam iuris-
dictionem spiritualem et ecclesiasticam in civitatem et diocesim
Lincoln' per reverendum in Christo patrem et dominum dominum
Henricum dei gracia Cantuar' archiepiscopum totius Anglie
primatem et apostolice sedis legatum pro tempore visitationis sue
metropolitice in dictis civitate et dioc' pendentis inexplete
sufficienter deputati.**

Acolytes in religious orders. John Heyton, Carmelite friar of Nottingham. Thomas Denton, canon of Croxton. Alexander Laverok, Austin friar of Stamford. William Langton, William Brunne, friars minor of Stamford. Reginald Kene, Carmelite friar of Lincoln.

Unbeneficed acolytes. Richard Paynfoule. John Smyth. John Kykelpeny. Robert Holand. Robert Nefwyk. Robert Grysby. John Thixhull. William Clerk. William Walton. William Prentyce. John Grygges. Simon Daws. Robert Hamond. Robert Hook. Henry Smyth. John Barkeworth. Thomas Stonehous. William Valens. William Wulston. John Swalowdale. Reginald Scotte. William Attylburgh. Thomas Bylman. Robert Wace. John Damlet. Thomas Cokson. John Wyseman. [fo. 188r] John FrCeys of Calais (*Cales*'), of Térouane (*Morinen*') dioc., by letters dimissory. Simon Touwold. John Stokton. John Sempar. Nicholas Marchall. William Burton. William Boye. John Fen. Richard Barlaston. Richard Brymyngton. John Hall. John Laghton. Robert Clerke. John Oston. John Clynt. John Selby. John Plummer. Thomas Coryour.

Subdeacons in religious orders. John Barton, Carmelite friar of Nottingham. John Burbache, canon of Canons Ashby. Thomas Enderby, John Kele, William Spyllesby, monks of Revesby. William Ermyn, friar minor of Grantham. Roger Chaumberleyn, John Steventon, friars minor of Stamford. John Boston, Carmelite friar of Lincoln. Richard Assheton, John Yorke, William Morton, monks of Peterborough. William Lincoln, canon of Newhouse.

Unbeneficed subdeacons. Robert Beek of *Syston*, t. Shelford. John Grantham of Boston, t. Newstead by Stamford. Robert Lorymer of Barton upon Humber, t. Newhouse. William Smyth, t. Gokewell. Thomas Kyrgate of Burgh on Bain, t. Barlings. Geoffrey Oustwyk of *Upton*, t. Newstead on Ancholme. John Rygdon of *Marston*, t. Shelford. John Peek, t. St Mary, Leicester. Richard Campsale, t. hospital of St John Evangelist, Leicester. John Ewer of Leicester, t. St Mary, Leicester. Roger Herry, t. Ulverscroft. Robert Whitebrede of Surfleet, t. Sempringham. John Gygur of *Claxton*, t. Newbo. John Geffys, t. Cold Norton. Robert Gowdlak of *Depyng*, t. Bourne. Thomas Wylde of West Ravendale, t. Louth Park. William Syston, t. Ulverscroft. Robert Moller of Habertoft, t. Markby. Thomas Hermer of Bedford, t. Caldwell. Robert Segdyke of Kirkby by Bolingbroke, t. Revesby. John Coke of Hatcliffe, t. Louth Park. John Tamson of Moulton in Holland, t. Spalding. John Ramsowe of Durham dioc., by letters dimissory, t. Easby St Agatha. John Chaumberleyn of Oundle, t. Cotterstock. Thomas Chyveler, t. Markby.

Deacons in religious orders. John Weirton, John Forman, canons of Croxton. Thomas Thorp, Carmelite friar of Lincoln. Richard Litlyngton, canon of Newnham. Thomas Makesey, monk of Peterborough.

Unbeneficed deacons. William Smyth of *Foterby*, t. Dorchester. Richard Cowyk, t. Louth Park. Thomas Vele of Tetford, t. Louth Park. John Sargeant, t. St Katherine by Lincoln. Walter Mochande of East Keal, t. Revesby. John s. Robert Wryght of Clee, t. Grimsby. Thomas Dereford, t. Canwell. John Battesford, t. Bushmead. Thomas Canke, t. Notley. Robert Randolfe, t. Croxton. John atte Kyrke of Claythorpe, t. Markby. John Copuldyke of *Kyrketon*, t. St Michael by Stamford. Thomas Derby of Swineshead, t. Swineshead. Richard Gannok, t. Revesby. Thomas Wodecok, t. Ulverscroft. William Smyre of *Wylugby*, t. Hagnaby. John Cadeby, t. St Katherine outside Lincoln. Richard Hare of *Gayton*, t. Markby. Thomas Roxton, t. Elstow.

Priests in religious orders. John Bachyler, Robert Somercotes, canons of Wellow. John Markeby, canon of Nocton Park. Robert Walsyngham, canon of Canons Ashby. Richard Durham, Alan Whaplode, monks of Pipewell. John Assheby, Austin friar of Stamford. John Cleydon, William Nocton, Everard Pappe, friars minor of Stamford. John Whyte, Austin friar of Leicester. John Lesyngham, monk of Peterborough.

Unbeneficed priests. Thomas Barton of Cadney, t. Fineshade. Robert West of Conisholme, t. Sempringham. Robert Clerke of *Somercotes*, t. Alvingham. William Sygge of Conisholme, t. Alvingham. Robert Luthburgh of *Luthburgh*, t. Kyme. William Goslyn of Thornton by Horncastle, t. Tupholme. John Toutheby of Thoresthorpe, t. Markby. John Clerk of *Staunton*, of Coventry and Lichfield dioc., by letters dimissory, t. Dale. Nicholas Melton of Wigston Magna, t. Ulverscroft. Henry Crosse of Melchbourne, t. Bushmead. William Kysby of Alwalton, t. St Michael by Stamford. John Manypeny of Godmanchester, t. Hinchingbrooke. Roger Baker of Kirby Bellars, t. Shelford. Thomas Smyth of Bourne, t. Swineshead. John Dere of Hughenden, t. Irthlingborough. Thomas Amys of Wymington, t. Harrold. John Syvely of Stamford, t. St Michael by Stamford.

Facta collatione concordat cum rotulis. Colstone.

[fo. 188v]

501. Ordination celebrated by John, bp *Ancoraden'*, in prebendal church of Liddington, 24 March 1425.

Ordines celebrati in ecclesia prebendali de Lidyngton' Linc' dioc' die sabbati qua cantatur Sitientes videlicet ix^no kalendas Aprilis anno domini millesimo CCCC^mo xxiiij^to per venerabilem patrem dominum Johannem Ancoraden' episcopum de mandato et auctoritate honorabilis viri magistri Roberti Leek officialis et commisarii supradicti.

Acolytes in religious orders. Robert Freston, John Wysbech, William Toynton, Carmelite friars of Boston. John Okham, John Wotton, friars minor of Boston. Henry Grene, friar minor of Stamford. John Aswardeby, friar minor of Grantham. William Ryslee, David Hokyn, Dominican friars of Stamford.

Unbeneficed acolytes. James Conyclyffe. Richard Soney. William Harison. John Dunyngton. John Jonson. John Challey. John de Lincoln. John Smeton. John de Ulceby. Walter Lokyng. Robert Rumpayn. Walter Rawson. Henry Depyng. Thomas Webster. John de Kyrkeby. Thomas Derby. Hugh Halton. Richard Walsh.

Beneficed subdeacons. Walter Fouler, rector of Stoke Talmage. William Tybard, rector of Middleton Stoney.

Subdeacons in religious orders. John Brant, Austin friar of Boston. John Ayton, Carmelite friar of Nottingham. Richard Clerk, Carmelite friar of Boston. Reginald Kene, Carmelite friar of Lincoln. William Langton, William Brunne, friars minor of Stamford. Thomas Mapelbek, friar minor of Grantham. John Coventre, monk of Eynsham.

Unbeneficed subdeacons. John Molle, t. Alvingham. William s. Robert Prentys of Lincoln, t. Barlings. Richard Barlaston of *Belton*, t. Ulverscroft. Thomas de Luda, t. Sixhills. Robert Holand of Long Bennington, t. Shelford. John Damlet, t. Croxton. John de Rouceby, t. Broadholme. William Burton of Lincoln, t. Revesby. John Fenne of *Steneby*, t. Vaudey. John Grygg of *Multon*, t. hospital of St John Baptist, Northampton. William Fermer s. Robert Fermer of *Eston*, t. Bradley. Henry Wryght, t. Legbourne. John Wysman, t. Caldwell. William Coston of *Castre*, t. St Michael by Stamford. John Clynt of York dioc., by letters dimissory, t. Grimsby. John Fraunceys of Calais (*Cales*'), of Térouane (*Morinen*') dioc., by letters dimissory, t. Croxton. William Boy, t. St Michael by Stamford. Nicholas Marchall of *Wystowe*, t. Sulby. John Smyth of *Rothewell*, t. hospital of St John Baptist, Northampton. John Weston, t. Notley. Robert Hamond of Necton, t. Blackborough. John Cook of *Flete*, t. St Michael by Stamford.

Beneficed deacon. M. Robert Moreton, rector of Thenford.

Deacons in religious orders. John Lynne, Austin friar of Boston. John Kynyardeby, monk of Louth Park. John Boston, Carmelite friar of Lincoln. Roger Chaumberleyn, friar minor of Stamford. William Ermyn, friar minor of Grantham. John Gulle, Dominican friar of Stamford.

Unbeneficed deacons. John Ewer of Leicester, t. St Mary, Leicester. Thomas Kyrkegate of Burgh on Bain, t. Barlings. Richard Campsale, t. hospital of St John Evangelist, Leicester. John Goudelake of *Depyng*, t. Bourne. John Rygdon of *Merston*, t. Shelford. Robert Segdyke of Kirkby by Bolingbroke, t. Revesby. John Gygur of *Claxton*, t. Newbo. Robert Whitebrede of Surfleet, t. Sempringham. Thomas Hermer, t. Caldwell. Robert Becke of *Syston*, t. Shelford. John Holte, t. Bicester. Richard Bayly, t. Biddlesden. John Geffys, t. Cold Norton. Robert Lorymer of Barton upon Humber, t. Newhouse. John Grantham of Boston, t.

Newstead by Stamford. Robert Moller of Habertoft, t. Markby. John Tomson of Moulton in Holland, t. Spalding. John Chaumberleyn of Oundle, t. Cotterstock.

Beneficed priest. Roger Buckeby, rector of two parts of Clipston.

Priests in religious orders. William Depyng, Austin friar of Northampton. Thomas Thorp, Carmelite friar of Lincoln. John Islep, canon of Cold Norton.

Unbeneficed priests. Richard Cowyk, t. Louth Park. Thomas Vele of Tetford, t. Louth Park. Thomas Desford of Coventry and Lichfield dioc., by letters dimissory, t. Canwell. John Copuldyk of *Kyrketon*, t. St Michael by Stamford. John Battesford, t. Bushmead. Robert Randolfe, t. Croxton. Thomas Roxton, t. Elstow. William Smyth of *Foterby*, t. Dorchester. Thomas Eland of Durham dioc., by letters dimissory, t. Bruern. William Smyre of *Wylugby*, t. Hagnaby. Richard Gannoke, t. Revesby. Thomas Tank, t. Notley. Thomas Wilford of *Burlee*, t. Newstead by Stamford.

Facta collatione concordat cum rotulis. Colstone.

[fo. 189r]

[Institutions carried out by M. Robert Leek, commissary of Henry [Chichele], archbp of Canterbury during his metropolitical visitation of the city and diocese of Lincoln.]

502.   Institution of M. William Paynell Lic.C.&Cn.L. to church of Withern; patrons, Richard Hawe, John Manby, Thomas Spenser and John Tilney, feoffees of the lands and advowsons of lord Wellys – and of Thomas Tylney, in person of M. Thomas Colston his proctor, to church of Aston, dioc. York; patrons, Thomas Clarell, Geoffrey Paynell and Richard Wyntworth, esquires, feoffees of the lands and advowson of John Melton kt. Exchange, by authority of commission of W[illiam], dean, and chapter of York, *sede vacante* (dated at the chancery of York, 13 April 1425). Liddington, 20 April 1425.

[fo. 189v]

503.   Institution of William Cleche, priest, in person of Henry Bronne his proctor, to church of Thorpe Malsor, vac. by death of William Thrustynton; patron, lady Isabella Penbrugge. Thame, 11 April 1425. Note that an inquiry was held, by which it was found that the said Isabella Penbrugge held the right of presentation by reason of a feoffment made to her for her life of the manor and advowson of Thorpe Malsor by Fulk Penbrygge kt, and that Petronilla Trussell presented the said William Thrustynton at the last vacancy.

504.   Institution of John Mons, priest, in person of William Bagge of Yarburgh, chaplain, his proctor, to church of St Peter, Mablethorpe, vac. by death of Simon Malberthorp; patron, Robert de Wylughby, lord of Eresby, kt. Liddington, 19 April 1425.

505. Certificate of institution, by William Admondeston B.Cn.&C.L., vicar-general of William [Heyworth], bp of Coventry and Lichfield *in remotis*, of Robert Baron to vicarage of Tugby, vac. by res. of Thomas Flynderkyn; patron, A. and C. of St Mary, Croxden. Exchange, by authority of commission of M. Robert Leek, Official of Consistory and commissary-general during archbp's visitation (dated at Thame, 15 April 1425) with vicarage of Leek Wootton, dioc. Coventry and Lichfield. Lichfield, 18 April 1425. Received at Liddington, 26 April 1425.

[fo. 190r]

506. Institution of William Malberthorp, priest, in person of William Port his proctor, to church of Denton, vac. by res. of John Malberthorp; patron, Thomas Greneham. Liddington, 28 April 1425.

507. Institution of John Anneys, priest, to vicarage of Geddington, vac. by death of William Taylour; patron, A. and C. of Pipewell. Liddington, 9 May 1425.

508. Institution of John Pennys, priest, to vicarage of Middle Rasen Drax, vac. by res. of Robert Sparowe; patron, P. and C. of Drax. Liddington, 12 May 1425.

[fo. 190v]

509. Certificate of Stephen Monyden, clerk, commissary-general of Henry [Chichele], archbp of Canterbury, in the archdnries of Huntingdon and Bedford, for the time of his metropolitical visitation of the city and diocese of Lincoln. In accordance with a commission of Robert Leek, Official and archbp's commissary (addressed to him jointly with the prior of Huntingdon, and dated at Liddington, 15 March 1424/5) he has held an inquiry in the church of Yelling into the presen-tation of John Dally, bp of *Stephanen'*, by the P. and C. of Merton, dioc. Winchester, to the ch. of Yelling. It was found that the church was vac. by the death of John Penneryth the last rector (who died at Yelling aforesaid on 10 March), and that there was no impediment to the institution of the presentee. He therefore instituted the said John to the church. The following were present at the inquiry: Edmund Hungerford, rector of Offord Cluny; Richard Edhous, rector of Offord Darcy; John Almot, rector of St John, Huntingdon; Thomas Blakemore, rector of St Bene-dict, Huntingdon; William Ade, vicar of Godmanchester; and John Wadno, vicar of Hemingford Grey. Dated at Huntingdon, 20 March 1424/5.

[fo. 191r]

510. Institution of Richard Castelakyr to vicarage of Billingborough; patron, P. and C. of Sempringham – and of John Brampcote to church of Nuthall, dioc. York; patron, John Cokefeld of Nuthall, esquire. Exchange, by authority of commission of D. and C. of York *sede vacante* (dated at York, 24 May 1425). Liddington, 1 June 1425.

[fo. 191v]

511. Institution of Thomas Cosle, priest, to vicarage of Kirkby Green, vac. by res. of Robert Fyssher; patron, P. and C. of Thurgarton. Liddington, 19 May 1425.[71]

512. Institution of Robert Fyssher, priest, to church of Blankney, vac. by death of Thomas Mufyn; patron, P. and C. of Thurgarton. Liddington, 19 May 1425.

513. Certificate of Philip [Morgan], bp of Worcester. In accordance with commission of Robert Leek (dated at Liddington, 21 April 1425), he has instituted William Andrewe to vicarage of Ashby St Ledgers, vac. by res. of John Baron; patron, P. and C. of Launde. By exchange with vicarage of Aston Cantlow, dioc. Worcester. London, 31 May 1425. Received at Liddington, at the hands of John Broune, substitute of John Turvey, original proctor of the said William Andrewe, 7 June 1425.

[fo. 192r]

514. Memorandum that a commission was issued to the prior of Huntingdon, M. Stephen Wylton D.Dec., and M. Stephen Monyden, commissary-general of Henry [Chichele], archbp of Canterbury, in the archdnries of Huntingdon and Bedford, to inquire into the vacancy of the church of Abbots Ripton and into the merits and person of the presentee, and to admit Thomas Pulter to the same; patron, A. and C. of Ramsey. Liddington, 3 April 1425.

515. Institution of M. Thomas Hill, priest, to the twelfth prebend in the new collegiate church of St Mary, Leicester, vac. by death of William Broun; patron Queen Katherine. Liddington, 19 June 1425.

516. Admission of br. William Schroesbury, canon of Kenilworth, as prior of Brooke, vac. by res. of br. John Streeth; patron, P. and C. of Kenilworth. Liddington, 25 June 1425.

[fo. 192v]

517. Institution of William Torald, in person of M. John Hoggesthorp, notary public, his proctor, to vicarage of Swarby; patron, P. and C. of Kyme – and of William Wace to vicarage of East Stoke (*Stoke iuxta Newerk*), dioc. York; patron, Richard Burnham M.A., preb. of Stoke and Coddington (*Cotyngton*) in Lincoln cath. Exchange, by authority of commission of D. and C. of York, *sede vacante* (dated at York, 8 June 1425). Liddington, 26 June 1425.

---

[71] Cause of vacancy inserted in the margin.

[fo. 193r]

518. Institution of Robert Yerburgh, priest, to vicarage of Swinford, vac. by res. of Robert Bolton; patron, br. Henry Crounhale, preceptor of Eagle and lieutenant of br. William Hulles, prior of Hospitallers in England, *in remotis*. Liddington, 29 June 1425.

519. Institution of John Wryght, priest, to church of Denton, vac. by res. of William Malberthorp; patron, Thomas Greneham. 29 June 1425 [place not specified].

[fo. 193v]

520. Ordination celebrated by John, bp *Ancoraden'*, in prebendal church of Liddington, 3 March 1425.[72]

Ordines generales celebrati in ecclesia prebendali de Lidyngton' Lincolnien' dioc' die sabbati quatuor temporum in prima septimana quadragesime videlicet quinto idus[73] Marcii anno domini millesimo CCCC^{mo} xxiiij^{to} per venerabilem patrem dominum Johannem Ancoraden' episcopum de mandato et auctoritate honorabilis viri magistri Roberti Leek legum doctoris offic' consistorii Lincoln' ac commissar' ad exercendum omnem et omnimodam iurisdictionem spiritualem et ecclesiasticam in civitate et dioc' Lincoln' per reverendum in Christo patrem et dominum dominum Henricum dei gracia Cantuarien' archiepiscopum tocius Anglie primatem et apostolice sedis legatum pro tempore visitationis sue metropolitice in eisdem civitate et dioc' pendentis inexplete sufficienter deputati.

Acolytes in religious orders. John Hayton, Carmelite friar of Nottingham. Thomas Denton, monk of Croxton. Alexander Laverok, Austin friar of Stamford. William Langton, William Brunne, friars minor of Stamford. Reginald Kene, Carmelite friar of Lincoln.

Unbeneficed acolytes. Richard Paynfoule. John Smyth. John Kykelpeny. Robert Holland. Robert Nefwyk. Robert Grysby. John Thyxhull. William Clerc. William Walton. William Prentyce. John Grygges. Simon Dawys. Robert Hamond. John Hoke. Henry Smyth. John Berkworth. Thomas Stonhous. William Valens. William Vulston. John Swalowdale. Reginald Scott. William Attylburgh. Thomas Bylman. Robert Wace. John Fraunceys of Calais (*Cales'*), of Térouane (*Morinen'*) dioc., by letters dimissory. John Damlet. Thomas Cokson. John Wyseman. Simon Tomwold. John Stokton. John Sempar. Nicholas Marchall. William Burton. John Fen. Richard Barlaston. Richard Brymmyngton. John Hall. John Laghton. John Oston. John Clynt. John Selby. John Plummer. Thomas Coriour. William Boye. Robert Cleve.

---

[72] This entry is a copy of no 500 above.
[73] An error for 'nonas'.

Subdeacons in religious orders. John Barton, Carmelite friar of Nottingham. John Burbache, canon of Canons Ashby. Thomas Enderby, John Kele, William Spillesby, monks of Revesby. William Ermyn, friar minor of Grantham. Roger Chaumberleyn, John Steventon, friars minor of Stamford. John Boston, Carmelite friar of Lincoln. Richard Assheton, John York, William Morton, monks of Peterborough. William Lincoln, canon of Newhouse.

Unbeneficed subdeacons. Robert Beek of *Syston*, t. Shelford. John Grantham of Boston, t. Newstead by Stamford. Robert Lorymer of Barton upon Humber, t. Newhouse. William Smyth, t. Gokewell (*Gowxhill*). Thomas Kyrgate of Burgh on Bain, t. Barlings. Geoffrey Owstwyk of *Upton*, t. [Newstead on] Ancholme. John Rygdon of *Marston*, t. Shelford. John Peek, t. St Mary Delapré, Leicester. Richard Campsale, t. hospital of St John Baptist, Leicester. John Ewer of Leicester, t. St Mary Delapré, Leicester. Roger Herry, t. Ulverscroft. Robert Whytebrede of Surfleet, t. Sempringham. John Gygur of *Clauston*, t. Newbo. John Geffys, t. Cold Norton. Robert Gowdlak of *Depyng*, t. Bourne. [fo. 194r] Thomas Wylde of West Ravendale, t. Louth Park. William Syston, t. Ulverscroft. Robert Moller of Habertoft, t. Markby. Thomas Hermer of Bedford, t. Caldwell. Robert Sygdyk of Kirkby by Bolingbroke, t. Revesby. John Coke of Hatcliffe, t. Louth Park. John Tomson of Moulton in Holland, t. Spalding. John Ramsow of Durham dioc., by letters dimissory, t. Easby St Agatha. John Chaumberleyn of Oundle, t. Cotterstock. Thomas Chiveler, t. Markby.

Deacons in religious orders. John Weyrton, John Forman, canons of Croxton. Thomas Thorp, Carmelite friar of Lincoln. Richard Lythyngton, canon of Newnham. Thomas Maksey, monk of Peterborough.

Unbeneficed deacons. William Smyth of *Foterby*, t. Dorchester. Thomas Vele of Tetford, t. Louth Park. John Sergeaunt, t. St Katherine by Lincoln. Walter Mochande of East Keal, t. Revesby. John s. Robert Wryght of Clee, t. Grimsby. Thomas Dereford, t. Canwell. John Battesford, t. Bushmead. Thomas Cank, t. Notley. Robert Randolf, t. Croxton. John atte Kyrk of Claythorpe, t. Markby. John Copuldyk of *Kyrketon*, t. St Michael by Stamford. Thomas Derby of Swineshead, t. Swineshead. Richard Gannok, t. Revesby. Thomas Wodecok, t. Ulverscroft. William Smyre of *Wylughby*, t. Hagnaby. John Cateby, t. St Katherine by Lincoln. Richard Hare of *Gayton*, t. Markby. Thomas Roxton, t. Elstow.

Priests in religious orders. John Bacheler, Robert Somercotes, canons of Wellow. John Markeby, canon of Nocton Park. Robert Walsyngham, canon of Canons Ashby. Richard Dorham, Alan Whappelode, monks of Pipewell. John Assheby, Austin friar of Stamford. John Cleydon, William Nocton, Everard Pappe, friars minor of Stamford. John Qwyte, Austin friar of Leicester. John Lesyngham, monk of Peterborough.

Unbeneficed priests. Thomas Barton of Cadney, t. Fineshade. Robert West of Conisholme, t. Sempringham. Robert Clerc of *Somercotes*, t. Alvingham. William Sygge of Conisholme, t. Alvingham. Robert Luthburgh of *Lughburgh*, t. Kyme. William Goslyn of Thornton by Horncastle, t. Tupholme. John Toutheby of Thoresthorpe, t. Markby. John Clerc of *Staunton*, of Coventry and Lichfield dioc., by letters dimissory, t. Dale. Nicholas Melton of Wigston Magna, t. Ulverscroft. Henry Cros of Melchbourne, t. Bushmead. William Kysby of Alwalton, t. St Michael by Stamford. John Manypeny of Godmanchester, t. Hinchingbrooke. Roger Baker of Kirby Bellars, t. Shelford. Thomas Smythy of Bourne, t. Swineshead. John Dere of Hughenden, t. Irthlingborough. Thomas Amys of Wymington, t. Harrold. John Sybly of Stamford, t. St Michael by Stamford.

521. Ordination celebrated by John, bp *Ancoraden'*, in prebendal church of Liddington, 24 March 1425.[74]

Ordines generales celebrati in ecclesia prebendali de Lidyngton predict' die sabbati qua cantatur officium in ecclesia Dei Sitientes anno domini millesimo CCCC^{mo} vicesimo quarto per dictum venerabilem patrem Episcopum Ancoraden' de mandato dicti honorabilis viri Magistri Roberti Leek Officialis et commisarii supradicti.

Acolytes in religious orders. Robert Freston, John Wysbeche, William Toynton, Carmelite friars of Boston. John Okham, John Wotton, friars minor of Boston. Henry Grene, friar minor of Stamford. John Aswardby, friar of Grantham. William Rysle, David Hokyn, Dominican friars of Stamford.

Unbeneficed acolytes. James Conyclyffe. Richard Soney. William Hanson. John Donyngton. John Jonson. John Challey. John de Lincoln. John Smeton. John de Ulceby. Walter Lokyng. Robert Rumpayn. Walter Rawson. Henry Depyng. Thomas Webster. John de Kyrkeby. Thomas Derby. Hugh Walton. Richard Walsh.

Beneficed subdeacons. Walter Fouler, rector of Stoke Talmage, t. his benefice *de [quo] reputavit se contentum..* William Tybard, [rector of] Middleton Stoney.

[fo. 194v] *Subdeacons in religious orders.* John Brant, Austin friar of Boston. John Ayton, [Carmelite] friar of Nottingham. Richard Clerc, Carmelite friar of Boston. Reginald Kene, Carmelite friar of Lincoln. William Langton, William Brunne, friars minor of Stamford. Thomas Mapylbek, friar minor of Grantham. John Coventre, canon of Eynsham.

Unbeneficed subdeacons. John Molle, t. Alvingham. William s. Robert Prentyce of Lincoln, t. Barlings. Richard Barlaston of *Belton*, t. Ulverscroft. Thomas de Luda, t. Sixhills. Robert Holand of Long Bennington, t. Shelford. John Damlet, t. Croxton. John de Rouceby, t. Broadholme. William Burton of Lincoln, t. Revesby. John Fenne of *Stenby*, t. Vaudey. John Grygg of *Multon*, t. hospital of St John Baptist, Northampton. William Farmer s. Robert Fermor of *Eston*, t. Bradley. Henry Wrygh, t. Legbourne. John Wysman, t. Caldwell. William Coston of *Castre*, t. St Michael by Stamford. John Clynt of York dioc., by letters dimissory, t. Grimsby. John Frаunceys of Calais (*Cales'*), of Térouane (*Morinen'*) dioc., by letters dimissory,

[74] This entry is a copy of no 501 above.

t. Croxton. William Boye, t. St Michael by Stamford. Nicholas Marchall of *Wystow*, t. Sulby. John Smyth of *Rothewell*, t. hospital of St John Baptist, Northampton. John Weston, t. Notley. Robert Hamond of Necton, t. Blackborough. John Cooke of *Flete*, t. St Michael by Stamford.

Beneficed deacon. M. Robert Moreton, rector of Thenford, t. his benefice *de quo reputavit se contentum*.

Deacons in religious orders. John Lynne, Austin friar of Boston. [John] Kynyerdby, monk of Louth Park. John Boston, Carmelite friar of Lincoln. Roger Chaumberleyn, friar minor of Stamford. William Ermyn, friar minor of Grantham. John Gulle, Dominican friar of Stamford.

Unbeneficed deacons. John Ewer of Leicester, t. St Mary Delapré, Leicester. Thomas Kyrkegate of Burgh on Bain, t. Barlings. Richard Campsale, t. hospital of St John Baptist, Leicester. John Gowdelake of *Depyng*, t. Bourne. John Rygdon of *Marston*, t. Shelford. Robert Segdyke of Kirkby by Bolingbroke, t. Revesby. John Gygur of *Clauston*, t. Newbo. Robert Whytebred of Surfleet, t. Sempringham. Thomas Hermer, t. Caldwell. Robert Beck of *Syston*, t. Shelford. John Holt, t. Bicester. Richard Bayly, t. Biddlesden. John Geffys, t. Cold Norton. Robert Lorymer of Barton upon Humber, t. Newhouse. John Grantham of Boston, t. Newstead by Stamford. Robert Moller of Habertoft, t. Markby. John Tomson of Moulton in Holland, t. Spalding. John Chaumberleyn of Oundle, t. Cotterstock.

Beneficed priest. Roger Bulkeby, rector of two parts of Clipston.

Priests in religious orders. William Depyng, Austin friar of Northampton. Thomas Thorp, Carmelite friar of Lincoln. John Islep, canon of Cold Norton.

Unbeneficed priests. Richard Cowyk, t. Louth Park. Thomas Vele of Tetford, t. Louth Park. Thomas Desford of Coventry and Lichfield dioc., by letters dimissory, t. Canwell. John Coupyldyk of *Kyrketon*, t. St Michael by Stamford. John Battesford, t. Bushmead. Robert Randolf, t. Croxton. Thomas Roxton, t. Elstow. William Smyth[75] of *Foterby*, t. Dorchester. Thomas Eland of Durham dioc., by letters dimissory, t. Bruern. William Smyre of *Wylughby*, t. Hagnaby. Richard Gannok, t. Revesby. Thomas Tank, t. Notley. Thomas Wilford of *Burlee*, t. Newstead by Stamford.

[fo. 195r]

522. Ordination celebrated by John, bp *Ancoraden'*, in prebendal church of Liddington, 2 June 1425.

Ordines generales celebrati per dictum Reverendum patrem dominum Johannem Ancoraden' Episcopum vice et auctoritate dicti Reverendi patris domini Cant' Archiepiscopum &c. et de mandato

---

[75] MS 'Symth'.

dicti honorabilis viri Magistri Roberti Leek Officialis et Commissarii supradicti in ecclesia prebendali de Lidyngton' Lincolnien' diocesis die sabbati quatuor temporum in vigilia sancte Trinitatis videlicet quarto Nonas Junii anno domini millesimo CCCC^{mo} xxv^{to}.

Acolytes in religious orders. Lambert de Myddylburgh, Austin friar of Leicester. Simon Silveron, William Hawdon, Dominican friars of Stamford.

Unbeneficed acolytes. Robert Wrygh. Henry Knyth. William Eston. Thomas Billyngham. Nicholas Capell. Adam Malkynson. William Paton. Robert Joce. Thomas Prentys. Richard Harwod. Robert Pysale. Robert Leton. John Warner. John Robynson. Alexander Chathewell. John in the Herne. Ellis North. John de Lyn. John Richardson. John Otyr. John Coke. John Leche. William Walker. John Burgeys. Robert Joye. John Browne. Richard Mydilbroke. John Wellyngdon.

Beneficed subdeacon. William Lathys of Tadcaster, archdn of Shropshire in Hereford cath., by letters dimissory.

Subdeacons in religious orders. William Lowthgbero, Austin friar of Leicester. Walter Rysley, Dominican friar of Stamford. Thomas Bascote, John Prescote, monks of Wroxton. Thomas Bradar, John Kyllyngholm, monks of Louth Park. Alexander Laverok, Austin friar of Stamford. John Spaldyng, canon of Barlings. William Hayhyrst, John Wykyngeston, canons of Leicester.

Unbeneficed subdeacons. William Attilburgh of *Wenge*, t. Launde. Thomas Basse of *Croft*, t. Kyme. Robert Doughty, t. Louth Park. John Burton, t. Caldwell. Robert Clerc of Great Bowden, t. Sulby. Robert Careby of *Morton*, t. Bourne. Robert Gonelde of *Irby*, t. Nun Cotham. Robert Nefwyk of North Kelsey, t. Newhouse. Thomas Dygby of *Haugh*, t. Markby. John Parysh of *Haghthorp*, t. Ormsby. John Aleyn, t. Owston. John Feversham of Higham Ferrers, t. Harrold. Stephen Brasyer of Higham Ferrers, t. Harrold. John Kyng, t. Chacombe. Henry Garbray of Bracebridge, t. Barlings. John Stalyngburgh, t. Barlings. Walter Kyrkeby of Sloothby, t. Markby. Simon Dawes of Hanging Houghton, t. hospital of St John Baptist, Northampton. John Mychell of *Multon*, t. Crowland. John Leek of Hagworthingham, t. Markby. Henry Depyng, t. Owston.

Deacons in religious orders. Richard Spaldyng, John Boston, monks of Spalding. William Bentley, Carmelite friar of Leicester. John Brantte, Austin friar of Northampton. William Langton, William Brunne, friars minor of Stamford. John Coventre, monk of Eynsham.

Unbeneficed deacons. John Grygges of *Multon*, t. hospital of St John Baptist, Northampton. William s. Robert Prentys, t. Barlings. William Smyth, t. Gokewell. Robert Smyth, t. Thornholm. John Rauceby, t. Broadholme. Henry Wryght, t. Legbourne. Geoffrey Owstewyk of *Upton*, t. [Newstead] on Ancholme. John Damlet, t. Croxton. Thomas de Luda, t. Sixhills. John Fenne of *Stenby*, t. Vaudey. John Mille, t. Alvingham. Robert Hamond of Necton, of Norwich dioc., by letters dimissory, t. Blackborough. John Frraunceys of Calais (*Cales'*), of Térouane (*Morinen'*) dioc., by letters dimissory, t. Croxton. Thomas Wylde of West Ravendale, t. Louth Park. William Burton of Lincoln, t. Revesby. John Coke of Hatcliffe, t. Louth Park. [fo. 195v] Robert Holand of Long Bennington, t. Shelford. Nicholas Marchall of *Wystowe*, t. Sulby. Thomas Chyvaler, t. Markby. William Syston of Leicester, t. Ulverscroft. John Weston, t. Notley. William Boye, t. St Michael by Stamford. Richard Barlaston of *Belton*, t. Ulverscroft. John Smyth of *Rothewell*, t. hospital of St John Baptist, Northampton.

Beneficed priest. M. Robert Moreton, rector of Thenford.

Priests in religious orders. Robert Malton, canon of Ormsby. William Flemyng, Dominican friar of Leicester. John Sylyard, Dominican of Stamford. Robert Byrys, Henry Midelham, friars minor of Lincoln. John Kynardeby, monk of Louth Park. John Lyn, Austin friar of Boston.

Unbeneficed priests. Richard Graunte, t. St Mary Delapré, Leicester. John s. Robert Wryght of Clee, t. Grimsby. Richard Campsale, t. hospital of St John Baptist, Leicester. John Ewer of Leicester, t. St Mary Delapré, Leicester. Thomas Derby of Swineshead, t. Swineshead. John Tomson of Moulton in Holland, t. Spalding. Thomas Kyrkegate of Burgh on Bain, t. Barlings. Walter Mochand of East Keal, t. Revesby. Robert Gawdelake of *Depyng*, t. Bourne. John Geffys, t. Cold Norton. Richard Hare of *Gayton*, t. Markby. John Cadeby, t. St Katherine by Lincoln. Robert Segdyke of Kirkby by Bolingbroke, t. Revesby. Robert Lorymer of Barton upon Humber, t. Newhouse. John atte Kyrke of Claythorpe, t. Markby. John Gygur of *Clauston*, t. Newbo. Richard Bayly, t. Biddlesden. Thomas Forster of Metheringham, t. Kyme. Robert Moller of Habertoft, t. Markby. John Clynt of York dioc., by letters dimissory, t. Grimsby. John Rygdon of *Marston*, t. Shelford. John Holt, t. Bicester. Robert Bekke of *Syston*, t. Shelford. John Grantham of Boston, t. Newstead by Stamford. Thomas Wodecote, t. Ulverscroft.

[fo. 196r]

Duodecimo die mensis Februarii anno domini millesimo quadringentesimo vicesimo quarto incipient institutiones expedite per honorabilem virum magistrum Robertum Leek' legum doctorem officialem consistorii Lincoln' ac commissarium ad exercendum omnem et omnimodam iurisdictionem spiritualem et ecclesiasticam in civitate et dioc' Lincoln' per reverendum in Christo patrem et dominum dominum Henricum dei gracia Cantuar' Archiepiscopum tocius Anglie primatem et apostolice sedis legatum pro tempore visitationis sue metropolitice in eisdem civitate et dioc' pendentis inexplete sufficienter deputatum.

523.   Institution of John Fourneys priest to vicarage of Ravensthorpe, vac. by res. of William Reve; patron, br. Henry Crounhale, preceptor of Eagle and lieutenant of br. William Hulles, prior of Hospitallers in England. Liddington, 3 March 1424/5.

[fos 196r–197r]

524. Certificate of M. Andrew Sutton, rector of Greetham. In accordance with commission of M. Robert Leek, commissary as above (addressed to him jointly with M. John Spencer B.Dec. and dated at Liddington, 7 March 1424/5), he has carried out an inquiry into the presentation by John Aungevyn of Theddlethorpe, esquire, of Robert Broun priest to the church of West Keal. The inquiry was held in full chapter in the said church on 10 March 1424/5, in the presence of Robert Kyrkeby rector of Bolingbroke, John Couper rector of Mavis Enderby, Thomas Kyrkeby and William Wragby rectors of [medieties of] East Keal, Thomas Beker rector of Miningsby, Walter Woderoff rector of Lusby, John Burdon vicar of Stickford, Robert Segdyk vicar of Kirkby and William Smyth vicar of Hagnaby. It was found that the church was vac. through the death of John Spryngthorp the last rector, who died in London on Ash Wednesday (*die cinerum*) last past; that the said John Aungevyn esquire had the right of presentation for this turn by hereditary right, as appeared by certain charters shown to them; and that the abbot and convent of Crowland presented John Spryngthorp at the last vacancy, by their right on alternate turns. It was also found that the said Robert Broun was of good fame and honest conversation, in priest's orders, and not beneficed elsewhere. Finding no impediment, therefore, he has instituted Robert Broun to the church. He has sealed the present certificate with the seal of the official of the peculiar jurisdiction of the prebend of Louth, the care of which office he bears at present, together with the seals of the aforesaid inquisitors. West Keal, 10 March 1424/5.

[fo. 197r]

525. Memorandum of a commission to M. William Symond, commissary-general in archdnry of Oxford, to inquire into the presentation of Henry Boxe by Thomas Chetewode kt to church of Begbroke. He is to inquire in particular of William Hawkyng, lately presented by the said Thomas to the same church. If there is no impediment, he is to admit the said Henry to the church. Liddington, 6 March 1424/5.

526. Institution of Thomas Taillour to church of Caldecote, vac. by death of William Maxey; patron, A. and C. of St Albans. Liddington, 12 March 1424/5.

527. Certificate of John [Fordham], bp of Ely. In accordance with commission of M. Robert Leek, commissary as above (dated at Liddington, 12 March 1424/5), he has instituted John Baxter, in person of John Zoll his proctor, to church of Colsterworth, vac. by res. of Stephen Monynden, in person of Richard Barton his proctor; patron, M. John Southam, preb. of Grantham Australis in Salisbury cath. By exchange with church of Rampton, dioc. Ely. Downham, 14 March 1424/5. Received at Liddington, 20 March 1424/5.

[fo. 197v]

528. Memorandum of a commission to official of archdn of Huntingdon to inquire into the vacancy of the vicarage of St John, Hertford, and into the presentation of John Nicoll to the same by P. and C. of St Mary, Hertford. If there is no impediment, he is to admit the said John to the vicarage. Liddington, 14 March 1424/5.

529.   Institution of William Jewster priest to vicarage of Chacombe; patron, P. and C. of Chacombe. Liddington, 15 March 1424/5.

530.   Institution of Robert Holewylle priest to church of Cuxham, vac. by death of M. Thomas Chilmart; patron, warden and scholars of Merton College, Oxford. Liddington, 18 March 1424/5.

[fo. 198r]

531.   Institution of Robert Sturdy of *Sclypton*, priest, to vicarage of Anwick, vac. by res. of John Colson of Leasingham; patron, P. and C. of Haverholme. Liddington, 23 March 1424/5.

532.   Institution of John Chaumberleyn priest to vicarage of Great Paxton; patron, subdean and chapter of Lincoln (dean being absent). Liddington, 23 March 1424/5.

533.   Certificate of John [Wheathampstead], abbot of St Albans. In accordance with a commission of M. Robert Leek, commissary as above (dated at Liddington, 21 March 1424/5), he has collated vicarage of Steeple Claydon, vac. by res. of M. William Gorcote, to Peter Braunch. By exchange with vicarage of Winslow, dioc. Lincoln and in the jurisdiction of St Albans. St Albans, 23 March 1424/5. Received at Liddington, 25 March 1425.[76]

[fo. 198v]

534.   Institution of John Bailly priest, in person of Richard Pyghtesley clerk, his proctor, to church of St Andrew, Huntingdon, vac. by res. of Robert Vyncer; patron, A. and C. of Ramsey. Liddington, 29 March 1425.

535.   Institution of Richard Stryngsale priest to vicarage of Eaton, vac. by res. of John Colyns; patron, A. and C. of St Mary Delapré, Leicester. Liddington, 20 April 1425.

536.   Institution of John Tychemersh priest, in person of John Warde literate, his proctor, to church of Broughton, vac. by res. of Thomas Pulter; patron, A. and C. of Ramsey. Liddington, 19 April 1425.

537.   Institution of John Cobard priest to church of Teigh, vac. by res. of John Muston; patron, Robert Barowe, *domicellus*. Liddington, 25 February 1424/5.

---

[76] The commission states that Braunch was presented to Steeple Claydon by A. and C. of Osney; the certificate, however, is clear that the vicarage was collated.

538. Institution of Laurence Stafford clerk to church of Grendon Underwood, vac. by res. of Walter Chycon; patron, Eleanor, lady St Amand, widow of Amauri de St Amand kt. Thame, 15 April 1425.

539. Institution of Thomas William priest to church of Warpsgrove; patron, A. and C. of Dorchester. Thame, 13 April 1425.

540. Institution of John Fuller priest to chantry of St Mary the Virgin in church of Newport Pagnell, vac. by death of John Wenge; patron, John Barton the younger, lord of Thornton by Buckingham. Northampton, 19 April 1425.

[fo. 199r]

541. Ordination celebrated by John, bp *Ancoraden'*, in prebendal church of Liddington, 2 June 1425.[77]

Ordines generales celebrati in ecclesia prebendali de Lidyngton' Linc' dioc' die sabbati quatuor temporum in vigilia sancte Trinitatis videlicet iiij^{to} Nonas Junii anno domini millesimo CCCC^{mo} xxv^{to} per venerabilem patrem dominum Johannem Ancoraden' Episcopum auctoritate et mandato honorabilis viri Magistri Roberti Leek' legum doctoris officialis et commissarii prox' prescripti.

Acolytes in religious orders. Lambert de Middelburgh, Austin friar of Leicester. Simon Sylveron, William Hawden, Dominican friars of Stamford.

Unbeneficed acolytes. Robert Wryght. Henry Knayth. William Eston. Thomas Byllyngham. Nicholas Capell. Adam Malkynson. William Paton. Robert Joce. Thomas Prentyce. Richard Harwode. Robert Pysale. Robert Leton. John Warner. John Robynson. Alexander Shathewell. John in the Herne. Elias North. John de Lyme. John Rychardson. John Oter. John Cooke. John Leche. William Walker. John Burgeys. Robert Joye. John Browne. Richard Midylbroke. John Wellyngdon.

Beneficed subdeacon. William Lathys of Tadcaster, archdn of Shropshire in Hereford cath., by letters dimissory.

Subdeacons in religious orders. William Lughtburgh, Austin friar of Leicester. Walter Rysley, Dominican friar of Stamford. Thomas Bascote, John Prescote, canons of Wroxton. Thomas Bradar, John Kyllyngholme, monks of Louth Park. Alexander Laverok, Austin friar of Stamford. John Spaldyng, canon of Barlings. William Hayhirst, John Wykyngston, canons of Leicester.

Unbeneficed subdeacons. William Attilburgh of *Wenge*, t. Launde. Thomas Basse of *Croft*, t. Kyme. Robert Doughty, t. Louth Park. John Burton, t. Caldwell. Robert Clerk of Great Bowden, t. Sulby. Robert Careby of *Morton*, t. Bourne. Robert

[77] This entry is a copy of no 522 above.

Gunneld of *Irby*, t. Nun Cotham. Robert Nefwyk of North Kelsey, t. Newhouse. Thomas Dygby of *Hagh*, t. Markby. John Paryssh of *Hagthorp*, t. Ormsby. John Aleyn, t. Owston. John Feversham of Higham Ferrers, t. Harrold. Stephen Brasyer of Higham Ferrers, t. Harrold. John Kyng, t. Chacombe. Henry Garbray of Bracebridge, t. Barlings. John Stalyngburgh, t. Barlings. Walter Kyrkeby of Sloethby, t. Markby. Simon Dawes of Hanging Houghton, t. hospital of St John Baptist, Northampton. John Michell of *Multon*, t. Crowland. John Leek of Hagworthingham, t. Markby. Henry Depyng, t. Owston.

Deacons in religious orders. Richard Spaldyng, John Boston, monks of Spalding. William Benteley, [Carmelite friar] of Leicester. John Brante, Austin friar of Northampton. William Langton, William Brunne, friars minor of Stamford. John Coventre, monk of Eynsham.

Unbeneficed deacons. John Grygges of *Multon*, t. hospital of St John Baptist, Northampton. William s. Robert Prentys, t. Barlings. William Smyth, t. Gokewell. Robert Smyth, t. Thornholm. John Rauceby, t. Broadholme. Henry Wryght, t. Legbourne. Geoffrey Owstwyk of *Upton*, t. Newstead on Ancholme. John Damlet, t. Croxton. Thomas de Luda, t. Sixhills. John Fenne of *Stenby*, t. Vaudey. John Mylle, t. Alvingham. Robert Hamond of Necton, of Norwich dioc., by letters dimissory, t. Blackborough. Thomas Wylde of West Ravendale, t. Louth Park. William Burton of Lincoln, t. Revesby. John Cook of Hatcliffe, t. Louth Park. Robert Holand of Long Bennington, t. Shelford. Nicholas Marchall of *Wystowe*, t. Sulby. Thomas Chyvaler, t. Markby. William Syston of Leicester, t. Ulverscroft. John Weston, t. Notley. William Boye, t. St Michael by Stamford. Richard Barlaston of *Belton*, t. Ulverscroft. John Smyth of *Rothewell*, t. hospital of St John Baptist, Northampton. John Fraunceys of Calais (*Calesia*), of Térouane (*Morinen'*) dioc., by letters dimissory, t. Croxton.

Beneficed priest. M. Robert Moreton, rector of Thenford.

Priests in religious orders. Robert Malton, canon of Ormsby. William Flemyng, Dominican friar of Leicester. John Sylyard, Dominican friar of Stamford. Robert Byrys, Henry Midelham, friars minor of Lincoln. John Kynyardeby, monk of Louth Park. John Lynne, Austin friar of Boston.

Unbeneficed priests. [fo. 199v] Richard Graunt, t. St Mary de Pratis, Leicester. Richard Campsale, t. hospital of St John Evangelist, Leicester. Thomas Derby of Swineshead, t. Swineshead. Thomas Kyrkegate of Burgh on Bain, t. Barlings. Robert Goudelake of *Depyng*, t. Bourne. Richard Hare of *Gaytton*, t. Markby. Robert Segdyke of Kirkby by Bolingbroke, t. Revesby. John atte Kyrke of Claythorpe, t. Markby. Richard Bayly, t. Biddlesden. Robert Moller of Habertoft, t. Markby. John Rygdon of *Merston*, t. Shelford. John Becke of *Syston*, t. Shelford. Thomas Wodecote, t. Ulverscroft. John s. Robert Wryght of Clee, t. Grimsby. John Ewer of Leicester, t. St Mary de Pratis, Leicester. John Tomson of Moulton in Holland, t. Spalding. Walter Mochaunde of East Keal, t. Revesby. John Geffys, t. Cold Norton. John Cadeby, t. St Katherine by Lincoln. Robert Lorymer of Barton upon Humber, t. Newhouse. John Gygur of *Claxton*, t. Newbo. Thomas Forster of Metheringham, t. Kyme. John Clynt of York dioc., by letters dimissory, t.

Grimsby. John Holt, t. Bicester. John Grantham of Boston, t. Newstead by Stamford.

Facta collatione concordat cum rotulis. Colstone.

542. Note that on the Ordination Saturday next after the Feast of St Matthew, 22 September 1425, the see of Lincoln being vacant, Henry [Chichele], archbp of Canterbury, to whom the right appertained by reason of the said vacancy, celebrated personally a general ordination in the parish church of Higham Ferrers.

[fo. 200r is blank.]

[fo. 200v]

543. Ordination celebrated by Bp Fleming in the parish church of Holbeach, 23 February 1426.

Ordines generales celebrati in ecclesia parochiali de Holbeche Lincoln' dioc' per reverendum in Christo patrem et dominum dominum Ricardum dei gracia Lincoln episcopum die sabbati quatuor temporum in prima septimana quadragesime septimo videlicet kalendas Marcii anno domini millesimo quadringentesimo vicesimo quinto.

Acolytes in religious orders. Thomas Weston, monk of Spalding. Wyntryngham,[78] Robert Torkesey, Thomas Brygge, Stephen Scothorn, Carmelite friars of Lincoln. Thomas Westfeld, Robert Umfray, canons of Wellow. John Appulton, William Titteshale, Austin friars of Boston.

Unbeneficed acolytes. John Everard. William Wroo. William Pyterell. William Jonson. John Pynk. William Wytham. John Walker. Ambrose Smyth. Richard Tapyter. William Lewlyn. William Styward. William Waynflete. Thomas Wryght. John Cooke. John Sewale. Thomas Elyot. John Wace. Robert Burwell. John Renge. John Bayly. Thomas Wyllymay. John Londe. Edward Clerke. William Andrewe. John Thornehyll. Richard Noblot. William Hopkyns. Constantine Gretham. Richard Prowet. Stephen Garner. William Freman.

Beneficed subdeacon. Thomas Fynden, minister in Lincoln cath., t. chapter.

Subdeacons in religious orders. Nicholas Sutton, John Spaldyng, William Stokes, Thomas Weston, monks of Spalding. Robert de Halton, canon of Hagnaby. Robert Botheby, John Trewman, Carmelite friars of Stamford. George Playford, Dominican friar of Stamford. Walter Skegnes, Richard Wynthorp, John Ramsey, John Wylughby, monks of Swineshead. John Appulton, William Tateshall, Austin friars of Boston. John Tolson, canon of Wellow. John Askotys, John Brawby, Richard Neucastell, William Hull, canons of Thornton.

---

[78] Christian name not given.

Unbeneficed subdeacons. Robert Pysall of *Keleby*, t. Nun Cotham. William of the hous of *Leek*, t. St Michael by Stamford. William Thurlby of Fotheringhay, t. St Michael by Stamford. Thomas Wryght, t. Vaudey. Roger Cowper of Lincoln, t. Stixwould. John Cooke junior of Northampton, t. Barnwell. William Cusson, t. Haverholme. Laurence Schole, t. Langley. Ambrose Felowe of Colesden, t. Bushmead. Robert Burwell, t. Revesby. Henry Waryndre of *Keston*, t. Stonely. Bartholomew Neyll of Shepshed, t. Garendon. William Wroo of *Lokyngton*, t. Shelford. Richard Gudhyne of *Kele*, t. Kirkstead. Ralph Sarson of Fotheringhay, t. Cotterstock chantry. Henry Hopkyns of *Gretham*, t. St Michael by Stamford. John s. Walter in the Hyrne of Fulstow, t. Louth Park. Thomas Dynet, t. St Mary, Nuneaton. Ralph s. Richard Barkere of Grimsby, t. Grimsby.

Deacons in religious orders. Thomas Inglond, canon of Croxton. William Stokys, Carmelite friar of Stamford. Thomas Enderby, John Kele, William Spyllesby, monks of Revesby. Richard Clerk, Thomas Ecton, Richard Lambe, Carmelite friars of Lincoln. Robert Leek, canon of Tupholme. Henry of St Neots, Richard of St Neots, monks of St Neots. William Irby, William Conyngeston, canons of Thornton. John Spaldyng, canon of Barlings.

Unbeneficed deacons. Thomas Webster of *Brampton*, t. Bradley. Ralph Prat of North Kilworth, t. hospital of St John Baptist, Northampton. John Esyngwold of York dioc., by letters dimissory, t hospital of Jesus and Mary, Fossegate, York. Thomas Byllyngham of Wappenham, t. Biddlesden. [fo. 201r] William Wygotte of Yarburgh, t. Louth Park. William Fermer s. Robert Fermer of *Eston*, t. Bradley. Robert Day, t. Legbourne. Alexander Tathewell, t. Heynings. Roger Harry, t. Ulverscroft. John Challey of Theddlethorpe, t. Irthlingborough College. Robert Haykham, t. Sempringham. William Kendale of Shepshed, t. Garendon. John Fenton s. John Fenton of Oakham, t. Bradley. Richard Cost of Harborough, t. Pipewell. John Oldeney, t. Launde. William Raufson of Huttoft, t. Markby. Thomas de Flete, t. Revesby. William Weddale of Crowland, t. St Michael by Stamford.

Beneficed priest. Richard Beche, minister in Lincoln cath., t. chapter.

Priests in religious orders. John Boston, Carmelite friar of Lincoln. Walter Rysle, Dominican friar of Stamford. John Stafford, Dominican friar of Northampton. Reginald Donyngton, canon of Bradley. Thomas Feltwell, canon of Kyme. John Leycestre, Richard Skegnes, monks of Crowland. John Goldesmyth, John Alesby, canons of Wellow.

Unbeneficed priests. Robert Kyggys, t. Markby. Walter Jonson of *Bekyngham*, t. Thornton. Thomas Smyth of *Bowdon*, t. Sulby. Robert Doughty, t. Louth Park. Geoffrey Owstwyk of *Upton*, t. [Newstead on] Ancholme. Simon Dawes of Hanging Houghton, t. hospital of St John, Northampton. John Parys of *Awthorp*, t. Ormsby. John Cooke of *Flete*, t. St Michael by Stamford. Thomas Symund of *Yerdeley*, t. Lavendon. Thomas Cooke of High Toynton, t. Revesby. John Pake of *Norburgh*, t. Ulverscroft. John Damlet, t. Croxton. Thomas Gosberkyrk of Low Toynton, t. Revesby. John Cooke of Hatcliffe, t. Louth Park. Robert Goneld of *Irby*, t. Nun Cotham. John Motte, t. Stonely. John Jhonnysson of *Manby*, t. Bourne.

Henry Malkyn of Oakham, t. Launde. William Syston of Leicester, t. Ulverscroft. John Robyn of Mixbury, t. Bicester. William Harecourt of Coventry and Lichfield dioc., by letters dimissory, t. Littlemore.

544.   Ordination celebrated by Bp Fleming in the parish church of Boston, 16 March 1426.

Ordines celebrati in ecclesia parrochiali de Boston' Lincoln' dioc' per reverendum in Christo patrem et dominum dominum Ricardum dei gracia Lincoln' ecclesie humilem servum die sabbati qua cantatur in ecclesia dei officium Sitientes videlicet xvij^mo kalendas Aprilis anno domini millesimo quadringentesimo vicesimo quinto.

Acolytes in religious orders. John Kelsey, Carmelite friar of Lincoln. John Roos, Carmelite friar of Boston. Walter Thorneton, canon of Barlings. Thomas Chabworth, William Burgh, friars minor of Boston. Robert Pygot, canon of St Katherine by Lincoln. Richard Sele, Robert Holme, Dominican friars of Boston. John Hole, monk of Bardney.

Unbeneficed acolytes. Richard Dawson. John Ryngot. John Wylly. Richard Barbour. Ralph Skynner. John Amwyk. Thomas Wade. John Gedney. John Barker. William Abram. Alexander Segdyke. William Toly. John Pynchebek. John Browne. William Byllyngey. Richard Webster. William Awbrey. Richard Wytton. Richard Munke. Thomas Garton. William Cole. Thomas Croxton. Thomas Taylour. William Wynerton. Richard Honyngton. William Kylworth. John Purle. Robert Benet. William Tatersall. Roger Wodeward. William Carter. John Lyon. Nicholas Jakson. Lambert Maddy. Richard Luk. Roger Greyve. James Warwyk. Henry Fysscher. Roger Baret. William Halle. John Halle. John Proktour. William Danney. Thomas Walmesger. John Jonson. Robert Steresman. Hugh Altoft. Thomas Colvyll. Nicholas Frende. Richard Laxton. William Poynton. John Careman. Richard Rampayn.

Subdeacons in religious orders. Robert Welle, canon of Markby. Robert Freston, John Wysbeche, Carmelite friars of Boston. [fo. 201v] William Toynton, Carmelite friar of Boston. Walter Thornton, canon of Barlings. William Selby, friar minor of Boston. Henry Wandysford, Robert Pygot, canons of St Katherine by Lincoln. William Randall, Edmund Leek, monks of Kirkstead. John Hole, monk of Bardney.

Unbeneficed subdeacons. John Amwyk of Sutterton, t. Swineshead. John Ruston of Boston, t. Swineshead. John Babulon of Stow Longa, t. Bushmead. Richard Tapyter of *Askeby*, t. Louth Park. John Weston, t. Osney. John Bewmerys of *Merston*.[79] Thomas Lamkyn of *Staynton*, t. Kyme. William Rouceby of Stamford, t. St Michael by Stamford. William Jonson of Wyberton, t. Spalding. William Kylworth of *Creek*, t. St Mary Delapré by Northampton. William Wynerton, t. Owston. John Sewale of Castle Bytham, t. Bourne. William Wytham of *Botelesford*,

---

[79] The title (to the subdiaconate only) is not specified.

t. Shelford. William Byllesdon, t. Owston. Thomas Stonehows of Lincoln, t. St Leonard, Torksey. Robert s. Robert Pye of Grimsby, t. Grimsby. John Tykylpeney of Market Deeping (*Estdepyng*), t. St Michael by Stamford. John Berkeworth, t. Fosse. Richard Nobyllet of Barton upon Humber, t. Broadholme.

Deacons in religious orders. Robert de Halton, canon of Hagnaby. Thomas Braydar, John Kyllyngholm, monks of Louth Park. Henry Grene, friar minor of Stamford. John Appylton, William Tateshale, Austin friars of Boston. Nicholas Sutton, John Spaldyng, William Stokes, Thomas Weston, monks of Spalding. William Wayn-flete, William Yorke, monks of Bardney. Walter Skegneys, Richard Wynthorp, John Ramsey, John Wylugby, monks of Swineshead.

Unbeneficed deacons. Robert Burwell, t. Revesby. William Thurlby of Fotheringhay, t. St Michael by Stamford. Ralph Sarson of Fotheringhay, t. Cotterstock chantry. Henry Bedell of Norwich dioc., by letters dimissory, t. Norton. Roger Cowper of Lincoln, t. Stixwould. William Wrooe of *Lokyngton*, t. Shelford. Achard Sythewell of Coventry and Lichfield dioc., by letters dimissory, t. Croxton. John Trevele of Worcester dioc., by letters dimissory, t. Holy Trinity, London. Henry Hopkyns of *Gretham*, t. St Michael by Stamford. Bartholomew Neyll of Shepshed, t. Garendon. Thomas Wryght, t. Vaudey. John s. Walter in the Hyrne of Fulstow, t. Louth Park. John Bucke of Aldwincle, t. St Michael by Stamford. William of the hows of *Leek*, t. St Michael by Stamford. William Cusson, t. Haverholme. Robert Godhyne of *Kele*, t. Kirkstead.

Beneficed priest. John Burdeux, rector of Sparham, dioc. Norwich, by letters dimissory.

Priests in religious orders. Richard Lame, Carmelite friar of Lincoln. Thomas Ingland, canon of Croxton. Richard Holme, friar minor of Stamford. Robert Leek, canon of Tupholme. Richard Beaver, canon of Kirby Bellars. William Leverton, monk of Kirkstead.

Unbeneficed priests. William Wygote of Yarburgh, t. Louth Park. Thomas Byllyng-ham of Wappenham, t. Biddlesden. Richard Cost of Harborough, t. Pipewell. Thomas Yowlot of Whittlesey, t. St Michael by Stamford. John Scotton of York dioc., by letters dimissory, t. Sulby. William Weddale of Crowland, t. St Michael by Stamford. Robert Day, t. Legbourne. William Kendale of Shepshed, t. Garendon. John Oldeney, t. Launde. Robert Careby of *Morton*, t. Bourne. Thomas de Flete, t. Revesby. John Smeton of *Foxton*, t. Sulby. John Esyngwold of York dioc., by letters dimissory, t hospital of Jesus and Mary, Fossegate, York. John Chamberleyn of Oundle, t. Cotterstock. Ralph Prat of North Kilworth, t. hospital of St John Baptist, Northampton. Alexander Thathewell, t. Heynings. William Raufson of Huttoft, t. Markby. John Challey of Theddlethorpe, t. Irthlingborough College.

[fo. 202r]

545. Ordination celebrated by Bp Fleming in the parish church of Fishtoft, 30 March 1426.

Ordines generales celebrati in ecclesia parochiali de Toft iuxta Boston' Lincoln' dioc' per reverendum in Christo patrem et dominum dominum Ricardum dei gracia ecclesie Lincoln' humilem ministrum sabbato sancto pasche iij° videlicet kalendas Aprilis anno domini millesimo quadringentesimo vicesimo sexto.

Unbeneficed acolytes. Thomas Skynner. John Whyte. Paul Grene. Robert Bees. Thomas Buteler. Henry Fyssher.

Beneficed subdeacon. Thomas Butteler, fellow of University College, Oxford, t. his college.

Unbeneficed subdeacons. John Rawlyn of Kislingbury, t. hospital of St John Baptist, Northampton. John Halywode of *Preston*, t. St Michael by Stamford. Stephen Boston of Heckington, t. Kyme. John Carman, t. Stixwould. Robert Baston of Boston, t. Stixwould.

Unbeneficed deacons. John Bewmerys of *Merston*, t. (deacon and priest) Haverholme. Thomas Lamkyn of *Steynton*, t. Kyme. Ralph s. Richard Baker of Grimsby, t. Grimsby. Richard s. Robert Pye of Grimsby, t. Grimsby. William Kylleworth of *Creek*, t. St Mary Delapré by Northampton. John Weston, t. Osney. William Wynerton, t. Owston. John Tykylpeny of Market Deeping (*Estdepyng*), t. St Michael by Stamford. John Amwyk of Sutterton, t. Swineshead.

Unbeneficed priests. William of the hows of *Leek*, t. St Michael by Stamford. John Tulke of Salisbury dioc., by letters dimissory, t. college of St Edmund, Salisbury. Robert Burwell, t. Revesby. John Leton of Welborne, of Norwich dioc., by letters dimissory, t. Catley. Bartholomew Neyll of Shepshed, t. Garendon.

546. Ordination celebrated by Bp Fleming in the parish church of Boston, 25 May 1426.

Ordines generales celebrati in ecclesia parrochiali de Boston' Lincoln' dioc' die sabbati quatuor temporum in vigilia sancte Trinitatis viij videlicet kalendas Junii per reverendum in Christo patrem et dominum dominum Ricardum dei gracia ecclesie Lincoln' humilem ministrum anno domini millesimo CCCC^mo vicesimo sexto consecrationis sue anno septimo.

Beneficed acolyte. M. William Colyng, fellow of Balliol College, Oxford.

Acolytes in religious orders. Henry Lincoln, Thomas Hale, Thomas Elkyngton, monks of Bardney. John Pare, Thomas Nelson, Dominican friars of Boston. Walter Lilyston, friar minor of Nottingham. Simon de Lincoln, canon of Thornholm.

Richard de Burgh, canon of Thornholm. John Gamston, friar minor of Grantham. John Twayte, Thomas Swan, Austin friars of Lincoln. John Garnon, John Goderyk, Richard Man, Austin friars of Boston. Thomas Colman, William Bysshop, Robert Bartylmewe, Alan Wryght, Austin friars of Boston.

Unbeneficed acolytes. John Blessett. William Cake. Richard Sayer. John Hugate. Robert Lorde. William Gudery. Richard Tydd. William Fletcher. William Cawnse. William Dyam. John Salford. William Hornse. William Goderood. Richard Osgod. William Smyth. John Haynson. John Clerk. John Musgrove. John Bolton. John Brereley. John Salford.

[fo. 202v] *Beneficed subdeacons.* Laurence Stafford, rector of Grendon Underwood. John Messyngham, vicar choral of Lincoln cath., t. chapter. M. William Collyng, fellow of Balliol College, Oxford, t. his college.

Subdeacons in religious orders. Henry Lincoln, Thomas Hale, Thomas Elkyngton, Richard Parteney, monks of Bardney. William Hamsterle, William Hagys, Gerard Harlem, William Holme, William Seel, Dominican friars of Boston. John Pare, Thomas Nelson, Dominican friars of Boston. Simon de Lincoln, Richard de Burgh, canons of Thornholm. Robert Burgh, William Ouresby, canons of Haverholme. John London, canon of St Katherine by Lincoln. Robert Newerk, William Botry, canons of Sixhills. John Gamston, friar minor of Grantham. Thomas Chaworth, friar minor of Boston. Walter Lilyston, friar minor of Nottingham. Thomas Colman, Austin friar of Boston.

Unbeneficed subdeacons. Richard Blaston of Sleaford, t. Nocton Park. Robert Wryght, t. Waltham. Thomas Prentys of Norwich dioc., t. dean and chapter of Stoke by Clare. John Browne of Aswardby by Langton, t. Revesby. John Kyrkeby of *Freston*, t. Crowland. John Coke of Lowesby, t. Charley. John de Lynn of Claypole, t. Shelford.[80] John Hugate, t. Newbo. Robert Lorde, t. Haverholme. Richard Harwode of *Barton*, t. Newhouse. John Kyrsewell of York dioc., by letters dimissory, t. St Andrew in the suburb of York. Walter Styrton of Louth, t. Kirkstead. John Salford, t. Cold Norton. John Clerk of Salisbury dioc., by letters dimissory, t. Cotterstock chantry. John Browne of Duns Tew, t. Cold Norton. John Lumner s. Richard Lumner of Lincoln, t. Newstead in Sherwood. John Brereley, t. Kirkstead.

Beneficed deacon. Thomas Butteler, fellow of University College, Oxford, t. his college.

Deacons in religious orders. Henry Ruston, canon of Bullington. Denis Mannyng, Dominican friar of Boston. Robert Freston, Carmelite friar of Boston. John Asfordeby, John Karby, friars minor of Nottingham. Henry Wansford, canon of St Katherine by Lincoln. Nicholas Welesenbek, friar minor of Grantham. William Selby, friar minor of Boston. John Bedford, John Ampthyll, canons of Caldwell. William Ortsale, John Moubrey, canons of Thurgarton.

[80] MS 'Sleford'.

Unbeneficed deacons. John Carman, t. Stixwould. William Jonson of Wyberton, t. Spalding. Richard Tapyter of *Askeby*, t. Louth Park. William Walker, t. Owston. John Cooke junior of Northampton, t. Barnwell. Ambrose Felowe of Colesden, t. Bushmead. John Dabulon of Stow Longa, t. Bushmead. Thomas Stonehous of Lincoln, t. Torksey. William Rowceby of Stamford, t. St Michael by Stamford. John Goldesmyth of Olney, t. Harrold. Stephen Boston of Heckington, t. Kyme. William Byllesden, t. Owston. John Sewale of Castle Bytham, t. Bourne. Robert Pysall of *Keleby*, t. Nun Cotham. William Wytham of *Bottelesford*, t. Shelford.[81] Robert Baston of Boston, t. Stixwould. Thomas Dynet, t. St Mary, Nun Cotham. John Rawlyn of Kislingbury, t. hospital of St John Baptist, Northampton. Henry Waryner of *Keston*, t. Stonely. Laurence Schole, t. Langley. Richard Nobyllet of Barton upon Humber, t. Broadholme.

Priests in religious orders. Thomas Forster, John Tyryngton, canons of Bullington. Roger Chaumberleyn, William Brunne, friars minor of Stamford. Dominic Serwyter, Dominican friar of Boston. Michael de Dyst, friar minor of Grantham. John Appylton, Austin friar of Lincoln.

Unbeneficed priests. John Weston, t. Osney. Thomas Lamkyn of *Steynton*, t. Kyme. Achard Sythewell of Coventry and Lichfield dioc., by letters dimissory, t. Croxton. Henry Bedell of Norwich dioc., by letters dimissory, t. Norton. John Bewmerys of *Merston*, t. Haverholme. John Rouceby, t. Broadholme. John Stalyngburgh, t. Barlings. [fo. 203r] William Wroe of *Lokyngton*, t. Shelford. William Wynerton, t. Owston. Robert s. Robert Pye of Grimsby, t. Grimsby. Richard Godehyne of *Kele*, t. Kirkstead. John Wyseman, t. Caldwell. Thomas de Luda, t. Sixhills. Thomas Hermer, t. Caldwell. Roger Harry, t. Ulverscroft. Robert Joce, t. Stainfield. John s. Walter in the Hyrne of Fulstow, t. Louth Park. William Kylleworth of *Creek*, t. St Mary Delapré by Northampton. John Slory, t. Haverholme. John Buk of Aldwincle, t. St Michael by Stamford. William Fermer s. Robert Fermer of *Eston*, t. Bradley. John Fenton s. John Fenton of Oakham, t. Bradley. Henry Hopkyns of *Gretham*, t. St Michael by Stamford. Thomas Wryght, t. Vaudey. Roger Couper of Lincoln, t. Stixwould.

547. Ordination celebrated by Bp Fleming in prebendal church of Sleaford, 21 December 1426.

Ordines generales celebrati in ecclesia prebendali de Sleford' per reverendum in Christo patrem et dominum dominum Ricardum dei gracia Lincoln' ecclesie servum humilem et ministrum die sabbati quatuor temporum in festo sancti Thome apostoli duodecimo videlicet kalendas Januarii anno domini millesimo quadringentesimo vicesimo sexto anno translationis sue secundo.

Acolyte in religious orders. Robert Northcotes, canon of Elsham.

---

[81] MS 'Sleford'.

Unbeneficed acolytes. Robert Lovell. Laurence Aylemer. Nicholas Aunger. Simon Welles. Thomas de Loughton. Thomas Grene. Thomas Drayton. John Dodde. William Olyer. William Inman. John Smyth. John Walter. John Gowbe. Thomas Laurence. William Wode. John Goudeby. Robert Steven. Robert Crabbe. William Knyght. William Bysshop.

Subdeacons in religious orders. William Thornton, Thomas Assheton, canons of Newhouse. Robert Northcotes, canon of Elsham. Ralph Neport, canon of Ravenstone. Richard Hylberworth, Dominican friar of Stamford.

Unbeneficed subdeacons. Thomas Beverley, t. Owston. William Fletcher, t. Owston. Thomas Bennet of Wardley, t. Launde. William Wode, t. Ravenstone. John Frost of Segenhoe, t. Dunstable. John Well of Great Dalby (*Dalby Chacombe*), t. Chacombe. William Waynflete of Wainfleet, t. Kyme. Simon Wellys of Eynesbury, t. Bushmead. John Thorp of Bigby, t. Newhouse. William Knyght of Peterborough, t. Crowland. John Lincoln of Theddlethorpe, t. Revesby. John Taberner of Swaffham (*Swaffham Market*), t. Bromehill, dioc. Norwich. John Conam of Kyme, t. Kyme.

Deacons in religious orders. William Lughburgh, Austin (hermit) friar of Leicester. Alexander Laveroke, Austin (hermit) friar of Stamford. Richard Seel, Dominican friar of Boston. Thomas Lowys, Gerard Laurence, Dominican friars of Stamford. John Brokelesby, canon of Newhouse.

Unbeneficed deacons. Roger Clerk, t. nuns of Chatteris, dioc. Ely. William Franckyse, t. Newhouse. John Glover, t. hospital of St John, Ely. John Lond of Great Gransden (*Grantesden Magna*), t. St Mary, Huntingdon. Walter atte Plattes of Wainfleet, t. Hagnaby. Richard Tydd of Long Bennington, t. Sempringham. Walter Lokkyng of Mumby, t. Markby. Simon Flegard of Wainfleet, t. Revesby. William Lewlyn of Mumby, t. Markby. William Myll of Harmston, t. St Katherine by Lincoln. John Smyth, t. Polesworth. Robert Addyson of Kirkby Thore, of Carlisle dioc., by letters dimissory, t. Shelford. John Purle of Mablethorpe, t. Markby. John Fylhous of Glinton, t. St Michael by Stamford. John Frost of *Ethrop*, t. Bicester. John Hall, t. Polesworth. William Waynflete, t. Markby. Richard Crowe, t. Newstead by Stamford. William Cryps of Turvey, t. Harrold. [fo. 203v] John Pyttys of Exeter dioc., by letters dimissory, t. Newnham. William Date of Spalding, t. Spalding. John Freman of Carlisle dioc., by letters dimissory, t. Gokewell. John Howtour of Hoby, t. Garendon. Thomas Elyoth, t. St Mary, Leicester. Ambrose Gaywode, t. Catley. John Hedon.

Priest in religious orders. Richard Coton, Austin friar of Stamford.

Unbeneficed priests. John de Lynn of Claypole, t. Shelford. Robert Wryght, t. Waltham. Richard Nobyllet of Barton upon Humber, t. Broadholme. Thomas Prentys of Norwich dioc., by letters dimissory, t. dean and chapter of Stoke by Clare. John Hugate, t. Newbo. William Jonson of Wyberton, t. Spalding. William Thurlby of Fotheringhay, t. nuns by Stamford. M. William Waynflete, t. Spalding. John Haliwode of *Preston*, t. St Michael by Stamford. John Cooke of Lowesby, t. Charley. John Rawlyn of Kislingbury, t. hospital of St John Baptist, Northampton. John Ruston of *Benyngton*, t. St Michael by Stamford. Richard Blaston of Sleaford,

t. Nocton Park. John Salford, t. Cold Norton. John Kyrkeby of *Freston*, t. Crowland. John Browne of Aswardby.[82] John Browne of Duns Tew, t. Cold Norton.

548. Ordination celebrated by Bp Fleming in prebendal church of Sleaford, 21 September 1426.

Ordines generales celebrati in ecclesia prebendali de Sleford' Lincoln' dioc' die sabbati quatuor temporum in festo sancti Mathei apostoli videlicet sexto[83] kalendas Octobris anno domini millesimo quadringentesimo vicesimo sexto per reverendum in Christo patrem et dominum dominum Ricardum dei gracia Lincoln' episcopum anno translationis sue secundo.

Acolytes in religious orders. John Langton, monk of Pipewell. John Towthorp, John Myrabell, Dominican friars of Lincoln. Thomas Sewestern, canon of Owston.

Unbeneficed acolytes. Thomas Kareby. Richard Crowe. William Redmer. Richard Smyth. John Dryngeston. William Clerk of *Thuresby*. William Stevenson. John Thorp. Edmund Hadylsay. Stephen Lakoke. John Frost. William Sleyght. Richard Gedney. John Spethyng. Robert Addyson. John Westam. Richard Rydwale. William Cryps. John Hannewode. John Hamerton. Philip Conam. Walter Warde. Thomas Daddy. William Feryby. John Walshe. Thomas Persebryg.

Subdeacons in religious orders. Thomas de Denton, canon of Croxton. John Langton, monk of Pipewell. Richard Laghton, canon of Leicester. Thomas Sewestern, canon of Owston.

Unbeneficed subdeacons. John Hedon of York dioc., by letters dimissory, t. Felley. Ambrose Gaywode, t. Catley. John Glover, t. hospital of St John, Ely. Roger Clerk, t. Chatteris, dioc. Ely. William Frankyse, t. Newhouse. Richard Tydd of Long Bennington, t. Sempringham. William Clerk of *Cosyngton*, t. Ulverscroft. William Myll of Harmston, t. St Katherine by Lincoln. Walter atte Plattes of Wainfleet, t. Hagnaby. John Warner of Raunds, t. (subdeacon) Harrold. John Purle of Mablethorpe, t. Markby. John Fylhous of Glinton, t. St Michael by Stamford. John Smyth, t. Polesworth. John Howtour of Hoby, t. Garendon. [fo. 204r] William Lewlyn of Mumby, t. Markby. Simon Flegard of Wainfleet, t. Revesby. Robert Rumpayn, t. Markby. John Hall, t. Polesworth. John Lond of Great Gransden, t. St Mary, Huntingdon. William Date of Spalding, t. Spalding. Thomas Elyoth, t. St Mary, Leicester. Richard Crowe, t. Newstead by Stamford. William Waynflete, t. Markby. Robert Addyson of Kirkby Thore, of Carlisle dioc., by letters dimissory, t. Shelford. John Frost of *Ethrop*, t. Bicester. William Cryps of Turvey, t. Harrold. John Frefman of Carlisle dioc., t. Gokewell.

Beneficed deacons. Walter Wodeward, rector of Hallaton (*Halughton'*), t. his benefice *de quo reput' se contentum*. M. William Collyng, fellow of Balliol College, Oxford, t. his college.

---

[82] Title not specified.
[83] An error for 'undecimo'.

Deacons in religious orders. Henry Lyncoln, Thomas Hole, John Hole, Thomas Helkyngton, Richard Parteney, monks of Bardney. Robert Burgh, William Ouresby, canons of Haverholme. Robert Newerk, William Botery, canons of Sixhills. Robert Well, canon of Markby. William Hayhyrst, John Wygyneston, canons of Leicester. Thomas Colman, Austin friar of Boston. John Ascutys, John Brawby, Richard Neucastell, William de Hull, canons of Thornton. John London, canon of Sempringham.

Unbeneficed deacons. John Brown of Aswardby (*Aswardeby iuxta Langton*), t. Revesby. Robert Wryght, t. Waltham. John Halywode of *Preston*, t. St Michael by Stamford. Thomas Prentys of Norwich dioc., by letters dimissory, t. dean and chapter of Stoke by Clare. John de Lynn of Claypole, t. Shelford. Richard Harworde of *Barton*, t. Newhouse. Walter Styrton of Louth, t. Kirkstead. John Kyrkeby of *Freston*, t. Crowland. John Lumner s. Richard Lumner of Lincoln, t. Newstead in Sherwood. John Coke of Lowesby, t. Charley. John Salford, t. Cold Norton. Richard Blaston of Sleaford, t. Nocton Park. John Ruston of *Benyngton*, t. St Michael by Stamford. John Barkeworth, t. nuns of Fosse. Robert Lorde, t. Haverholme. John Hugate, t. Newbo. John Browne of Duns Tew, t. Cold Norton.

Beneficed priest. John Repyngdon, v. of Hook Norton.

Priests in religious orders. Thomas Weston, monk of Spalding. William Waynflete, William York, monks of Bardney. Thomas Glubwell, John Wertone, John Forman, canons of Croxton. John de Spaldyng, canon of Barlings. John Powmery, Robert Stanton, canons of Leicester. John Stacheden, canon of Newnham. Richard Leycestre, William de Oselveston, canons of Owston. John de Sancto Ivone, William Castre, canons of Huntingdon. Nicholas Wynter, Dominican friar of Lincoln.

Unbeneficed priests. John Cooke of Northampton junior, t. Barnwell. John Conys of *Rusheden*, t. Harrold. William Cusson, t. Haverholme. William Wytham of *Bottelesford*, t. Shelford. Stephen Boston of Heckington, t. Kyme. Ralph s. Richard Barker of Grimsby, t. Grimsby. Laurence Schole, t. Langley. John Goldsmyth of Olney, t. Harrold. William Rouceby of Stamford, t. St Michael by Stamford. Thomas Dynet, t. Nun Cotham. Richard Tapyter of *Askeby*, t. Louth Park. Ralph Sareson of Fotheringhay, t. Cotterstock chantry. Robert Smyth of Lincoln, t. Thornton. Thomas Webster of *Brampton*, t. Bradley. William Walker, t. Owston. John Sewale of Castle Bytham, t. Bourne. John Dabulon of Stow Longa, t. Bushmead. William Byllesdon, t. Owston. Henry Depyng, t. Owston. Henry Waryner of *Keston*, t. Stonely. Robert Baston of Boston, t. Stixwould. Ambrose Felowe of Colesden, t. Bushmead.

[fo. 204v is blank.]

INDEX OF PERSONS AND PLACES

(Note: Numbers refer to entries in the text.)

Bedford, archdnry (*cont.*)
  suffragan in, *see* Dally
Bedford, 243, 476, 479–480, 485–486, 488,
    500, 520
  churches
    All Saints, 233, 257
    St Cuthbert, 260
  friaries
    Franciscan, friars, *see* Barnevyll, Barry,
      Bedford, Berenveyle, Darby,
      Godfray
Bedford, Bedeford
  John, canon of Caldwell, deac., 546
  John, friar minor of Bedford, ord., 493,
    495
  Richard, acol., 481
  Thomas, friar minor of Bedford, acol.,
    473
Bedminster, Somerset, hospital, orders
    conferred to title of, 488
Beeby, Leics., 489, 491–492
  church, 10
Beek, *see* Bek
Bees
  John, of Pinchbeck, rector of East
    Horndon; vicar of Great Paxton,
    145
  Robert, acol., 545
Beeston, Notts., vicarage, 92
Beford, John, of Grimsby, ord., 472, 476
Begbroke, Oxon., church, 297, 355, 525
Bek, Becke, Beek, Beke, Bekke
  James, vicar choral of Lincoln cath.,
    ord., 478–479, 486
  John, ord., 472, 482, 485–486
  John, rector of St Michael at the North
    Gate, Oxford, 336
  Richard, rector of Maids' Moreton, 415
  Robert (or John), of *Syston*, ord., 500–
    501, 520–522, 541
  William, of *Carleton*, ord., 491–493, 495
Beker, Thomas, rector of Miningsby, 524
Bekeryng, Thomas, 155
Bekke, *see* Bek
Bekyngham [unidentified], 543
Bekyngton, M. Thomas
  rector of Hatfield, 181
  rector of Sutton Courtenay, subd., 481
Belchford, Lincs., 471–472
Belgrave, Leics., church of St Peter and St
    Paul, 62
Belgrave
  Richard, vicar of Lincoln cath., pr.,
    476

William, 105
Bele, William, of Leicester, ord., 472, 476
Belesby, Thomas, Carmelite friar of
    Lincoln, pr., 492
Bell, Belle
  Henry, of *Merston*, ord., 480–482
  John, of Oakham, ord., 480–482, 486
  M. Walter, rector of Bletchingdon, 314
Belton, Rutland, chapel, 396
Belton [unidentified], 471, 474, 476, 485,
    501, 521–522, 541
Belton
  Thomas, preb. of Empingham in Lincoln
    cath., 458
  Thomas, vicar choral of Lincoln cath.,
    pr., 479
  M. William, rector of Rearsby, 24
Belvoir, Lincs., priory
  patron, 7
Benebruk, Robert, rector of Withcote, 76
Benett, Benet, Bennet
  Robert, acol., 544
  Thomas, of Wardley, subd., 547
  Thomas, rector of Bix Gibbewin, 349
Bengeo, Herts., church of St Leonard,
    vicarage, 125
Bennet, *see* Benett
Bennington, Long, Lincs., 501, 521–522,
    541, 547–548
Bentley, Benteley
  Thomas, minister in Lincoln cath., ord.,
    491, 495, 498
  William, Carmelite friar of Leicester,
    deac., 522, 541
Benynton, Bynyngton [unidentified], 472,
    488–489, 491–493, 495, 547–548
Benyngton
  Ralph, 163
  Ralph, of York dioc., ord., 471
  Richard s. William, ord., 493, 498
Bereford, Berford [unidentified], 495, 498
Berenveyle, Richard, friar minor of
    Bedford, subd., 473
Berewell, Berwell, Nicholas, canon of
    Notley, ord., 492
Berford [unidentified], see *Bereford*
Berford, M. William, preb. of Marston St
    Lawrence in Lincoln cath., 460
Berkeworth, *see* Barkworth
Berkhamsted, Little, Herts., rector, *see*
    Barkworth
Berkworth, *see* Barkworth
Bermondsey, Surrey, abbey of St Saviour,
    34, 125, 304

Thomas, acol., 547
Drewe, John
  rector of Northwold, 141
  rector of Therfield, 136, 141
Driby [unidentified], 471–472
Drie, William, rector of 'Henton', 280
Dryngeston, John, acol., 548
Dryver, Roger, vicar of Segenhoe, 226
Ducklington, Oxon.
  advowson, 346
  church, 278, 346
  manor, 346
Dudyngton, Dodyngton, Nicholas, canon
  of Fineshade, ord., 472, 480
Duffeld
  John, rector of Asfordby; rector of
    Branston, 16
  M. John, *see* Scarle
  M. Thomas, chancellor of Lincoln, 464
  M. William, 373
Dughty, Robert, acol., 480
Dullyng, *see* Dallyng
Dunholme, Lincs., prebend of Dunham in
  Lincoln cath., 440, 449
Dunkan, Thomas, presented to
  Ducklington, 346
Dunnyng, John, vicar of North Stoke; vicar
  of St John in the Isle of Thanet, 344
Dunstable, Beds., 27, 153, 304, 478–479,
  481, 486
  friaries
    Dominican
      conventual church, ordination in,
        473
      friars, *see* Astwell, Bosco Ducis,
        Burnham, Bylyngdon, Edwyn,
        Lawles, Merydyth, Nettelden,
        Stelyng, Waneford
  priory, 63, 209, 226, 260, 262
    canons of, *see* Burre, Eyton, Legger,
      Rysle
    orders conferred to title of, 478–479,
      481, 486, 489, 491–492, 547
Dunston, Duston, William, of Elstow, ord.,
  471–473
Dunton, Bucks.
  church, 407
  manor and advowson, 407
Dunyngton, Donyngton
  John, acol., 501, 521
  Reginald de, canon of Owston, deac.,
    483
  Reginald, canon of Bradley, pr., 543
  Stephen, acol., 480

Durant, Dorhand, Richard, Carmelite friar
  of Stamford, ord., 492–493
Durem, Thomas, 424
Durham, bp of, *see* Langley
Durham, dioc., ordinands from, 480–482,
  493, 495, 500–501, 520–521
Durham, cathedral priory, monk, *see*
  Pomfrett
Durham, Dorham
  Richard, monk of Pipewell, ord., 491–
    492, 500, 520
  Thomas, canon of Kyme, pr., 476
Durnell, Thomas
  chaplain of chantry, Colney, 388
  rector of Shenley, 3
Duston, *see* Dunston
Dyam, William, acol., 546
Dyer
  John, 381
  Robert, rector of Britwell Salome; vicar
    of Great Kimble, 291, 379
Dygby, Thomas, of *Haugh*, ord., 495, 522,
  541
Dyke, *alias* Langton, M. John, rector of Fen
  Ditton; rector of Langton, 85
Dykelun, Richard, of *Northburgh*, ord., 486,
  491, 498
Dykes, Dykys, M. Robert
  rector of Glenfield, 59, 100
  rector of Wethersfield, 100
Dylney, William, vicar of Segenhoe,
  226
Dymmok, Dymmoke, Richard, ord.,
  485–486
Dynet, Thomas, ord., 543, 546, 548
Dyngdale, Richard, vicar of Little Dalby,
  102
Dyst, Michael de, friar minor of Grantham,
  pr., 546

Eagle, Lincs., preceptor, *see* Crounhale
Easby, Yorks., abbey of St Agatha, orders
  conferred to title of, 500, 520
Eaton, Leics., vicarage, 44, 106, 535
Eaton Socon, Beds., vicarage, 243
Eburton, John, rector of Wigginton, ord.,
  473, 485
Eccleshall, Staffs., church, 285
Echard, Robert, ord., 493, 496
Ecton, Thomas, Carmelite friar of Lincoln,
  deac., 543
Edenham, Lincs., 476, 480–481
Edenham
  Robert de, canon of Bourne, pr., 471

Hildeston, Hyldeston, Robert, canon of
   Thornton, ord., 486
Hill, Hyll
   John othe, of Ropsley, ord., 480,
      482–483, 485
   M. Thomas, 451
      preb. of Newark college, Leicester,
         108, 515
   Thomas, rector of Alphamstone; rector
      of Tingrith, 263
   William, 124
Hilton, Robert, of Bangor dioc., deac., 474,
   476
Hinchingbrooke, Hunts., priory of St
      James, 138
   nun, *see* Brynkle
   orders conferred to title of, 481, 486,
      488–489, 491–493, 495, 498, 500,
      520
   prioress, *see* Brynkle
Hinckley, Leics., vicarage, 35
Hitchin, Herts., 140, 237
Hobkyn, Richard, rector of Wyke Dyve,
   ord., 488–489
Hobkyns, *see* Hopkyns
Hoby, Leics., 547–548
   church, 5
   lord of, *see* Howby
Hoby, Hevy, Thomas, of Middle Rasen,
   ord., 471, 480
Hockliffe, Beds., hospital, 253
Hogg, Hogge
   John, rector of Datchworth; rector of
      Watton at Stone, 184
   Thomas, vicar of Upton, 375
Hogges, John, chaplain of St Mary chantry,
   Chipping Norton, 340
Hoggesthorp, M. John, 146, 255, 358, 378,
   517
Hogham, Hogh [unidentified], 491–493
Hoke, *see* Hook
Hokyn, David, Dominican friar of
   Stamford, acol., 501, 521
Holand, Holland
   Joan, countess of Kent, lady Wake, 142,
      162
   John, Austin friar of Northampton, acol.,
      493
   John, monk of Crowland, ord., 485–486
   Robert, of Long Bennington, ord.,
      500–501, 520–522, 541
   Thomas, acol., 473
   Thomas, monk of Bardney, ord., 480
   see also Lovel

Holbeach, Lincs., church, ordination in,
   543
Holbech, Holbeche
   James, acol., 471
   Nicholas, canon of Launde, pr., 471
   Simon, monk of Spalding, ord., 492,
      495, 498
Holbek, William
   rector of mediety of Beachampton, 366,
      396
   vicar of Wardley, 69, 396
Holcote, Halcote, Thomas, Carmelite friar
   of Northampton, ord., 493
Hole
   John, monk of Bardney, ord., 544, 548
   Thomas, monk of Bardney, deac., 548
Holewyll, Holewylle, Robert, rector of
   Cuxham, 356, 530
Holland, *see* Holand
Holme
   Richard, friar minor of Stamford, ord.,
      493, 544
   Robert, Dominican friar of Boston, acol.,
      544
   William, Dominican friar of Boston,
      subd., 546
   Thomas, 71
   William, rector of Swepstone, 14
Holt [unidentified], 485–486
Holt, Holte, John, ord., 501, 521–522, 541
Holygoste, Bartholomew, vicar of
   Willington, 215
Holywell, Hunts., church, 182
Homme
   John, rector of South Molton, ord., 493
   Richard, of Hereford dioc., ord.,
      473–474, 476
Honyngton, Richard, acol., 544
Hook, Hoke
   John, acol., 520
   Robert, acol., 500
   Robert, citizen and grocer of Lincoln,
      149
Hoper
   Robert, ord., 472–474
   M. William, 186
      rector of St Michael at the South
         Gate, Oxford, 324
   William, rector of portion of
      Waddesdon, pr., 491
Hopkyns, Habkyns, Hobkyns
   Henry, of *Gretham*, ord., 495, 543–544,
      546
   William, acol., 543

Alice, wife of, 397

Thornborough, Bucks., vicar, *see* Hardyng

Thornebury, Thomas, canon of St
  Frideswide, Oxford; vicar of
  Headington, 327

Thorneham, *see* Thornham

Thornehyll, John, acol., 543

Thornerton, Nicholas, vicar of Whaddon,
  432

Thorneton [unidentified], 486, 488

Thorneton, *see* Thornton

Thorney, Cambs., abbey, 114, 167

Thornham, Thorneham, William, canon of
  Newhouse, ord., 491–492, 498

Thornholm, Lincs., priory
  canons, *see* Burgh, Lincoln, Thorp
  orders conferred to title of, 496, 522, 541

Thornsby, *see* Thoresby

Thornton, Bucks.
  church, 415
  lord of, *see* Barton

Thornton, Leics., vicarage, 79

Thornton, Lincs., abbey
  canons, *see* Ascutys, Brawby,
    Conyngeston, Hesell, Hildeston,
    Hull, Irby, Neucastell
  orders conferred to title of, 471, 476,
    478–483, 486, 543, 548

Thornton by Horncastle, Lincs., 492–493,
  498, 500, 520

Thornton, Thorneton
  M. John, preb. of Norton Episcopi in
    Lincoln cath., 459
  Walter, canon of Barlings, ord., 544
  William, canon of Newhouse, subd., 547
  William, of Kirton in Holland, ord.,
    471–473

Thorp
  John, acol., 548
  John, canon of Thornholm, pr., 471
  John, of Bigby, subd., 547
  John, of *Willugby*, ord., 493, 495
  John, monk of Kirkstead, pr., 486
  John, preb. of Corringham in Lincoln
    cath., 450
  M. Ralph, rector of Hampton Poyle, 279
  Thomas, Carmelite friar of Lincoln, ord.,
    492, 500–501, 520–521
  Thomas, of Noseley, ord., 478–480, 482
  William, acol., 482

Thorpe by Daventry, *see* Thrupp

Thorpe by Norwich, Norfolk, 70, 111, 141

Thorpe Malsor, Northants.
  church, 503

manor and advowson, 503

Thrapston, Edmund, vicar of Hemel
  Hempstead, 113, 170

Throbber, John, vicar of Little Houghton;
  vicar of Oakley, 245

Thrupp (Thorpe by Daventry), Northants.,
  491–493

Thrustynton, William, rector of Thorpe
  Malsor, 503

Thuresby [unidentified], see *Thoresby*

Thurgarton, Notts., priory
  canons, *see* Mowbray, Ortsale
  orders conferred to title of, 471–473,
    476–477, 480
  patron, 511–512

Thurlaston, Leics., church, 97

Thurlby, Thurleby
  John, acol., 486
  Thomas, canon of Markby, ord., 472,
    480
  William, of Fotheringhay, ord., 543–544,
    547

Thurleby [unidentified], 471–473

Thurleby, *see* Thurlby

Thurleigh, Beds.
  church, 403
  vicarage, 402–403
    house, 403
    ordination of, 403

Thwaytes, Thwaytys, Twaytes
  Robert, master of St James and St John
    hospital, Aynho, 343
  Robert, rector of Terrington, ord., 491,
    495

Thymelby, John, vicar of Beeston; vicar of
  Evington, 92

Tickford, Bucks., priory
  monks, *see* Bredon
  orders conferred to title of, 481, 485–
    486

Tilbrook, Hunts., 471
  church, 217, 228, 250

Tillett, William, rector of Thornton, 415

Tilney, Tylney
  John, 502
  Thomas, rector of Aston; rector of
    Withern, 502

Tilsworth, Beds., vicarage, 362

Tilton, Leics., 482–483, 486

Tilton, Thomas, rector of Skeffington, 103

Tingewick, Bucks., church, 218

Tingrith, Beds.
  church, 263
  manor, lord of, *see* Brokkele

Walden, Essex, abbey, orders conferred to
    title of, 483
Wale
  John, 340
  Robert, 340
  William, 340
Walker
  John, acol., 476
  John (another), acol., 543
  John s. John, of High Toynton, ord.,
    495, 498
  John s. Richard, of Horncastle, ord., 471
  Simon, ord., 476, 481–482, 485
  Thomas, vicar of Beckley, 352
  William, ord., 522, 541, 546, 548
Wallingford, Berks., priory, 301, 337, 351
Walmesger, Thomas, acol., 544
Walscheborne, John, rector of Great
    Comberton; vicar of Broadwell, 282
Walsh, Walshe
  John, acol., 548
  Richard, acol., 501, 521
Walsyngham
  M. James, 137
  Robert, canon of Canons Ashby, ord.,
    493, 495, 500, 520
Walyngton, John, rector of Baldock, 172
Walter, rector of Creslow, 433 rector of
    Creslow, 433
Walter
  John, acol., 547
  William son of, of Claxby, ord., 482–
    483, 485
Waltham, Essex, abbey of Holy Cross
  orders conferred to title of, 474, 476–
    477, 546–548
  patron, 152, 263
Waltham, Lincs., rector, *see* Frende
Waltham on the Wolds, Leics.
  church, 72
  rector, *see* Fenton
Waltham, Thomas, friar minor of Lincoln,
    pr., 495
Walton, Bucks., church, 361
Walton on the Wolds, Leics., church, 94
Walton, Wood, Hunts., 124, 176
  church, 111, 173
  lord of, *see* Bevyll
Walton, Halton
  Hugh, acol., 501, 521
  Thomas, of Leicester, subd., 472
  M. Thomas, preb. of Leighton Buzzard
    in Lincoln cath., 204
  William, acol., 500, 520

Walyngford
  John, canon of Notley, pr., 473
  Thomas, canon of Notley, ord., 492, 495
Wandysford, Henry, *see* Wansford
Waneford, William, Dominican friar of
    Dunstable, acol., 473
Wansford, Wandysford, Henry, canon of St
    Katherine outside Lincoln, ord.,
    544, 546
Wapelode, *see* Whaplode
Wappenham, Northants., 543–544
Warboys, Hunts., 163
  church, 163
Ward, Warde
  John, 199, 536
  John, master of collegiate church,
    Northill, 252
  Richard
    rector of mediety of Beachampton,
      366
    rector of Maids' Moreton, 363
  Robert, vicar of Bringhurst, 54
  Walter, acol., 548
Wardele, John, rector of Clothall, 149
Wardley, Rutland, 547
  chapelry, *see* Belton
  vicarage, 69, 396
Wardon, Beds., abbey, monks, *see* Sondey
Wardon [unidentified], 495–497
Wardon, John, acol., 492
Ware, Herts., priory, 23
Waresley, Hunts., vicarage, 126, 143, 212
Warfeld, John, 349
Warmwell, Dorset, church, 232
Warmyngton, Wermyngton [unidentified],
    471–473
Warner
  John, of Raunds, ord., 522, 541, 548
  John, rector of Marlow, 370
  William, of Boston, ord., 476, 482, 485
Warpsgrove, Oxon., church, 268–269, 302,
    357, 539
Wartre, Richard, rector of Glooston;
    warden of chantry, Sapcote, 78
Warwick, church of St Mary, chapter, 299,
    331
Warwick, earl of, *see* Beauchamp
Warwyk, James, acol., 544
Waryn
  John, ord., 496
  Robert, of Bedford, ord., 485, 488
  Thomas, of Banbury, ord., 485
Waryner, Waryndre, Henry, of *Keston*, ord.,
    543, 546, 548

INDEX OF SUBJECTS